FOREWORD BY STEVE SJOGREN

ELMER TOWNS   ED STETZER
WARREN BIRD

11 INNOVATIONS IN THE LOCAL CHURCH

How Today's Leaders Can Learn, Discern and Move into the Future

11 INNOVATIONS IN THE LOCAL CHURCH

Forty years ago, I read Elmer Towns's cutting edge book *The Largest Sunday Schools in America*. He's still at it, except this time he has added Ed Stetzer and Warren Bird who, like Towns, are dedicated to the future of the church yet grounded on the Word of God. I recommend this book.

Tommy Barnett
Senior Pastor, First Assembly Phoenix
Phoenix, Arizona
www.phoenixfirst.org

There are ways of doing church that no one has thought of yet. Ed Stetzer, Warren Bird and Elmer Towns don't just point the way—the stories and models they share will take you on a journey to the future and help you discover your unique "churchprint." This book is a must-read for anyone serious about reaching the next generation for Christ.

Mark Batterson
Senior Pastor, National Community Church
Washington, D.C.
www.theaterchurch.com

Preserve the essence; change the form. We live in a time when it seems history is moving beneath our feet like a rolling sidewalk; even the status quo is in motion! This book looks at 11 church types, explains the innovations, gives examples and then reviews pros and cons of each innovation so that readers can consider whether to look further into the innovation— or, if it is not for them, to be more understanding toward those who want to implement those innovations.

Bob Buford
Author, *Halftime* and *Finishing Well*
Founder, Leadership Network
Dallas, Texas
www.leadnet.org

God is doing something new and radical in our day, and these men are checking the pulse on the Body of Christ. When you open this book, you will begin to see some of the new stuff emerging. Some of it will prod you, some of it will provoke you, and some of it may even propel you into a more productive ministry—but all of it is real and happening right now.

Neil Cole
Author, *Organic Church: Growing Faith Where Life Happens,*
Cultivating a Life for God and *TruthQuest*
Director, Church Multiplication Associates
Signal Hill, California
www.cmaresources.org

If you care about where God is at work in the church today, you must read *11 Innovations in the Local Church*. This is a handbook for all of us who want to be innovators and early adopters to what God is doing next!

Dave Ferguson
Lead Pastor, Community Christian Church
Naperville, Illinois
www.communitychristian.org

11 Innovations in the Local Church doesn't promise answers to every question about how to effectively build the kingdom of God, nor does it provide 11 easy steps to ensure future growth and prosperity in our faith communities. Rather, it inspires us to believe that there are questions worth asking and that there is a God capable of revealing all that we need to know in order to build the kind of church He desires at each of our unique locations. This book allowed me to consider new ways of sharing God's timeless message of hope.

Teresa J. McBean
Minister, NorthStar Community
Richmond, Virginia
www.northstarcommunity.com

This insightful book fills a huge void. You could spend thousands of dollars visiting hundreds of churches and still not gather one-tenth of the insights contained in this book. Our entire church staff is going to read, digest and discuss it. Towns, Stetzer and Bird have done a great service for church leaders.

Nelson Searcy

Lead Pastor, The Journey Church (New York City)
Founder, www.ChurchLeaderInsights.com

The journey toward innovation began for me when, as a 22-year-old pastor-wannabe, my wife gave me a copy of a book called *All Originality Makes a Dull Church*, detailing creative churches of that time. Reading it nudged my thinking outside of the box a bit. Perhaps *11 Innovations in the Local Church* will spark ideas in other hungry young innovators who will, in turn, trust God for more than they could possibly ask or imagine.

Greg Surratt

Senior Pastor, Seacoast Church
Mt. Pleasant, South Carolina
www.seacoast.org

ELMER TOWNS   ED STETZER
WARREN BIRD

11 INNOVATIONS IN THE LOCAL CHURCH

*How Today's Leaders Can Learn, Discern
and Move into the Future*

Regal

**From Gospel Light
Ventura, California, U.S.A.**

Published by Regal Books
From Gospel Light
Ventura, California, U.S.A.
Printed in the U.S.A.

Library of Congress Cataloging-in-Publication Data
Towns, Elmer L.
11 innovations in the local church / Elmer L. Towns, Ed Stetzer, and Warren Bird.
    p. cm.
Includes index.
ISBN 0-8307-4378-2 (trade paper)
1. Church renewal. 2. Non-institutional churches. I. Stetzer, Ed. II. Bird, Warren. III. Title. IV. Title: Eleven innovations in the local church.
BV600.3.T69 2007
250—dc22   2006101225

1 2 3 4 5 6 7 8 9 10 / 10 09 08 07

Rights for publishing this book in other languages are contracted by Gospel Light Worldwide, the international nonprofit ministry of Gospel Light. Gospel Light Worldwide also provides publishing and technical assistance to international publishers dedicated to producing Sunday School and Vacation Bible School curricula and books in the languages of the world. For additional information, visit www.gospellightworldwide.org; write to Gospel Light Worldwide, P.O. Box 3875, Ventura, CA 93006; or send an e-mail to info@gospellightworldwide.org.

CONTENTS

FOREWORD

Publishers usually don't like writers to mention popular culture references. Why? Because the phenomenon lasts only a year or two, and once it passes away, the book at hand seems somewhat dated.

With this in mind, I am about to take a risk—which is what this book encourages its readers to do. There is a show that my wife, Janie, and I have begun to follow recently that has become one of the most popular TV shows in this decade. It is simply called *Heroes*. The show is ironic in its title in that each of the "heroes" is both very human (more human than you or me probably!) but also *super-gifted* in some spectacular way that makes him or her an unforgettable person.

I mention this show because the book you hold in your hand has been written by three of the heroes in my life. Each is an unforgettable person in his own way. This is saying something honestly, considering the source. If you knew me, you would realize that I am a scrutinizer. I'm not skeptical, but in a world that is ruled by the Peter Principle (which states that we tend to grow into positions of our greatest incompetence in organizations), it is good to know that the real thing is still out there.

All three of these guys are very human yet amazingly gifted and insightful. In fact, I would go so far as to say that each of them is at the top of his game in this generation of leaders in their areas of insight and leadership. This sort of insight doesn't come through mere cleverness or through the development of a mental muscle—these are the gifts of God. Realizing that truth is humbling.

The 11 areas that this book picks up on are the sorts of insights that aren't obvious to any but the most careful students of human behavior. I have made note more than once that many

"Christian" leadership books are of dubious value in that they simply state the obvious. Not so with this work.

As you read this book, I pray that you will be touched in two specific ways: (1) Your skill set will be remarkably enhanced, expanded and challenged; and (2) You will see yourself as a doer of these strategies and as an up-and-coming communicator of these lessons as you do the deeds of Jesus—not simply a thinker of great thoughts.

Toward the opening of the book, the authors state, "Let's not enter the future only to look back later and observe, 'The culture changed—and even our church changed, but no one told us!'" The following pages will help you not only to see what's ahead but also to size up the pros and the cons of each innovation. Some of the ideas presented in this book may not be right for you, but at least you will now understand what they're about and the spiritual motivation behind them. Other innovations presented will represent a step of faith that God is calling you and your church to explore further.

In fact, maybe God is calling you to be a hero—a leader in a church that tries something new to show God's love in practical and compelling ways.

Steve Sjogren
ServantEvangelism.com
CoastlandTampa.com

AUTHORS' PREFACE

Suppose you were a first-time missionary sent to an unreached people group. You would no doubt ask, "What can I learn from *other* missionaries pioneering in similar areas, especially missionaries working with groups who have responded positively to the gospel?" Missionaries know there are many biblical ways to present the gospel, and they're on the lookout for clues about what God might be using to reach each particular culture.

That's the idea behind this book. The better we understand what God seems to be blessing, the better we can learn an approach that's appropriate for our own settings. Likewise, the more we can identify the most influential heartbeat behind other churches, the more intentional we can be in asking if this is the direction God is trying to take us.

In the early twentieth century, H. Richard Niebuhr wrote a book named *Christ and Culture*. He observed that most churches take on a particular attitude (Christ *against* culture, Christ as *transformer* of culture, Christ *of* culture, and so forth), which influenced the pattern and direction of their growth. He called them church *types*; no church fit the model perfectly, but many churches were a close match.[1]

This book takes a similar approach. By learning from 11 different church *types*, readers can be more intentional about exploring what God might want to bless and then cooperate with God to move in that direction, as appropriate.

The structure is simple: The first section briefly introduces the need for innovative churches. It argues that Jesus came to seek and save lost people, and if our current methods are not working, maybe we need to try something new. The second section—the bulk of the book—presents 11 different types of churches that have found a breakthrough in reaching people and making disciples. As we profile each innovation, we illustrate it with many different churches. Along the way, we continually review the pros and cons of each method. The third section asks what these church types together teach us. We draw together the common themes behind all the innovations explored in the book.

You certainly don't need to be the senior pastor to benefit from this book. If you love your church and want to see God work through you to make more and better disciples of Jesus Christ, then this book is for you.

The Holy Spirit has empowered your church to be an effective witness for Jesus Christ. May God use this book to dare you to discern the Spirit's promptings to be both faithful and fruitful in this era.

THE CHURCH CHANGED, AND NOBODY TOLD US

As part of an experiment, I (Ed) encouraged all members of a 35-attendee congregation, which had a median age of 68 years, to visit 5 churches that had proven to be effective in reaching younger adults through their worship services. These members wanted to reach young adults, so it made sense for them to see what success in that area could look like. Most of the 35 went on the outing with clipboards in hand and minds relatively open.

The visits were conducted over a two week period; three services the first week, two the next. These little old ladies and a few old men took notes ranging from the types of musical instruments the churches used to the churches' nursery programs, preaching styles and topics, singing, and just about everything else.

During a Wednesday night service after the team had concluded their research, we had "the meeting." Everyone gathered to talk about what the team had seen—and indeed they had seen a lot! They were all accustomed to the pattern from the '70s—two hymns, an offering, another hymn and possibly a chorus, followed by a certain style of preaching. None of the churches that were visited, however, followed that particular model. In fact, they were all completely different from the familiar old format.

The first comment was a classic—and everyone agreed with it. One of the older ladies stood up and announced almost indignantly, "Preacher, the church changed, and nobody told us!"

The Goal Is to Reach People for Christ

You may get a chuckle about a church so obviously unaware that times have changed. But what if the median age in my church had been 38 rather than 68—could we also have lost our relevance and evangelistic edge and not noticed it? Could we, like the classic frog-in-the-cooking-kettle story, have missed the changes in our environment and unwittingly begun to slide into extinction? What if our church, instead of being stuck in the '70s, had been stuck in the '80s or '90s—or even stuck in certain patterns from *last year* that had led us nowhere? If our church had made no impact for Christ outside of our membership last year, should we remain content to do the same things *this* year?

Most churches need to change because they're showing little or no statistical growth (numerical, spiritual or otherwise) and minimal impact on the surrounding culture. Too many are struggling just to keep their doors open, and yet they tend to keep replaying what they did "last year."

American churches have the money and resources to seek new and alternate ways to revitalize their lethargic outreach. Yet instead of looking for a breakthrough, churches across the country are slowly dying because too many tend to value tradition over expanding God's reach.

Innovation or death? Too many churches choose death over innovation. The choice we make today will impact the church of our children.

No More Fines for Falling Asleep in Church

A recent PBS series on colonial life in America in 1622 was a great reminder about how much the norms for "church" in our country have changed during the last 400 years. In the 1600s, sermons were regularly more than two hours long and people were fined for falling asleep in church! It was even *required* that everyone in town attend church weekly. Musical instruments such as the organ were considered worldly. Steeples or outdoor crosses on church buildings were looked down on as inappropriate. Playing golf on Sunday could get you put into the stocks, and having the "wrong" view about topics such as baptism could get you kicked out of the colony! Aren't you glad that at least some of those ways of doing church have changed?

On a more serious note, American churches have not suffered—for the most part—the pain experienced by many churches around the world. The idea of an underground church, a persecuted church, or even a church with modern-day martyrs is largely non-existent in North America. Other countries generate news such as, "400 churches closed! Pastors killed and imprisoned!" Instead, American churches are moving in the sad direction of, "400 churches closed because communities don't want them around!"

What America needs today is a culture-impacting revival. According to Philip Jenkins in *The Next Christendom: The Coming of Global Christianity*, a shift is occurring that places the vibrant, growing edge of Christianity not in North America or in Europe but in places like Asia, Africa, Central America and South America.[1] Today, the only continent where Christianity is not growing is North America. That's a fact we dare not ignore.

Distinguishing Method from Principle

11 Innovations in the Local Church takes a look at new innovations and methods that are taking place in churches across America, proving true an old saying:

> Methods are many
> Principles are few,
> Methods may change
> But principles never do.
> —Anonymous

Two of my (Elmer's) previous books in the field of church growth examined specific methods that God was blessing at the time they were written.[2] This present book examines new and unique methods that are being used at the beginning of the twenty-first century, methods that God seems to be blessing in this new era. Interestingly, many of the churches I previously wrote about continue to use the same methods that now no longer work as well—and, not surprisingly, their evangelistic outreach has declined and attendance at a number of them has dropped precipitously. The message to us all is this: When culture changes, adjust your methods or you will lose your effectiveness . . . but never change your message or your principles! When methods no longer work, don't blame the harvest as being unreachable; instead, ask God if it's time to change your methods!

Too Much Innovation?

It seems as if the Church has come up with more innovative ways to do ministry today than ever before. Is this good, bad— or both? Do you feel, like Dickens, that it is the best of times and it is the worst of times?

We propose that today is the best of times because each church has the freedom—as leaders and members follow the guidance of the Holy Spirit—to use the huge toolkit of options at their disposal. Churches today are using *more* methods to do *more* ministry in *more* different ways to accomplish *more* different results to reach *more* people and to involve *more* workers. If this is the case, who wouldn't expect to see more harvest for Christ?

But could this also be the worst of times? Does God want us to do *more*, even if we use people who are unspiritual, use methods that are not taught or sanctioned in Scripture, get results that are not mandated in the Bible, or are diverted from the Great Commission and all that's implied in the final command of Jesus to us? Today's culture affirms that *more* is generally better. The computer is approaching unlimited memory, science is approaching unlimited cures, the world thinks it has unlimited resources to solve all its problems, and Christians continue to imagine new ways to tell the "old, old story." Is this good or bad?

Think about King David, who had a great-sounding idea: He would build a great Temple for God. But according to 2 Samuel 7 and 1 Chronicles 17, God reminded David that He did not ask for a great Temple and that He in fact, did not want a man of war like David to build Him one. Oops.

Or consider those misguided people in Genesis 11 who tried to please God by making a ziggurat. They were making a tower tall enough to physically climb into heaven, a pyramid dedicated to their man-made worship of who they thought was God in heaven. But "the Lord came down to look at . . . the tower" (Gen. 11:5) and didn't like what He saw. One of God's criticisms was, "This is just the beginning. Soon they will be able to do anything they want" (v. 6). The story of the tower of Babel didn't end well. God changed the language of the people and construction stopped.

The point is this: We need to constantly ask, "Will God be pleased with our innovations?" Life isn't about what *we* can do—it's about obeying what *God* wants us to do. We must make sure our actions are right in His eyes.

It is important to keep in mind that not everything that people today refer to as a "church" is in fact a church. For example, some may refer to a *pub* as a church because a church sponsors a discussion group in the bar. But this is not a church—it might be the evangelistic outreach of a church or maybe a preaching location, but it's not an actual church. A halftime Bible study on an asphalt court in an inner-city neighborhood is not a "basketball church"—it is simply an evangelism arm that reaches out to meet the needs of lost teenagers. We must be careful not to call everything we do "church," nor must we call anytime Christians assemble together a "church." When we use the word "church" to describe the outward gathering of Christians into a local body that reflects the heavenly and spiritual body, then we please God.

Our working definition of church is "an assembly of professing believers, uniquely indwelt by Jesus Christ, under the discipline of the Word of God, administering the ordinances and led by spiritually gifted leaders."[3] This definition of church is an irreducible minimum. We need to measure all innovations by the seed of this truth and ask the question, "Does this innovation bear the marks of a New Testament Church?"

All three of us have had the privilege of learning from Peter Drucker, a well-known business writer who devoted much energy to helping churches and other non-profits. Drucker has two favorite questions: "What business are you in?" and "How is business?" When we think about church innovations, it might be helpful to explore this perspective. In church terms, the question might be, "How is the business of mission that God has called your church to?"

If the primary business of the Church is to glorify God by obeying the Great Commandment (see Matt. 22:34-40) and carrying out the Great Commission (see Matt. 28:19-20), we ask you to evaluate how business is faring. From a historical perspective, most innovations have arisen when the Church has failed to reach the lost, failed to teach Christians and failed to be a testimony to God in this dark world. These failures demanded fresh innovations.

We can ask the same question about the innovations explored in this book—how's business? Is the "motorcycle church" reaching hog riders? Is the "cowboy church" reaching cowboys? Is the organic house church making disciples of the household? Are the innovations doing a better job than what they replaced? In short, is the business of the Church growing through the innovation?

Learn and Discern

As you prayerfully reflect on the innovations that follow, we ask that you be willing to hold the models loosely and Jesus firmly.

It's easy to *agree* with that statement, but do you know who has the hardest time *practicing* it? People who have seen God do amazing things in the past. Those who are most successful in the *last* paradigm often have the most difficulty moving ahead into the next. Why? Because they know that if next year could be 1972 (or 1952, or 2002) all over again, they would be ready! They saw God work powerfully through a particular model of ministry (maybe that's even how they personally came to faith in the Lord), so they're just certain that they should hang onto it—even if it seems to have lost its ability to connect with people. Their logic goes like this: God blessed a particular method in the past, so we can count on Him to continue to do so into the future. They don't realize that the "how" of ministry is influenced by the "who," "when" and "where" of culture.

Our premise offers an alternative. Sometimes, having had a success in the past can limit openness to a different approach for the future, especially if the winds of the Holy Spirit start to blow in a new direction.

We three authors have a strong bias that it takes all kinds of churches to reach all kinds of people. It has been both fascinating and disturbing to watch the "paradigm wars" of the North American Church. Churches are arguing about what is appropriate and what is not, and they tend to do so based more often on their personal preference than on the teachings of Scripture. It's like reading the book of Acts, picking a favorite chapter and throwing away the rest! Acts clearly demonstrates a wide variety of methods that the Holy Spirit used to grow the Church.[4] Therefore, it seems to make sense that God, the Author of creativity, would continue to bless a wide variety of methods for conveying His timeless, unchanging gospel. If, like snowflakes, no two people are alike, then it makes sense that there would be biblical variety between the methods God uses in different churches.

We believe that God is using a wide variety of churches, but we also believe that it is crucial that churches function biblically. We are aware that some innovations could possibly compromise or confuse biblical fidelity. We are also aware that many approaches to "church"—even many of those pioneered by a godly visionary with a very high view of Scripture—present themselves not as a model but as *the* New Testament standard (and, to be fair, each tends to define its approach in a distinctive way with a solid appeal to relevant Scripture). For example, Wolfgang Simpson, a major organic (house) church leader, tells us that through the house church, "God is restoring HIS pattern for HIS church so that the Holy Spirit can come and REMAIN."[5]

Meanwhile, the Purpose Driven (PD) folks explain on their site, "PD is about being biblical and eternal. The five purposes, rooted in the Great Commandment and the Great Commission, will never go out of style. The five PD purposes are based on the commands Jesus said were essential to the church."[6] Elmer Towns's book *Putting an End to Worship Wars* explores five other models of church, showing the biblical foundation for each.[7] Can all of these models be *the* right one?

Our belief is that we all need to recognize that God is using models we might not necessarily use, as well as models we might not even like. In some cases, God is even working in models that we think lack discernment (isn't God patient with us in our shortcomings?). To paraphrase the apostle Paul, sometimes we need to conclude, "Some are preaching about Christ because they are jealous and envious of us. Others are preaching because they want to help. They love Christ and know that I am here to defend the good news about him. But the ones who are jealous of us are not sincere. They just want to cause trouble for me while I am in jail. But that doesn't matter. *All that matters is that people are telling about Christ, whether they are sincere or not. That is what makes me glad*" (Phil. 1:15-18, emphasis added).

We believe the answer is to look to Jesus and not to models. Models may change, but God's truth never changes. Innovations should never detract from His plan for salvation but should instead help us fulfill that plan.

Learning Without Affirming

Evaluating innovations is the same as evaluating anything about a church. It starts with one simple question: *Is God in it?*

I (Elmer) often use the phrase "to touch God and be touched by Him" in my writings. Coming to worship is primarily about touching God—we want to feel His presence when we meet together. God promised us, "Later, I will give my Spirit to everyone" (Joel 2:28; Acts 2:17) and "Give up your sins, and you will be forgiven" (Acts 3:19). Just as you can feel moisture on your face on a cloudy day when it's not raining, so too you can feel the presence of the Lord like dew when you walk into certain Christian gatherings. You *know* God is there and you *know* He is going to do something in that church!

This may be a subjective criterion, but it is something felt by many Christians when they gather in the name of the Lord to do the work of the Lord according to the Word of the Lord. If you sense the presence of Christ in an innovation of a particular church, then that may very well be a confirmation of God's leading. If the innovation is for any other motive or purpose than to call attention to the power, plan and presence of the Lord, then back away. But if it lines up with Scripture and God is in it, then we affirm it.

Learn, Discern, Move Ahead

We have convictions and concerns about some of the churches that we profile in this book, but we try to describe them in as positive of terms as possible. This is because the purpose of this book is to help people learn, not to correct. (For some helpful ideas on boundaries, see Towns and Stetzer's earlier book *Perimeters of Light.*[8])

This book is intended to make you think. Our hope is that you will learn and discern as you read through the innovations listed.[9] Some of the innovations you will not like (we don't like them all either!). However, lives are being changed in these churches. Innovations, even problematic ones, have come and gone within the Church, but some have had a lasting impact on the Church, and their influence is often beneficial.

If our purpose is not to endorse the more than 50 different churches in these pages so much as to learn from them, then what is it that we want you to learn? For starters, churches need to ask themselves, "Are there any methods we're using that need to change?" While we don't celebrate any innovation that leads to compromise (and we think some do), we can still learn from churches that are trying their best to reach their communities. We did tend to stack the deck with examples of churches that are effectively showing people how Jesus can restore them from brokenness and lead them into eternal life. And we left out all the churches that tried really bad ideas and died as a result!

Our hope is that you will keep an open but prayerfully discerning mind as you thoughtfully study these 11 innovations. This does not mean that you should blindly accept everything described in the following pages. Instead, we ask that you consider what you can learn from these sincere fellow believers who are working to reach their community with methods they feel best suit the community they know best. We ask that you first *learn* what they are doing, then *discern* if it is appropriate scripturally, and finally *move ahead* with whatever God guides you to do with your church.

This book does not focus on 11 specific innovative churches but on 11 different *types* of innovation, with each chapter drawing from numerous churches as illustrations. So study these emerging church types to learn how to better conduct your ministry. Not everything described in this book will work in your particular setting, which is why we've included the "so what" material in each chapter to help you discern why an innovation may not work for your church. However, we believe that every innovation can help you think through issues in your church, even though in some cases the innovators may have gone farther than we think they should have. We lay out these innovators' stories, help you think them through and let you decide.

Your church stands at the open door of a wonderful era of ministry. Our prayer is that Jesus Christ will use this book to do two things: First, we hope it will deepen your faith in the unchanging message of the gospel; second, we hope it will empower you to make changes to reach more lost people than ever before and to incorporate them into your church.

We don't want you to have to say, "The church changed, and nobody told us!" We tell you in these pages how it is changing, but we also hope that you will learn to think through the innovations we describe, discern them through the lens of Scripture, and then move forward with God's best for your church.

CHAPTER 1

ORGANIC HOUSE CHURCHES

*Every day they spent time in the temple and in one home
after another. They never stopped teaching and telling
the good news that Jesus is the Messiah.*

ACTS 5:42

Meeting Neil Cole is, well, anticlimactic. Here is a guy who has
helped lead one of the more prolific church-planting networks
in the country.[1] He has written some significant books and he
speaks all over. So I (Ed) was pretty excited when I landed at
LAX and started driving over to his office.

Since getting lost in Los Angeles is as easy as falling asleep
in a church business meeting, I splurged and got myself a GPS
in the car. For each of the miles from the airport to Cole's office,
a nasally woman said "turn left" and "go three miles and take the
ramp on the right." (It's amazing that some people pay for what
my wife will do for free.)

Anyway, my trusty GPS eventually announced, still in nasal
tones, "arriving at destination." But there was nothing there.
No sign, no parking. I assumed the GPS was wrong, programmed
it again, and drove around the block. Again I heard, "arriving at
destination." So I gave up—when a woman tells you twice the
right directions, you better listen. I got out and knocked on the
door. And out came Neil Cole.

I don't mean to say that Cole himself is anticlimactic. Yes, he
shrugs a lot and is very laid back, but it was his surroundings,

not his persona, that gave me the letdown. You see, Cole—and everything he shapes—is "anti-slick." One of Cole's sayings is that "simple" empowers Christians. And he lives it too—his office is a mess, it's small and it's hot (air conditioning is too expensive to run, he says). The couch where we finally settled had seen better days.

Cole's simple approach is not because he lacks money (although he does and you should send him some). It is because he has passion: a passion that the best way to propagate the gospel is with the idea that the church can and should be simpler and more organic—like Cole. Like Jesus. Everything Cole does (quoting him here and throughout) "is not bound by a large gathering or service we could reproduce quickly." That's the point—church should be simple and easy to reproduce. Normal people, with small messy offices and threadbare couches, should plant and model planting churches led by ordinary people.

I asked Cole a lot about the numbers. I am a missiologist. I was born to count. I'm especially interested in new believers and new churches. But Cole explained, "If you are successful in a multiplication movement, than you cannot count them . . . if you can count them, you are not a multiplication movement." Cole is concerned about reaching people and making disciples, not with the number and longevity of his churches. "The greatest sin of today's church is self-preservation . . . if a church lasts one year and gives birth twice, it is a success."

Cole is the anti-attractional leader for the anti-attractional church (a concept we'll explore in chapter 11). And Cole likes it that way. He does not want a big church; he wants a reproducing one. He does not want a quality church; he wants a transforming one. He explains, "We must lower the bar of how we do church and raise the bar on what it means to be a disciple."

Talking to Cole is just odd. Usually it takes about five minutes for the typical pastor in a growing church to work the conversation around to the week's attendance. Not so with Cole. He is about people—and he tells a lot of stories about them. Many are transformative, and some are discouraging. "It hurts more to do church this way, but it's still worth it."

Cole could be pastoring a good-sized (what some would call "real") church, but he sees that as a flawed system. He boils the principles down to three simple ideas:

1. What we are doing isn't working.
2. What's really happening around the world tends to be in house churches.
3. If multiplication is our desire, it needs to be simple, transferable and ordinary.

For Cole, that simplicity boils down to the right DNA:

D—Divine Truth
N—Nurturing Relationships
A—Apostolic Mission

Cole believes we have created a culture of clergy codependency. The church leadership is the codependent, and the parishioners are the irresponsible dependent ones. What is needed is a radical detox. We have to stop relying on Christian leaders who tell us when to stand up, when to sit down and when to kneel.

Many house-church advocates take swings at what they call (usually with a smirk) the "institutional church." Not so with Cole. "I think the old wineskins should hold the old wine . . . not dismantle the old," he says. Instead, Cole believes we should "invest in apostolic architects, not in builders . . . and don't put a lot of money in it."

Cole lives it. His massive operation without a parking lot has a grand total of 1.5 employees but trains 2,000 people in

12 states and around the world. Not bad for a guy with a nasty hole in his couch.

Making an Important Distinction

In his book *Organic Church*, Cole observes that "the world is interested in Jesus; it is His wife (the Church is the bride of Christ) that they do not want to spend time with."[2] Lamenting that "the local church no longer has the influence to change the world," he observes, "Something is wrong with the way we are doing church here."[3] His assessment is that too many established, facility-based churches have "lost the plot" along the way.[4] "Attendance on Sundays does not transform lives; Jesus within their hearts is what changes people."[5]

That focus on people—especially other people—is what appeals to Cole. "The apostolic heart in our group," Cole says, "originating in changed lives, regularly reminds us that God works as ordinary people are called to do the extraordinary. We don't *go* to church; we *are* the church."

Cole left the world of the institutional church in an era in which this country's churches are the best organized in history, have some of the best facilities in history, have some of the best programs in history and have the best educational resources in history—all in order to belong to a house-based church with none of those advantages. Cole's path could be termed "reversion from excessive success," which means that American churches have more of everything and the best of all things, yet in an environment surrounded by American materialism, they overshadow the number-one thing in Christianity: that faith is all about the Person Jesus Christ and a day-by-day faith relationship with Him.

Cole is not alone. In *Revolution*, evangelical researcher George Barna claims that in the year 2000, most of the nation's organized religious activity took place at or through local churches.

Today, according to Barna, the action is increasingly shifting to forms of religious commitment that lack any connection to a local church. In a typical week, Barna reports, 9 percent of all adults participate in a house church. An even greater proportion (22 percent) engages in spiritual encounters that take place in the marketplace, with groups of people while they are at their workplace or recreational setting, or in other typical daily contexts. For some, this supplements involvement in a local church.[6]

This house-church trend—as evidenced by a major story in *Time* magazine and as reported on CNN and MSNBC in nightly news segments—is not going unnoticed. Many religious organizations have begun to take notice of the movement, including the organizations we serve.

At the Center for Missional Research (CMR), which I (Ed) lead, we sought to clarify the numbers on those involved in house churches by seeking to find those who were exclusively involved in a house church. CMR partnered with Zogby International and called more than 3,600 people to ask about their involvement in spirituality and alternative expressions of religion. In the survey, we asked respondents, "Do you meet weekly with a group of 20 people or less to pray and study Scriptures as your primary form of spiritual or religious gathering?" Surprisingly, 24.5 percent of Americans surveyed indicated that they met with a small group as their *primary* form of spiritual gathering!

Many of those could be church/synagogue/mosque small groups, Sunday School classes, and so forth. Yet a surprising number of those who rarely or never go to church/synagogue/mosque still attended a small group for spiritual nurturing as well.

When we cross-tabulated the small-group question with the church attendance question, we found that 50 out of the 3,600 adults surveyed attend a group of 20 or fewer and rarely

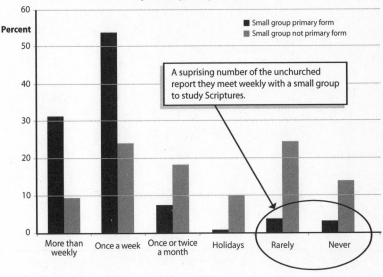

Frequency of Attendace at Place of Worship by Primary Group 20 or Less

- Small group primary form
- Small group not primary form

A suprising number of the unchurched report they meet weekly with a small group to study Scriptures.

or never attend a place of worship. If extrapolated, this is 1.4 percent of the American population and may represent the purest measure of those who are not involved in an organized church, synagogue, or mosque but are still involved in some alternative faith community like, in the Christian faith, a house church. That is about 4 million people—not a small number.[7]

For many, including an increasing number of evangelical Christians, church is not about a building, a program or budgets—it's about relationship and community. This also coincides with a trend in culture in which more and more people see themselves as spiritual but not religious. According to the same poll, 22 percent of respondents think of themselves as being spiritual but not religious. This is especially true of those who attend church rarely or never.[8]

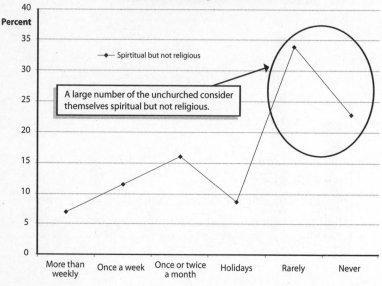

Frequency of Attendace at Place of Worship by Spiritual and Religious Self-assesment

Thus, for a rapidly growing number of Americans, a local church is no longer the place to go as their primary religious meeting place. Non-traditional forms of religious experience and expression are growing in popularity and drawing millions of people closer to God but farther away from involvement in a congregational church.

Looking at a Typical House Church

Research in late 2006 by George Barna's organization provided a unique profile of what takes place in the typical house church and who is involved. Barna's findings include the following:

- Most house churches (80 percent) meet every week, while 11 percent meet on a monthly basis. The most common meeting days are Wednesday (27 percent) and Sunday (25 percent), while 1 out of every 5 (20 percent) varies the days of the week on which they meet.

· The typical house-church gathering lasts for about two hours. Only 7 percent meet for less than an hour, on average, while only 9 percent usually stay together for more than 3 hours at a time.

· While most conventional churches follow the same format week after week, 4 of every 10 house churches (38 percent) say that the format they follow varies from meeting to meeting. Of those home gatherings that typically engage in spiritual practices:

   · 93 percent have spoken prayer during their meetings.

   · 90 percent read from the Bible.

   · 89 percent spend time serving people outside of their group.

   · 87 percent devote time to sharing personal needs or experiences.

   · 85 percent spend time eating and talking before or after the meeting.

   · 83 percent discuss the teaching provided.

   · 76 percent have a formal teaching time.

   · 70 percent incorporate music or singing.

- 58 percent have a prophecy or special word delivered.

- 52 percent take an offering from participants that is given to ministries.

- 51 percent share communion.

- 41 percent watch a video presentation as part of the learning experience.

- Most house churches are family-oriented. Two out of every 3 house churches (64 percent) have children involved. Those churches are divided evenly between those who have the adults and children together throughout the meeting (41 percent) and those who keep them separated (38 percent). The remaining churches divide their time between having everyone together and having time when the children and adults are separated.

- The average size of a house church is 20 people. In the home churches, that number includes children—there is an average of about 7 children under the age of 18 involved.

- The rapid growth in house-church activity is evident in the fact that approximately half of the people (54 percent) who are currently engaged in an independent home fellowship have been participating for less than 3 months. In total, 3 out of every 4 house-church participants (75 percent) have been active in their current gathering for 1 year or less. One out of every 5 adults has been in their house church for 3 years or more.[9]

Removing the Queen in Biblical Community

Cole gave me (Ed) permission to survey the attendees at his first-ever national "organic church" conference, which took place in February 2007 and drew several hundred participants. In one question of the survey, we asked people to describe their approach to church. The consensus idea was a small gathering around the life of Jesus. Respondents' phrases included "where real life happens" and "a home-based church that is missional rather than attractional." Participants characterized these faith communities as based on relationships and seeking authenticity. They emphasized an equality of all participants for the purposes of God's kingdom.

In my writings, I introduced a different term than "house church"—one that emphasizes the face-to-face community of house-church life. In *Planting Missional Churches*, I explain why I have begun to use the term *"koinos* church" as a more accurate description of the movement:

> The term "Koinos Church" is birthed out of a frustration. There is a need to describe this phenomenon often called "house church," but people in this movement do not like being identified by a "house." They point out that these churches do not just meet in a house, they also meet in a restaurant, business, or other settings. What defines these churches is not location, but emphasis . . . *Koinos churches* are churches that function completely by face-to-face relationship. If everyone cannot be "in common," the church is no longer a *Koinos Church* . . . The term "koinos" is used infrequently in Scripture, but we see it in Acts 2:44 where the believers had "all things in common." *Koinos churches* are churches that, at their core, have committed to

have face to face relationships in such a way that they truly live life together. This requires a commitment to community beyond larger churches in that they will always intentionally stay small so that people cannot be a part of the church without being truly connected in biblical community.[10]

According to the surveys, the goal of the movement is simple yet revolutionary. One respondent summarized it as the "growth of Christianity via decentralized church by reproduction of small house churches." Another survey said that reproduction of believers and groups is a "strategic function but is as natural as worship."

Alan Hirsch says that if you want to learn to play chess, the best way to do it is to remove the queen. When you do that, you learn to value and use all the other pieces. You become more holistic in your approach and less dependent on the "big thing." For Cole and organic churches, that queen is the Sunday morning experience—big, smooth, excellent and attractive. They believe that when the queen is removed, everyone else is empowered, and the kingdom of God will be better for it.

A Brief History of the House Church

The New Testament church was primarily a house-church movement. If the 5,000 men counted in Acts 4:4 represented 5,000 households and included women and children in the total number of converts, there could easily have been up to 25,000 in the Jerusalem church! Obviously, this megachurch couldn't possibly meet in one house but assembled in many different households. Thus, it would be considered a house church—the first "mega-house church."

House churches have existed since the days of the Early Church. Early Christian communities met in homes for centuries, not just the first few decades (the first known church building was not built until A.D. 201). Many continued to meet in homes even after the Roman Empire legalized Christianity in A.D. 313. This practice continued among Christian groups on the margins of society.

During the Middle Ages, Brethren of the Common Life gathered in homes to worship all over Europe. Many feel it was these house churches that were the foundation for both the Renaissance and the Reformation.[11]

Many Christians in America know only a little about house churches. They've heard something about the amazing growth of Christianity behind China's Bamboo Curtain. There are reports of more than 80 million believers in the underground church that meet in homes.[12] Some say there are more than 100 million believers in house churches!

When the Bamboo Curtain was slammed closed in 1947 against any Western influence—especially the Church—many observers felt that the world's largest nation was a spiritually lost cause until a time when China would reopen to outside influence. Yet in the 60 subsequent years, the Chinese house church has exploded exponentially. God did it without Western missionaries, Western money or Western guidance (but perhaps with the support of many Western-originated prayers). These house churches continue to grow without seminary-trained pastors, church buildings, denominational programs, Sunday School resources, and so forth. In many cases, they didn't even have a Bible; in some places, a single Bible was "loaned" from church to church![13]

In Bangladesh, thousands of new believers meet in Issu houses (Jesus houses) every Friday to sing about Jesus and pray to the Father through Jesus. In this dominant Islamic culture, they still dress according to Islamic traditions, but they gather on the Islamic holy day to worship Jesus in house churches.

These examples only begin to illustrate something that has been happening for two millennia. *Koinos churches* have been on the margins of Church and culture since the founding of the Church, and now they are growing in prominence in North America.

The House Church as Community

Most Christians in America would think very few house churches exist in the United States. Most would be absolutely shocked if they knew the full scope of the movement across America. The anti-organizational nature of people in many house churches makes it impossible to find them and count them. A Google search on the Internet lists at least 200 house-church organizations (individual house churches tied loosely together). Mike Steele, Director of DAWN (Disciple a Whole Nation), identifies almost 150 *networks* of house churches, each comprising many individual churches. For example, the Xenos Fellowship of Columbus, Ohio, has more than 110 house churches in that regional area.

One of the primary places where *Koinos church* enthusiasm is occurring is in Denver, Colorado. It is hard to know why, but perhaps the culture there is one of extremes—a Focus on the Family evangelicalism alongside hard-core cultural postmodernity. Thus, many who have rejected the values of the modern family and Church are not being reached by the megachurches of Colorado. Instead, they are being reached by alternative faith communities like house churches.

Why do individuals leave the institutional church to join smaller house churches? What brings them to seek the face-to-face community of a *Koinos* church? Usually they do so in a desire to experience closer fellowship with other believers. Some have left the large megachurch or the urban downtown church;

others have left the average neighborhood church. But one of the main reasons they leave is because they are looking for greater spiritual intimacy with others.

The following seven characteristics of a house church describe some of the spiritual dynamics that make a house church appealing to disenfranchised church members or to those who have never been in a church. This is not to say that all house churches meet these descriptions. On the contrary, there are many streams of the house-church movement—some charismatic, some focused on home school and home birth, some following a specific teacher, and some simply adrift doctrinally and spiritually. However, when we describe house churches, we are describing what we see as a *biblically faithful model* of such.

1. House Churches Are Communities of Convictions

When people become a part of a Christian community, they usually affirm their faith through an "interacted identity" with the faith-experience of the house-church community. They learn what the others in the group believe and experience the values and attitudes of others. But most important, they open themselves to life-changing situations that others have experienced. They become "one" with the house-church community—often at a greater level than that which occurs in larger facility-based churches.

Most house churches are not held together by written principles, and most do not have detailed standards of conduct or ask new members to sign a covenant or pledge. Rather, people typically become members of the community as they interact with the values and attitudes of other believers in the church. Hence, everyone in a house church grows into a deep commitment to the values and experiences of one another. In this sense, house churches become *communities of conviction*. They have a shared sense of how to live for God as they learn it from others. In a broader sense, this community of conviction is what makes a house church attractive to new members.

2. House Churches Are Learning Communities

Those who join a house church find a sense of family or oneness with other people and feel that they're a part of a faith-based community. They may even describe it as a "Christ-centered community."

The very nature of community is a shared experience of oneness by its members. Community is realized when all Christians share and then reciprocate by blessing and being blessed by others. Given the isolated nature of most individuals, those joining a house church open their lives to those in the community as others in the church relationally open up to them.

Oneness, *community*, is possible because each person has had the same profound experience in that he or she has met Jesus Christ, has become born-again and understands what is involved in that experience. Because they understand each other's inner life (those experiences they can't necessarily verbalize), they are able to interact with one another and learn from one another.

3. House Churches Are Faith-Formation Communities

Often, American Christians think they must learn faith in a classroom where a teacher communicates or explains a doctrinal statement. They may even imagine a schoolroom practice of students studying such a statement and committing it to memory. However, this educational process does not usually make that doctrine part of their lives.

The New Testament uses "faith" as both a noun and a verb. When faith is used as a noun, it is a reference to a doctrinal statement of faith—a concept to internalize. When faith is used as a verb, it suggests action, such as *trusting* in God, *obeying* His Word, and so forth.

Most house churches do not ask members to sign a doctrinal statement of faith, nor do they usually teach their beliefs in structured classes. Correct doctrinal faith (the noun) is acquired as a member exercises inner faith (the verb). These occur as facets of a person's overall response to God.

Both living faith and doctrinal faith are important and necessary. However, which comes first? In house-church contexts, living faith that is nurtured in a community comes first.

Usually, a person's faith is formed through reading the Scriptures, "then faith [comes] by hearing, and hearing by the word of God" (Rom. 10:17, *NKJV*). But a person also gains faith through interacting with God. When the formation of faith occurs in community, new believers observe older believers following Jesus Christ and, in the same way, they follow Jesus Christ. Many young believers see the older believers step out in faith, and they follow the same example. Thus, their faith is both formed and nurtured in community under the influence of others.

In community, young believers typically grow in their desire to serve God, and they begin to find places to serve Him. Usually, they start with small tasks in a house church and then grow to greater areas of responsibility and accountability. Therefore, it is in community that young believers discover their spiritual gifts and calling.

4. House Churches Are Value-Formation Communities

As the community becomes important to a new believer, its values become contagious. New believers find themselves aligning with others in the group. If others in the group model honesty in their business dealings, the new believers begin to value honesty. The same happens with purity of heart, obedience to God and service to other people. Taken together, these values create a sense of self-identity: I am a *follower* of Jesus Christ. Over time, these values help people discover how they are growing: I am a *fully committed* follower of Jesus Christ.

5. House Churches Are Mentoring Agents

When new Christians enter a house church, they are not initially taught what to believe nor are they taught how to practice the Christian life. These values and attitudes are assimilated through observation and non-verbal experiences, usually through one-on-one relationships. These mentoring relationships are need-driven rather than driven by the study of a prepared curriculum.

Because most house churches see themselves as a close-knit extended family, they often do not have formal statements of faith and practice—any more than we do with our biological families. New believers are accepted for who they are but soon feel pressure (and hopefully *desire*) to assume the attitudes of others in the house church, to live the way others are living and to prize the things the others value. As a result, it's usually not any one individual who leads them into acceptance in the house church; it is the community as a whole that becomes the mentoring agent.

6. House Churches Are "Belonging" Communities

The house church offers a network in which new Christians feel recognized for who they are as well as for who they are becoming in Christ. Therefore, the house-church community becomes a powerful focus for influencing the lives of new believers. In mentoring, the house-church community accomplishes two things: First, the house church, by its very nature of community, challenges new believers to enter into their shared experience; and second, the house-church community is supportive of its members no matter where they are in their spiritual pilgrimage of faith.

7. House Churches Give Self-identity

Just because people give themselves to community doesn't mean they lose their self-identity or sense of belonging. They still have other loyalties outside the house church that may not be related to the values of the house church.

Although community begins with the "born-again experience," this doesn't mean that every person in a house church will always agree with other believers in every aspect of life. However, because regeneration influences the central things valued in life and the principles under which Christians live, everyone in a house church who has had a similar experience shares those values and attitudes.

Community encourages hospitality. Each member of a house church serves one another, respects one another and, in a true sense of the Scriptures, loves one another. This means they accept each other as unique individuals within the community. As a result, there is freedom in community and, at the same time, there is oneness in the community.

Because those in a house church experience community, they seldom indoctrinate people to their doctrinal statement. Most house churches do not have a written creed or confessional. They do not demand agreement in order to become a part of the community, nor do they attempt to force everyone in the community to accept all of the tenets of their doctrinal position. This is because they realize that community is a greater "glue" that bonds them together than the glue of a doctrinal statement. Therefore, the community recognizes and values each other's individuality and personhood.

Kinds of House Churches

Many different attraction points draw people to the house church, and all kinds of glue causes them to stay, or "stick." Part

of the challenge with categorizing the house church is that many
readers of this book have already met people in a house church
and have discovered that certain members can seem a bit odd at
times. We have met house-church people who, for example, make
their own clothes, store food and firearms in their basement,
deliver newborn babies in their bathtub—and feel like doing
house churches is perfectly normal. (We are not sure if such
unusual ideas and lifestyles lead to the house church or the house
church leads to these more offbeat ideas . . . more on that later!)

There has been a tendency to call the recent proliferation of
house churches a "movement," but that term would be mis-
leading. The reason is because there are currently too many
variables and too few unifying principles within this approach
to doing church. If you look up "house-church groups" on the
Internet, you find a variety of issues that initiated them. They
include "deeper life" teachings, home schooling, separation
issues, anger with established churches, Pentecostal theology,
and even, yes, home birthing. We propose the following five
major categories of organic churches:

1. *Separatists:* These are groups that have come into
   existence because they hope to establish a culture
   that is distinct and separate from the world around
   them. This is evident in the groups that insist on
   home schooling and home births. Some of these
   groups look to ministries such as Bill Gothard's to
   gain insight for living separately from the world.

2. *Anti-establishment:* These are groups that hold a
   moderate to severe disdain for what is seen as a traditionally established church. Some are just plain
   angry, some are dissatisfied, and some are simply
   on a positive mission to do things differently. The

thought of a formal structure, building and hierar-
chy are anathema to them. They feel that the churches are adulterated and God is calling for a renewed
format of the church that involves owning no prop-
erty and having no programmatic structure. T. Austin
Sparks, a significant figure in this movement,
wrote, "What is the Church? It is Christ in living
union with His own. That is the Church."[14] Other important figures in this movement are Gene Edwards,
George Warnock, the Latter Rain movement and
Sam Fife.

3. *Deeper Understanding:* These are groups with thought
   leaders that include Watchman Nee and Witness Lee.
   The Living Stream Ministry also exists to perpetuate
   the teachings of these two men. In fact, they have
   even produced *The Recovery Version Bible* to spread
   their message. When reading Nee's and Lee's writings, there are similarities in that they call for home
   groups operating with prophesy, reading the Word
   in prayer sessions, and everyone participating in the
   speaking of truths to one another. In this final char-
   acteristic, they are much like Quakers.

4. *Expositional/Issue Group:* These groups are often
   barely more than a home Bible study. They may state
   their purpose as one of unraveling the mysteries of
   Scripture, but it is more likely a soapbox format for
   the leader of the group to air his or her opinions
   and debate the merits of others' perspectives who
   are not present in the study. The emphases of these
   groups range from end-time prophecy to various
   charismatic doctrines. In general, these groups

give little priority to reproducing themselves through other house groups.

5. *Spontaneous:* Some house churches aren't reacting against anything, nor are they following anyone's specific lead. Like other house churches, they say that they have sprung up by the sovereign hand of God, in this case because people simply like to meet and discuss spiritual matters, and finding a house-church environment is the most workable way to do so. Some of these groups include mature believers who can guide others to salvation in Christ, but some do not.

As you can see, there are many kinds of house churches. Not all are orthodox, nor are they filled with single-issue people—and it would be a mistake to place all house churches in any one category.[15]

What Can We Learn from Organic House Churches?

What can we learn from the house church? That may seem like an odd question, because for the first two centuries of Christianity (some would say its best two centuries) no other option existed. *All* believers met in homes, lived in biblical community and functioned relationally. The more important question today is what we need to *relearn* from house churches about church.

Let us challenge your thinking. Which of the following is more likely to see his or her life transformed by the power of the gospel: someone who attends church in a neighbors' home, lives life together with them in an accountability relationship and is intricately connected in each other's lives, or someone who attends the typical American facility-based church?

Here is how one house-church leader describes the community:

First, everyone in the church knows one another. And
quite well. We spend time together outside of religious
meetings. There is a fraternity of sorts among us. We are
like family in many ways . . . [E]veryone is free to lead a
song or request a song . . . [T]he ministry comes from
anyone who wishes to share . . . [A]nyone can ask a
question or add an insight when someone else is sharing.
This happens quite frequently and it is spontaneous and
very edifying . . . [W]e realize that all of us are responsible
to care for one another (we are the church). We make
decisions together as a Body. We plan our meetings, our
activities, and we decide how to handle our problems. We
decide how to use the money we give . . . [W]e exhort
one another in our meetings . . . My spiritual growth is
dependent on an entire Body of believers who minister
the Lord to me every week . . . We fellowship throughout
the week, and we mutually encourage each other.[16]

Conversely, the definition of "success" in the typical American
church is to lead a new believer to come to church, give a tithe
and take on a job assisting somehow in the church's ministry.
Most of our discipleship processes are intended to produce
those three things. They are important, but they can (and often
do) occur without the necessity of a life-changing impact within the Christian.

Something is wrong when the typical American Christian
does not experience powerful life change when encountering the
power of the gospel and the church. Yet, sadly, mediocrity happens more often than transformation. Those Christians who are
not part of the house-church movement can learn much from it:
Community is a central value of the church, discipleship is not a

class but a lifestyle in community, and authenticity requires community—not just sitting face forward listening to the dynamic communicator *du jour*.

Beyond the obvious lesson of needing more and better small groups, we would suggest several other lessons to learn and to discern from the house church:

- *The Christian life is more naturally lived in an authentic community.* The Christian faith is not a decision, class and membership card. For decades, Christians have talked about building community—and they probably have less community now than they did during the peak of the Sunday School movement of 50 years ago. Most small-group gurus would probably admit if pressed that small groups are not working as promised. We must find new ways to build community in established churches. (We think Randy Frazee has some good ideas to consider in his book *The Connecting Church*.[17])

- *Churches need to make a decision to create community.* Most churches simply have not paid the price necessary to build true community. Instead, many churches seem to work hard to make community impossible— well-intentioned programs that lack relational components, families separated for activities, expectations that a different family member will come out to church every night. It is difficult to live life together when your life is lived in non-relational programs and activities. Some churches have begun to realize that they need to stop doing certain things in order to do community well. Some have reduced their focus to two things: celebrative worship and cells in homes.

House churches have combined those into one experience—not a bad idea.

• *Church is way too complicated.* Tony and Felicity Dale call their approach "simple church." The term is appealing because most churches are far from simple—they are filled with committees, long-term plans, budget needs, and so on. Churches must find a way to become simple disciple-making communities, not large bureaucracies to perpetuate themselves. The church is not the end; it is God's chosen means to an end: the transformation of life by the power of the gospel. It needs to be simple enough to accomplish God's objective and complicated enough to follow the biblical teaching regarding how to accomplish it. (A helpful resource is the book *Simple Church* by Thom Rainer and Eric Geiger.[18])

• *We should not defend a system that produces such poor results.* With American Christianity as anemic as it is, it seems odd that some are afraid of the house church. It makes no sense to defend what is too often a dying and unproductive church. Christians need to learn that God can work through the house church again—particularly as we have moved into an emerging culture where anyone and everyone can be a spiritual leader. As we break down the unbiblical distinction between clergy and laity, we can see a new and more effective form of church birthed.

What We Need to Consider

As we write about the house church, we are excited about what God is doing. We also admire Christians who are willing to sacrifice the comforts of today's building-based church. The Constantinian model of Building + Clergy + Program = Church neither stands up to the biblical picture nor to the test of mission, and it has not led to a more godly culture or more godly people.

Is the house church the answer? Possibly. But there are challenges that need to be considered. First, there are 34 Western industrialized democracies with missionaries trying to catalyze a house-church movement, and so far none have broken through among majority peoples. There are many reports of church-planting movements in the West (as David Garrison described in his pamphlet and book *Church Planting Movements*[19]), but so far none stand up to scrutiny. As observers of the Church, we want and need to find that one breakthrough to report so that we can rally others to the cause. If house church is the tool God is using, more people need to know of it. Yet reports of such movements have always proven to be driven more by enthusiasm than by actual breakthroughs.

In a Western culture like ours in America, most people have become accustomed to a culture of specialization. We live in a post-labor era and segmented society. When your car breaks down, you go to your mechanic. When you are sick, you make an appointment to see a doctor. When you need legal help, you consult a lawyer. When you need spiritual guidance, well, you don't go to your mechanic. Instead, most people find a religious "professional." Furthermore, when Christians have the economic ability and freedom to do so, they tend to sit under more and more skilled leadership in larger and larger groups. That is a cultural reality, not just a skewed theology of clergy and laity. House churches simply have yet to make a great impact, not just because the establishment Church opposes them, but also because the culture is not quite accustomed or accommodating to the idea.

Some of the other challenges are a little more obvious. House churches tend to have more theological problems. (Obviously, institutional churches have their share!) Christians can, and should, trust the Holy Spirit and His missionary methods, but we have also observed that many Christians with odd theological beliefs seem to be attracted to house churches. (We believe that it is more likely that people with odd beliefs may be attracted to house churches rather than that house churches produce odd beliefs.)

We also believe there are elements of biblical church that are missing from many house-church models. For example, the fact that too many churches have poor leadership and institutional clergy does not mean that the Bible does not give guidance about the biblical roles of elder/pastor and deacon. If these did not matter, why does the New Testament give so much detail about leadership to the house churches of early Christianity?

Also, as important as community is, it is not the same as *covenant*. In the New Testament, the believers covenanted with each other in communities of faith. There was community, and even unbelievers were welcomed there. However, there was covenant community—and the Bible taught that people were to be removed (see 1 Cor. 5:9; 2 Cor. 2:6) and then readmitted (see 2 Cor. 2:7-8) to the covenant community.

Other concerns are important—the use of biblical ordinances, for example. The issue is simple: Much of what the Bible *describes* (particularly when it goes into great detail on subjects such as leadership, ordinances, discipline, covenant, and so forth) is *prescribed* because it is assumed as part of the Early Church. These prescriptions are not relics of the modern era; they're teachings birthed from the house churches of the New Testament. Thus, they are applicable to every church, then and now.

God Is Using the House Church

Make no mistake, God is using the house church. We want to tell that story. We also want you to consider your own church. Would people find the kind of community they need or desire in your church? Have you become a *koinos* community, living face to face and in common relationships? How can you tell?

If people in your church require prompting and nagging to care for each other, you may have a *system* of pastoral care but not a *community* of people who care. There is an important difference. People are not looking for a friendly church; they are looking for friends. People are not looking for a statement about caring; they are looking for caring friends. The church should be the place most people think of as a place of caring.

If our churches could become places of biblical and authentic community, the change would be significant and would have a powerful impact. If we live in community, we truly become a place where people are drawn to us and to Christ. We become much like what we teach our children in second grade Sunday School: "A new commandment I give to you, that you love one another; as I have loved you, that you also love one another. By this all will know that you are My disciples, if you have love for one another" (John 13:34-35). If that is done well in a house church, we rejoice. But if it is not done in your church and mine, we have not yet truly become a biblical church with real community, whether we meet in a house or in a brick megachurch.

CHAPTER 2

RECOVERY CHURCHES

He gives us more grace. That is why Scripture says:
"God opposes the proud but gives grace to the humble."
JAMES 4:6, *NIV*

Dale Ryan describes his upbringing as that of a nice kid raised
in a nice home that worshiped each week in a nice church. Ryan
earned a Ph.D. in biochemistry, but early in his career he sensed
a call of God to ministry, so he went to seminary.

As he prepared to graduate, Ryan recalls telling his wife,
"I'm looking for a nice church where nice people will be nice to
the nice pastor—and everything will be nice!" They both chuck-
led, but there was also an element of seriousness in his goal.

He did indeed find a church that looked just like what he
hoped. Mattel's Barbie and Ken would have fit in just fine. Even
the church facility looked nice, with a golf course across the street.

However, within the first hours of Ryan's first day as a pastor, he received a phone call about a sex abuse situation within one of the families of the church. Before the week was out,
he learned of another family privately struggling with alcohol.
The next week he encountered an issue of addiction to prescription drugs.

"It didn't take me long to suspect that something sys-
temic was going on," he says. As he looked around, however,
he couldn't find many resources to address all these hidden
pains. At one point his church sent out their volunteer hand

bell choir director to a two-week school. She came back equipped to lead the group—and eager to go to advanced training the next year. "I was frustrated to learn that there are far more resources for training someone to be a hand bell choir leader than to lead a recovery group!" Ryan lamented.

Like many Christian leaders, Ryan thought the addiction issues were limited to other people. Then he began to discover that he too had serious issues with anger, codependency, lack of vulnerability, and greater comfort in working from strength, rather than living by Jesus' Word that "My power is strongest when you are weak" (2 Cor. 12:9).

"Eventually, I realized I was too full of resentment to be a nice pastor. I too was damaged," Ryan said. "My passions were different from Jesus' passion. Most studies of sexual abuse project that 25 to 30 percent of women in any given church are victims of sex abuse. What would the Christian community look like if Jesus' followers made the at-risk harvest its central priority?"

One passage that hit home for Ryan was Luke 10:1-12, which describes Jesus' training plan before he sent out 72 of His followers. Verse 2 describes the basic condition under which all ministry takes place: "A large crop is in the fields, but there are only a few workers. Ask the Lord in charge of the harvest to send out workers to bring it in." What is Ryan's translation for "recovery ministry"? "Seas of addictions exist," he says. "Pain is everywhere. Every place in the world has a drunk tank. It is not hard to find people in recovery—a harvest that is clearly at risk. Too many churches don't even think about how many problem drinkers, drug abusers, or other addictions exist in their community—or in their own churches. Don't just look for it. Instead, ask God to send out workers—perhaps starting with you."

Today Ryan is Professor of Recovery at Fuller Seminary. In 1989 he founded the National Association of Christian Recovery (www.nacronline.com).

What's the Innovation?

While the name "recovery church" is new, the embryonic ministry is not. The Salvation Army, which began in 1865, was basically an attractional ministry (see chapter 11) using uniforms, martial music and military terminology to attract the neglected slum-dwellers of London. However, their original recovery ministry involved hospitals, homes for the unwed, shelters, rehabilitation centers for the homeless, prison work, and emergency disaster services. An early statement of purpose said social welfare services were provided for all persons, regardless of race, color, religion or depth of depravity—"church for the churchless."[1]

It seems like the church has always dealt with the alcohol issue. Perhaps it came to a head in the early 1900s with the establishment of rescue missions in the major cities of America. Its prominent focus was the Nineteenth Amendment of the Constitution that prohibited the manufacturing and sale of alcohol. The corporate American conscience concluded that alcohol addiction hurt families, especially the children.

Also, church groups have been famous for ministries to pregnant girls. This was perhaps the door that led to churches helping people with sexual addiction. However, recently an entire literature genre on addiction and codependency in general, and a willingness to talk openly about it, seems to have exploded in America much more than issues of alcohol and sexual addiction. Today people talk about addiction to work, drugs, Internet, pornography, food, sports and probably a dozen more "acceptable" things that become abusive to individuals when they are unable to control themselves and operate as healthy human beings.

Why so much addiction in the twenty-first century? Some say the lack of moral purpose by American individuals has resulted in a moral vacuum within the heart. And of course, all nature abhors a vacuum, so Americans fill it with habits that become addictive. Others would say that as the church loses its impact on our nation, American individuals lose their moral compass and cause addictions. Still others would say the Holy Spirit is being removed in these latter days before Christ returns (see 2 Tim 3:1-7; 1 Tim 4:1-3), hence, the light of God in the world is reduced so that darkness rushes in like a flood. Still others say addiction comes from more prosperity and a social acceptance of hedonism—doing what feels good.

As the explosive Freedom in Christ (www.FreedomIn Christ.com) ministry of Neil Anderson, author of such bestsellers as *The Bondage Breaker,* illustrates, addiction issues point to a huge cancer—not just in society, but also within the church.[2]

Churches *with* Recovery Ministry

Gil Smith grew up as a pastor's kid in a home where alcohol consumption was never a welcome guest. At age 15, however, some new friends offered him beer, and he accepted in order to belong. "That choice set me on a 33-year odyssey," Smith says. He quickly began to abuse alcohol and drugs, developing dependency and addiction even while graduating from seminary and serving as a local pastor.

In 1982, he informed his congregation of his "little" problem and entered the hospital, explaining that his doctor wanted him to be monitored during withdrawal from the painkillers. Looking back, he admits that his statement was a lie. "I should have come clean and said that I was taking about 30 prescription pills a day, that I have a serious addiction, and that I had become a fraud as a pastor," he says.

Smith's life continued its downward spiral. Stripped of his ministry credentials and defrocked, he entered a halfway house in Atlanta and got a job washing dishes and cleaning bathrooms at a Waffle House. During one of his lowest days, life began to change. He simply wanted to live. God's grace became his only gift, but it was enough!

He returned home by bus and checked into the Salvation Army as a homeless man. He then turned to Steve Sallee, a minister friend from seminary days. Sallee took Smith in, allowing him to live in the church building. The church loved him unconditionally and walked with him through his recovery. Smith stayed there three months, worked for a car dealer, and finally got a one-room apartment and a $750 car. Day by day, and grace upon grace, Smith began to recover and heal.

Today Smith heads a Christ-centered recovery ministry at that same church, Cokesbury United Methodist Church, in Knoxville, Tennessee. It is one of the largest in the country, drawing more than 500 people weekly to its meetings on Thursday nights.

"I offer an altar call every week," Smith comments. "It's usually full of people crying, holding on to each other, praying sobbing and laughing. We're living proof that there all broken people have hope and that God's grace is for real."

Slow, Steady Growth in Recovery Ministry

Smith's congregation is one of an estimated 2 percent of churches across the United States that help support at least one recovery-related group beyond merely providing space.

Recovery ministry is no longer a second-class, hide-them-in-the-basement affair. It has been steadily validated by a progression of Christian psychologists such as Clyde Narramore; clinics such as Rapha and Minerth-Meier; pastors such as David Seamands, author of *Healing for Damaged Emotions*; and high-visibility churches such as Saddleback Church in Lake Forest, California. Since 2004, Bible publishers have been promoting recovery Bibles containing verse highlights and testimonies of Christians struggling with various recovery-related issues.

Churches that Teach Recovery Ministry

Perhaps the highest-visibility recovery ministry today comes from Saddleback Church. The church has created a transferable curriculum called "Celebrate Recovery" and offers helpful conferences to train people in how to use it. Celebrate Recovery employs the Purpose Driven Church strategy that attracts and wins the unchurched, develops them to spiritual maturity, equips them for ministry, and helps them establish a life mission in the world.

Celebrate Recovery is the brainchild of John Baker, a staff pastor at Saddleback and a recovering alcoholic. Frustrated that he didn't feel comfortable talking about Jesus in A.A. meetings, his idea was to create a recovery program centered on the teachings of Jesus. The result was "Eight Recovery Principles" based on the Eight Beatitudes (see Matt. 5:3-10). These principles, together with the Twelve Steps from Alcoholics Anonymous, form the core of Celebrate Recovery.

Celebrate Recovery bills itself as an aid for people with "hurts, habits and hang-ups" of all stripes. Unlike specific Twelve Step groups—Alcoholics Anonymous, Gamblers Anonymous, Overeaters Anonymous, and so forth—Celebrate Recovery takes in people with problems across the board. Those with anger issues sit next to those who overwork, those who struggle with negative thinking and those addicted to alcohol, drugs or sex. "We are all broken," says Baker, on the Celebrate Recovery website. "We have all sinned. We have all missed the mark."[3]

A.A. participants identify themselves by saying, "My name is . . . and I'm an alcoholic." At Celebrate Recovery, however, they say, "My name is . . . and I'm a believer who struggles with alcohol."

In a two-hour Celebrate Recovery meeting, the first 45 minutes bring men and women together for worship and singing, followed by testimony from participants. Then the men and women separate into small groups, each with a leader, for 45 minutes of discussion of the Twelve Steps and the Eight Principles. Afterward, everyone gathers again for 30 minutes of socializing.

Saddleback's program launched with 43 people in 1991. As it grew, some 70 percent of its members came from outside the church. Eighty-five percent of the people who go through the program stay with the church and nearly half serve as church volunteers.

Churches that *Are* Recovery Churches

Some churches focus entirely on recovery. If you visit NorthStar Community, Richmond, Virginia, for example, you'll notice that everything about the gathering is shaped with the recovery community in mind. Yes, you'll encounter singing, teaching, children's ministry, ushers and other external evidences that this is a church, but curiously, you'll also notice that the church is named "community" rather than "church." More telling, the back cover of the printed worship bulletin of Northstar Community contains an adapted version of the Twelve Steps of AA. Even more overtly, the teaching is gospel-centered and constantly applies the Bible to day-to-day life, but it does so by consistently referencing one of the Twelve Steps.

"We're focusing this week on step four, and here is how God's Word can help," you might hear. From song selection to Bible application, it's as if almost everyone in the congregation is in recovery and wanting God's perspective on doing so—and indeed that is exactly the case. "Most of us are recovering from something," says Teresa McBean, who started the church as an outreach ministry of nearby Bon Air Baptist Church. "Overworking, overspending, fear, anxiety, addictions, perfectionism, gambling, overeating, grief, divorce, codependency, lying, anger, guilt, abuse, insecurity, hurtful relationships or something else."

The church has a tremendous outreach to the unchurched but also to long-time members of more traditional churches, which McBean calls the "church wounded." Adds McBean, "We are a really mixed bag of believers, searchers, and even those who are defensive and hostile toward church. Our common mark is coming to belong, and maybe along the way (we trust) coming also to believe."[4]

Smaller Churches Can Do Recovery

Can smaller churches offer recovery groups? "Absolutely," says Dale Ryan, "but you do it differently." One strategy is to constantly provide access to resources. Churches like this post sheets with locations of where various groups meet across town. The women's bathroom stalls have small cards with the phone number to the hotline for the battered women's shelter, and the name and number of a Christian counselor.

Ryan tells the story of a conference he led to teach smaller churches how to become recovery friendly. "I need help," one pastor confided to Ryan as the seminar was ending. "I'm in a church where moving the Communion table three feet will get me fired. I can't change anything. How can I develop a recovery ministry?"

Ryan chatted with him to ask if the man had any area of freedom in the worship services. "None," the man replied. Then almost as a joke he added, "Well, we do have a few moments for announcements, but I simply could not announce anything about a recovery group at that time. Besides no one listens to them anyway." They brainstormed together and decided that the pastor would change the greeting just once.

The next week the pastor included this statement in his announcement: "I went to a workshop this week and learned that a lot of people who come to church have deep hurts from the past. So I want to thank you for trusting us for coming here today."

To his surprise, people started calling him, not to complain, but to ask for help. "I don't know what to say, so I referred them," he told Ryan. Six months later he had a support group for survivors of sex abuse. It took years to develop a stable leadership team, but an irreversible step happened when he spoke the truth in a vulnerable way at a time when he thought no one would notice.

This pastor inadvertently empowered the grassroots. That's what can happen in a church of any size. Today, more than ever, the models and resources are available for any church to take the next step in developing a healthy recovery ministry.

"After all," says Ryan, "recovery at heart is simply hurting people helping other hurting people, a value that is one of God's central purposes for His church."

Things We Should Consider

Recovery churches are a diverse lot. Some do recovery ministry well, while others are actually built around recovery ministry. We think *all* churches should consider the former, and God might lead some to the latter. The gospel is all about recovery. The biblical kind of recovery, however, is not the same as the general recovery movement. Yes, we can admit that we are powerless over our addiction, just as in the recovery movement, but our addiction is bigger than just one sin. It is a life lived apart from God, and even in hostility toward God.

The recovery movement does reflect a reality that is helpful. To use Saddleback's phrase, all of us have hurts, habits and hang-ups that need help. The answer to struggles and problems is God in Christ, not some amorphous "higher power."

It should not surprise us that Christ-centered recovery programs are more effective than secular ones. It is the power of
Christ that truly changes lives. Several scientific studies have
shown the difference, including a study comparing Teen
Challenge to a control group of secular programs. The results
were clear and consistent:

Prevalence of Pretreatment Frequent Drug Usage in Teen Challenge Sample and Matched Comparison Group

(For alcohol, percent daily use during year before program; for other drugs, percent weekly use during year before program)[5]

Drug	Teen Challenge	Comparison Group
Cocaine	57.6	45.9
Alcohol	55.9	30.1
Marijuana	49.1	37.1
Stimulants	15.3	4.8
Hallucinogens	15.3	5.6
Opiates	10.2	5.6
Tranquilizers	10.2	13.0
Painkillers	6.8	12.8
Barbiturates	3.4	10.5
Other Drugs	5.1	0.0

Churches Need to Recognize that Most People Have Deep-seated Hurts, Challenges and Needs

It surprises many pastors and church leaders to discover just
how many problems people have. It's naïve to think that the better people look on the outside, the more their lives are in order.
Instead, with money and education, people merely become bet-

ter skilled at masking their issues. Recovery churches can minister to the whole person—since all of us are filled with needs.

Many pastors have been surprised to see how many people in their church are struggling with major issues. A line from the movie *Black Hawk Down* might be illustrative. The crusty Lt. Col. Danny McKnight sees the Humvee filled with blood and wounded soldiers, some of whom are dying. He points to Private Othic and yells, "You, get up there and drive!" Othic responds, "But I'm shot, Colonel!" McKnight's response is a metaphor for life: "Everybody's shot! Drive!" Recovery churches teach us that we live in a fallen world where "Everybody's shot."

For Too Long, Churches Have Not Recognized Deeper Issues

For a long time, churches made the assumption that if people just got "saved" their lives would be all "fixed." The irony is that most adults come to Christ because of a personal crisis, yet the church is not able to deal with the crises when they come for help.

Dan Morgan helped develop Saddleback's new-believer program. Morgan correctly points out that new believers need stability in three areas: spiritual stability, relational stability and functional stability. Churches often hold classes that provide the right teaching for spiritual training and connect people relationally. However, few help the new believer who just hit rock bottom from alcohol, just got divorced, or just lost a family member to a tragedy. Though these things often force a spiritual life change, most churches are unprepared to help new believers through the tumultuous changes to come. A financial bankruptcy may cause a crisis that leads a woman to faith in Christ, but she is still bankrupt after she meets Jesus. Many churches have found an answer in recovery ministry.

Sin Is a Complicated Issue

Not all recovery issues involve sin problems, but some do, and some sins are harder to overcome than others. Scripture often calls these "besetting sins." The reality is that it often takes steps, friends, time and commitment to overcome certain sins that beset us in life. Recovery churches have learned and applied these scriptural truths.

Pain Is Bigger Than Most of Us Think

Unless you have been through some of the pain associated with recovery ministries, the challenges can be difficult to understand. Many people wonder, "Why can't you just get over it?" The reality is that some things you don't "just get over" but instead have to work through. Working through such issues alongside God's people and in the power of the Holy Spirit can be a transforming experience.

Things We Should Be Concerned About

There are certainly challenges to consider about recovery ministries and recovery churches. Recovery ministries have historically not been connected to churches because churches, unfortunately, did not consider them necessary. The church believed that special programs for recovery were not needed because everyone was transformed by supernatural conversion. The past era's emphasis on regeneration that transformed new believers was thought to be enough to break alcohol, anger, or any other addiction. Some would ask, If our churches truly emphasized transforming regeneration, maybe we could minimize recovery programs?

Do Recovery Ministries Justify Sin?

It is an awkward question to ask, but when we call sin a "disease," do we justify sin? It is a hard question. Scientific studies have postulated some perceived links between alcoholism dependency and genetics. The Bible calls drunkenness a sin. Can it be both?

Theology recognizes that we all have a propensity toward sin, some toward one sin and some toward others. Propensity, however, does not mean activity. Good recovery churches and ministries recognize that we might have a propensity toward certain sins, but the cross covers all sin—even those of addictions. That's the point—we are powerless over them, but God is not.

Some Recovery Ministries Can Enable Rather Than Transform
In more than one case, people in recovery can use their recovery ministry to enable their struggle rather than to deal with it. If people confuse sin with disease and go to meetings where others reinforce that view, it can be easier to get "sick" again. The best recovery ministries hold each other accountable to get better in every sense of the word.

Churches Can Segregate Themselves If They Become Recovery Churches
Churches are known for many things—and this includes helping people out of sin and issues of hurt. Those churches that focus heavily on recovery need to make it clear that they are a welcoming place for *all* people, not just for those whose lifestyles have been affected, such as the alcoholic who cannot hold a steady job or whose chain smoking fills the church parking lot with cigarette butts. We all have needs, and we all need each other. Those without those pasts or addictions need to journey with those who still have them.

Combining Spirituality with Recovery

Recovery groups generally trace their roots to Alcoholics Anonymous. Interestingly enough, Alcoholics Anonymous was greatly influenced by the Oxford Group, a Christian renewal movement. Although the Oxford Group was not without problematic issues, many of the principles of recovery were built from scriptural teachings. Our hope is that they will become more so in the coming years.

CHAPTER 3

MULTI-SITE CHURCHES

And the message of salvation spread like wildfire all through the region.
ACTS 13:49, *THE MESSAGE*

"How can we do a better job of spreading the gospel to those who won't or can't come to our church?" Many churches answer that question with a "both/and" strategy. "Yes, let's do all we can to invite them to join us," they say. "But let's also take church to them." That is the attraction of the multi-site church.

My (Warren's) first exposure to a multi-site church was on a 1992 weekend business trip to California. I wanted to worship with the church that had given birth to the Jesus Movement: Calvary Chapel, in Santa Ana, led by Chuck Smith, Sr. I got there just before the 9:30 morning service, but the place was already packed. People were already congregating outside the sanctuary, peering inside through the full-length windows and listening to the loudspeakers positioned around the outside of the building.

As I walked around, trying to find an available outside seat, I noticed people in an adjoining building that seemed to house their own version of the worship service. There was a gigantic television screen against one wall, with the worship and preaching bigger than life. "This is a lot better than being on the outside edge of the outdoor chair sitters," I immediately decided.

I went in, sat in one of the chairs and noticed that the room was only about half full of chairs. The other half was an open space occupied by what looked to be a small stroller convention. Young mothers were watching the service on the screen while rocking their little ones back and forth in their strollers. Plus many of the moms were also drinking coffee, available from the pot at the rear of the room. "What a great idea!" I remember thinking, which is probably why I recall the experience so vividly even today.

Calvary Chapel had stumbled on an approach that did a great job of meeting a real need. I could imagine a pastor at another church selling the advantages of a similar, specialized worship venue: "Moms and Dads, when you bring your little ones to church, we want to give you the best cry-room arrangement imaginable. We'll give you a separate room off the crowded pathway, easily accessible, filled with potential friends, and supplied in a way that you can worship and grow spiritually while also caring for your baby."

Of course, a church doesn't have to target a niche group like parents who prefer to keep their baby with them rather than use the church nursery. It can videocast the sermon or drama or testimony or vocal artist to any group. Since my Calvary Chapel visit, I've heard of examples ranging from a church at a mall (a community-centered location) to a residential drug rehabilitation center (they're not allowed to leave premises, so why not bring church to them?).

This on-campus approach, which I've seen elsewhere as an *off*-campus approach as well, is today referred to as a "video venue." Most commonly it involves on-site worship, coordination by an on-site campus pastor, and teaching (pre-recorded or live) by videocast. It is one way people are extending their church beyond one location, but it is not the only way.

During my seminary days, my church was multi-site for a year or two without calling it such, embodying what people today call a "low-risk model." Our church building was less than a mile from a low-income housing project, and many at my church felt a spiritual burden to help the housing-project community feel welcome at our church. One approach was to bring Christ to them, so we did a Sunday evening service in the community room of the complex. Aspiring preachers from the nearby seminary, together with others from the congregation, led the services, which consisted of music, testimony and preaching.

The term "low risk" refers to low cost, low amount of administration, and low drain on the sponsoring church. Yet the potential return is high, both in the spiritual response from the housing-project community and also in the lives of the team that conducted the services.

Another church visit exposed me to what is today called a "partnership model" multi-site church. This involves a local church and a community organization establishing more than a simple rental arrangement. The idea is that each contributes to the other's goals. The first time I experienced it was at a church located on a college campus. They weren't renting the auditorium as just another tenant. The school had religious roots and the administration had welcomed the church's presence as a way of developing the whole person—spirit as well as intellect—for students and faculty alike. The school benefited from having the church there, and the church benefited from being located at the school.

Another type of multi-site is known today as a "teaching team" multi-site church. My first personal experience with this model was Mosaic, in downtown Los Angeles. I went to a Sunday morning service (at that time they were meeting in a rented high school), where lead pastor Erwin McManus spoke to a congregation that contained many artists. I also went to a Mosaic Sunday evening service in a rented nightclub, where Erwin's brother Alex McManus was the preacher, speaking to a congregation that contained many college students. It was interesting to compare similarities and differences in the teaching at each location. Both were Mosaic churches, yet each was contextualized to its particular location.

At another church excursion, my wife and I visited one of the Willow Creek regional campus sites in Chicago. We hung out after the service, talking with several couples who had made this their church home. They commented on the far shorter commute time from home to church, but not in a selfish way. "We're thrilled to be so close to where we worship because we're more able now to bring our unchurched friends," one couple said.

Many Models But Similar Goals

The idea of becoming one church in multiple locations is not new. Circuit-riding Methodist pioneer John Wesley did it by horseback back in the 1700s, with his followers doing likewise in the 1800s, helping Methodism spread faster than any other denomination. Methodists started classes that functioned as local churches but were under the oversight of a circuit rider who served several towns.

In the mid-1900s, Jack Hyles did it with buses, which became mobile chapels for thousands of children each week through First Baptist Church of Hammond, Indiana. In the 1970s, Atlanta pastor Paul Walker, profiled in *10 of America's Most Innovative Churches*,[1] did it by car as he finished his sermon at one campus of Mt. Paran Church of God and then raced a few miles to preach at another campus. Today pastors do it with many tools, including digital technology. The "it" is taking church to where the people are, developing multiple venues on one campus or developing two, three, four, or more different campuses.

Multi-site churches today can be found in churches that are urban, suburban and rural. They are represented by mainline churches and non-denominational churches. Leadership Network, which has made a list of more than 1,000 multi-site churches, has found multi-site churches in 49 states—and is confident New Hampshire will soon join the rest![2]

This approach goes by many names and variations: satellite campus, regional campus, extension site, video café, video venue, and others. A congregation that is one church but in many locations has the same core values, mission, administration and budget as a single-site church. Most of all, it presses forward because of an evangelistic heartbeat; a Leadership Network survey found that evangelistic outreach is overwhelmingly the number one reason churches go multi-site.[3] In fact, another Leadership Network survey found that 69 percent of multi-site churches report that by becoming multi-site, they've become *more* evangelistic.[4] As an article in Rick Warren's *Ministry Toolbox* commented, "Starting a second site without a compelling drive behind it is like trying to give birth without being pregnant."[5]

Interest and experimentation in multi-site approaches are mushrooming. In 2003, researcher Thom Rainer asked a random sample of churches across the United States whether they "moved or probably would be moving" in the direction of a multi-campus model. One out of 20 said yes. Two years later he did the same survey, and found that 1 out of 3 said yes.[6] Indeed, the phenomenon is gaining such interest that a Coast to Coast multi-site conference keeps selling out: 200 registrants in 2004, 500 in 2005, and 700 in 2006.[7] As a result of the growing interest across denominations and geographies, one multi-site pastor called it a "multi-site revolution" and wrote a 2006 book using that phrase as his title.[8]

The first book to devote an entire chapter to the multi-site movement is *Beyond the Box: Innovative Churches that Work*. Authors Bill Easum and Dave Travis identify multi-site churches as an approach that gets churches beyond their boxed-in limit. "Within the box, church leaders think location; beyond the box, they think mission. These leaders aren't tethered to one place. They are developing an untethered church. . . . For these congregations, space is never a limitation. Mission, rather than space, determines the agenda."[9]

In short, multi-site summarizes today's approach to church where geography is no longer the defining factor.

Other Churches Look to Join a Multi-site Congregation

The five models listed above, which are developed further in the book *The Multi-Site Church Revolution*, work well for churches that have enough forward momentum to start additional services, additional on-campus venues, or additional off-campus sites. Much good advice exists on how to go from one to two services, such as Elmer Towns's "How to Go to Two Services" kit.[10] Likewise, as outlined in books such as *How to Start a New Service: Your Church Can Reach New People* by W. Charles Arn, many churches have found good results by going with an alternate style service or alternate day service (such as Saturday evening or Sunday evening).[11] More recent books like *The Multi-Site Church Revolution* show how healthy and growing congregations can extend further, to the point of developing an entire movement of replicating campuses.

But what about churches that have experienced long-term decline? Tens of thousands of these exist across the United States. They may be full of good-hearted, praying people, but year after year they cannot find the breakthrough they need to begin a new cycle of spiritual life.

I (Warren) visited with Luke Dudenhoffer, pastor of a church that had been struggling for survival. We met in his church facility in a working-class neighborhood in Chicago's Near South

Side, with a very modest adjoining parsonage for his wife and young family. We walked into the sanctuary and I marveled at the beauty of the 22 handmade pews inside the 100-year-old building. Dudenhoffer agreed but lamented that they had remained largely empty every week for years.

"What happened since you came?" I asked.

"I came with a vision to reach Chicago for Christ," he replied, "a vision shared by several in the congregation. But I knew—and we knew—that we couldn't do it alone. How can a handful of people with a building we cannot even maintain make a difference for Christ?"

The answered prayer, as he sees it, came from joining the vision of Moody Bible graduate Mark Jobe, whose little urban mission church, known as New Life Community Church, had grown phenomenally and was expanding into satellite sites all over downtown Chicago.[12] To Dudenhoffer, becoming known as New Life's Bridgeport campus had several advantages:

- New Life offered a network of advisors—pastors in the New Life family—to mentor Luke as a young pastor. "People burn out in the city because they're alone," Dudenhoffer says. "Through the New Life movement, I'm expected to meet with our group every Monday morning, where I'm fed spiritually."

- The same team of pastors works together to develop sermon illustrations and biblical insights. "We each preach the same sermon series, using the same text, but we each vary our outline and applications," Dudenhoffer explains.

- New Life offers a discipleship model and plan. "The series of First Steps booklets they've developed help us

be more relational as a church, living more as a priest-
hood of believers," Dudenhoffer says.

• Another New Life congregation loaned the Bridgeport
  campus a vibrant couple that served as worship leaders and lay leaders when the church was beginning its
  turnaround. The couple made an initial six-month
  commitment but ended up staying two years.

• The New Life organization made a $35,000 loan for a
  facility-related payment. This amount represented 70
  percent of the Bridgeport budget at the time, so no
  bank would have considered the idea.

Today, the 22 handmade pews inside the century-old building are filled by about 150 people, many of them neighborhood
families in their thirties who belong to New Life Bridgeport.
The church once again offers youth programming and it feeds
15 to 30 people through its Bread of Life initiative on Mondays.
The transition to become a campus of New Life
Community Church did require a congregational vote and permission from the denomination (United Church of Christ).
Both occurred amicably in 2002. The discussions leading up to
the merger were intense, but the church knew that it would die
without change. "We have to do something different here," said
Dee, who has belonged to the church since 1942. When former
members phoned her with cautions about the potential merger, she responded by describing the good things that were happening. "The church is again full of excitement," she would say.
"I recently went to a baby shower there. I can't remember the
last time we had a baby shower."
According to Dudenhoffer, the biggest transition issue
involved the name of the church. "We were formerly known as

Doremus Congregational Church. People had the hardest time with the name change, fearing we would lose the memory of Doremus Scutter, the church's second pastor who became its first missionary."

The church nevertheless voted decisively to make the merger and is very glad it did so. It hasn't lost the memory of its past, but it also feels that its best days are yet to come. "We are big enough to make a difference and small enough to care," Dudenhoffer says. "It's great to be part of a larger network."

New Life, following the teaching team model introduced earlier, represents the willingness to take on a struggling or declining church and help it find a new cycle of life.

Advantages of Being Multi-site

The Multi-Site Church Revolution summarizes the following 13 advantages of becoming multi-site:

1. It brings together the best aspects of larger churches and smaller churches.
2. It increases the total number of seats available during optimal worship times.
3. It overcomes geographic barriers when a church facility is landlocked or tightly zoned.
4. It enables untapped talent to emerge each time a new venue or site is opened.
5. It mobilizes volunteers through an added variety of ministry opportunities.
6. It increases options of location and sometimes of worship style too.
7. It assists in reaching friends and family unwilling to travel a great distance to church.
8. It accelerates the climate for diversity, creativity and innovation in ministry.

9. It improves a church's stewardship of funds and resources.
10. It enables a church to extend itself into niches like a cancer ward or office complex.
11. It helps a congregation see evidences of how it's part of a larger Kingdom mission.
12. It models and trains people for church planting elsewhere.
13. It provides a pipeline for the development of emerging leaders and future staff.[13]

Implications for Church Planting

People who start new churches have emerged as one of the most responsive groups to the multi-site idea. The primary difference between expanding to multi-site and launching a totally separate new church (also known as church planting) is whether the group shares a common vision, budget, leadership and board.

Many new churches use multi-site as a "both/and" approach. They get started as an extension site of an existing church, enjoying the many advantages of being part of a multi-site, which include:

- Accountability
- Sharing of resources (stewardship)
- Infusion of trained workers
- Shared vision and core values
- Greater prayer support
- Pre-established network for problem solving
- Not needing to reinvent the wheel
- Connection with others doing the same thing[14]

Then, over time, the originating church or sponsoring denomination spins them off to become a self-governing, self-supporting congregation that can eventually replicate itself. Thus, multi-site serves as a very effective church-planting model. Some people (Ed in particular) have concerns that the multi-site model might hurt church planting, but it is too early to tell whether this will be the case. For now, most church-planting conferences feature a track on using a multi-site approach.

The Challenge of Cloning

Many people are concerned about church "cloning." Recently, a Christian satire site explained the new approach of a hypothetical congregation named Evergreen Community Church, saying:

> In 2001 Evergreen began gobbling up churches across the nation and turning them into Evergreen clones, with identical features, down to the doorknobs, ushers' jackets and sermons. Even the pulpits and Sunday school rooms are the same. "We're like Burger King or Subway— a solid, trustworthy business," says Evergreen brand manager Stefan Borcht.[15]

Some are worried about pastors projecting their image and their ministry approach outside of their communities—creating clones all over the country that are not contextualized to their communities. We recognize that this can be a problem, but we do not think it always needs to be.

Some have said that Acts 15 illustrates how Paul dealt with some of the organizational challenges of a multi-campus church. The Jerusalem campus felt that the congregation in Antioch wasn't doing things the right way—the way they were done at the "main" campus. As a result, several self-appointed leaders headed to Antioch to straighten them out. "This caused trouble, and Paul and Barnabas argued with them about this teaching"

(Acts 15:2). A decision was made to send Paul and Barnabas, along with some other church members, to Jerusalem to sort out the problem. At Jerusalem, they began working out organizational challenges, defining the essential core values of the new church and clarifying how best to communicate between the campuses.

The Early Church soon came to reflect the perspective that the needs of a congregation 20 miles away were different from the needs in the original community. The dynamics of a small campus are different than those of a larger congregation. The new campuses are often filled with people unfamiliar with the standard operating procedures of the original campus. And as seasoned staff members are moved to new sites, the original campus can be drained of the experienced and talented staff it once had.

Reproductive Necessities

The experiences of Acts 15 remind churches today that before they go around reproducing themselves as a church, they need to make sure they know *what* they're reproducing. Seacoast Church was a growing congregation in a growing suburb of Charleston, South Carolina. When the local zoning board soundly turned down their request to expand their worship facility, the church experimented by creating an off-site campus. Today the church has 10 different campuses—5 in the Charleston area and 5 in other cities. Many of them use movie theaters. Total worship attendance is 7,000 each weekend, which means two-thirds of the congregation have never been to the still-landlocked original campus on Long Point Road!

In developing new campuses, Seacoast faced the challenge of how to transfer its core values and vision from site to site and venue to venue. Is it a particular worship liturgy and music style that makes a church identifiable as being part of Seacoast?

Not really. Seacoast has learned that the essentials to transfer are practical life-giving messages, a sense of God's power in worship, a relaxed and non-threatening atmosphere, excellent children's ministry, and relational small groups. The common name (Seacoast Columbia, Seacoast Greenville, Seacoast Savannah) and common logo also help create a sense of shared identity.

Seacoast also does its teaching at the various campus sites by sending a DVD or downloadable file to its various branches. For videocast churches, shared teaching is often a leading factor in carrying the church's core values and vision from campus to campus, especially if sermon-based small groups reinforce the preaching. For churches that do not use videocast but instead have on-site teachers, it's a little harder to create a feel of being "one church in many locations." Such churches often use shared materials and similar sermons (such as the New Life example above).

For all multi-site churches, whether or not they use videocast teaching, success ultimately comes down to vision and core values. The list of "must have" pieces typically shrinks down to a handful of issues as churches discover ways the programming may look the same or different, yet the "one church in many locations" feel is still present.

What about specific roles? While there is a great deal of variety in how different multi-site churches approach staffing, several leadership roles are common to almost all successful models. *The Multi-Site Church Revolution* reports a widespread use of five such personnel positions:

1. *Multi-site Director.* This is the person who is responsible on a day-to-day basis for steering the multi-site mission. For churches starting their first or second site, the senior pastor or senior leadership team often wears the hat of this role. Over time, the need

for this position emerges, especially in cases of multiple campuses.

2. *Campus Pastor.* The key to any new startup is the campus pastor. This is the leader who will convey the core values and vision of the primary campus, recruit the core team, develop the new leaders and carry on the ministry once the campus is launched. If videocast teaching is used, the campus pastor role is still essential, even though this person does not preach. The qualities that make campus pastors most successful include:

   - A leader who completely buys into the church's vision and is loyal to its senior leadership;
   - A team player with strong relational skills;
   - A team builder who can reproduce vision in others;
   - A pastor (someone with a desire and heart to shepherd groups and individuals); and
   - A flexible entrepreneur.

3. *Worship Director.* In addition to the campus pastor, the worship director oversees the weekend experience at the new campus. This person is responsible for creating an authentic worship experience that reflects the atmosphere of the primary campus.

4. *Children/Youth Ministry Director.* After the overall weekend experience, the quality of the ministry to children often determines the success or failure of a new campus. Similar to the role of the worship director, the leaders in children's ministry strive to

replicate as much as possible the environment of the primary campus.

5. *Small Groups/Spiritual Life/Discipleship Director.* Often a volunteer in the beginning, this director is responsible for the spiritual development programs and ministries of the new campus.[16]

What's So New?

How are today's multi-site models different from the preaching points, mission stations, radio ministry, television ministry and other kind of outreach that churches have done in the past when trying to demonstrate that lost people matter to God? They are different in four primary ways:

1. *Relationship vs. rescue.* The attitude motivating most multi-sites is relational. The desire is to not only proclaim the gospel but to also establish a presence and a relationship. Even when they're trying to meet the needs of the poor, oppressed and forgotten, multi-sites are not to just go back home at the end of the day.

2. *Stepping-stone vs. limited-service mission.* A multi-site approach becomes a stepping-stone for greater local church involvement. A televised broadcast of a church service, for example, does nothing toward the creation of a local worshiping community, but a multi-site approach does. If a church has developed an off-site service at a local correctional facility, developing relationships in the process, when inmates are released from prison it will be natural for them

to become involved in the church that they've come to know. Likewise, if a church has developed an off-site service at a local firehouse, when firefighters have a day off on Sunday, it's a short step for them to join people they know at one of the full-service campuses of the church.

3. *Personalization vs. cookie-cutter.* Most multi-site locations designate someone as the campus pastor (a face to go with the place), who personalizes the church. This person, usually backed by a team of volunteers, helps adapt the church service to the unique local context.

4. *Lay empowerment vs. clergy dependency.* Multi-site niche churches are not just about touching new people but are also about growing a church's ministry capacity—deploying more volunteers. Multi-sites should not be looked at as just another task for the church staff's to-do list but as a means for more of the church's people to be involved spreading the gospel in their surrounding community and affinity groups.[17]

How Is It Funded?

If your church begins a prayerful discussion about joining the world of multiple-location churches, it is important to count the costs. As Jesus reminds us, "Suppose one of you wants to build a tower. What is the first thing you will do? Won't you sit down and figure out how much it will cost and if you have enough money to pay for it?" (Luke 14:28).

According to a Pastors.com article, multi-site churches have found a variety of financial sources.[18] The article lists the following ideas but emphasizes that the real savings are in the synergy of shared resources, as the expense of operating a second, third and fourth campus is often much less than operating the original site.

Special Offerings

When Life Church felt God calling them to open a fifth campus in Oklahoma City, they appealed to the people. Their first idea was to follow a traditional fundraising route, asking people to give money to fund the equivalent of chairs in the new site. But they felt that might limit people's vision for the new project. Pastor Craig Groeschel decided to simply take the vision to the people and see what would happen. With very little fanfare, he clearly shared what he felt God had called them to do and then asked the people to give. In one weekend, they gave their biggest one-day offering ever toward a campus they would never attend. Life Church opened their south campus in spring 2005 and is now reaching more than 2,000 additional people at this new site.

Pay It Forward

At Christ the King Church just north of Seattle, Washington, Pastor Dave Browning has developed what they call the "Pay It Forward" plan. From the beginning, each new campus pays 10 percent of their budget into the Pay It Forward fund. This fund is in turn used to cover the initial investment needed to start new campuses.

Pay It Locally

Sometimes a campus can be virtually self-sustaining from day one, especially if done as a low-risk approach. For example, Browning reports, "When our Samish Island Worship Center opened in 2003, nearly all the costs were absorbed by the core team of volunteers involved. They rented the community center.

They purchased sound and video equipment. They publicized the opening."

Tapping Into Grants
Healing Place Church in Baton Rouge, Louisiana, in conjunction with The Church United for Community Development (an organization it helped create), has secured more than $6 million in government grants to address the needs of the poor in their community from their faith-based perspective. "We're passionately committed to caring for hurting people," says Pastor Dino Rizzo, "whether they are AIDS orphans in Africa or those living in one of the nation's lowest-income communities in nearby Donaldsonville. We are here to serve them with the love of Jesus Christ."

Other Options
Some churches have made multi-site a part of a general capital campaign. Other churches have started their new sites from their operating budgets, much as they would begin new ministries. Some churches use a part of their designated missions money to start a new outreach into a new community.

Two, three or four campuses often share the same bookkeeper, the same videographer, and the same small-group pastor. All the bills can be paid from one business office; there is one insurance plan and one payroll system. At some churches, such as Seacoast, each campus is considered a separate entity in a sort of franchise model. While there is one master budget and one bank account, each campus is budgeted separately and pays part of its income to the central budget to cover operating costs and to help fund new campuses.

Where Would You Expand?

Seacoast Church is typical in how it identifies a potential new site and trains the volunteers and staff needed. In *The Multi-Site Church*

Revolution, Seacoast prayerfully asks three crucial questions for helping churches decide where to put the next campus:

1. *Are there people in the area with a connection to the church?* Seacoast's first step is to mine its database to find where people are coming from to attend an existing Seacoast campus. They look for communities with a high concentration of Seacoast attendees more than 10 minutes away from an existing campus.

2. *Is there a need in the community for this type of church?* Seacoast tries to avoid competition with other growing, like-minded churches in a community. They want to identify communities where unchurched people do not have a Seacoast-type ministry to attend.

3. *Is the campus located in a growing community?* Seacoast prefers to locate its new campuses in growing communities. The new people moving to an area can provide a start-up campus with needed leadership and growth without draining other churches in the area.[19]

"Once we have targeted a community for a new campus, we begin to narrow down our selection of the exact location within that community," says Geoff Surratt, Seacoast's senior pastor. "While the first key to a successful campus is the right leadership, a close second is the right location. A poor location can cripple a new campus. At Seacoast, we look for a site with high visibility in a growing area surrounded by housing developments."

Seacoast's ideal is for an auditorium that will seat a minimum of 300 adults and have space for at least 60 children, divided into four areas, with parking for 200 cars. Why those numbers? "A momentum kicks in if we can reach a certain critical mass in terms of size," says Surratt.

Once Seacoast has identified the right leaders and the right location for a new campus, the next step is to discern the right time. "We have found the optimum times to launch a new campus are in the fall right after school starts, at the beginning of a new year, and at Easter," says Surratt.

Countdown to Launch

Seacoast has five campuses in greater Charleston and five elsewhere in South Carolina and Georgia. Seacoast's experience of launching a new campus, when it's less than an hour from the sponsoring campus, is similar to adding an additional worship service: There is already a built-in group of people willing to be a part of the new campus. Sometimes, as Surratt notes, "our job is to help them realize they are willing."

Seacoast's first step, whether the campus is near or far away, is to identify a campus pastor. Ideally the candidate will already be a leader in the sponsoring campus. Once identified, the leader's task is to begin building a core team, drawing from family, friends and other contacts.

Within a few weeks of selecting a campus pastor, an informational meeting is held for people from the sponsoring campus. The idea is to share the vision and invite them to become a part of the new campus, ideally becoming core team members to work with the campus pastor. This group meets regularly for prayer and planning.

About one month prior to the launch of the new campus Seacoast holds a Vision Picnic, or equivalent. The idea is to invite anyone who has ever attended Seacoast and lives in the new community to attend the picnic. They share the vision for the new campus and try to give a taste of what a weekend service will be like. The goal at the Vision Picnic is to build a crowd for launch day and to recruit more volunteers for the ministry teams.

Launching a campus more than an hour's commute from the original campus is more like planting a new church than starting a new service. First and foremost is to train the campus pastor. At Seacoast, each campus pastor undergoes at least three months of mentoring at the original campus before being sent to the new community. The training regimen is a mixture of classes, hands-on experience and immersion in the Seacoast values and vision.

The second step is to start a small group or series of small groups designed to build a core of leaders for the new campus. The group meets weekly for prayer, vision casting, relationship building and outreach. Once the core group reaches 20 to 30 adults, they move to the worship café stage. A medium-size space is secured for weekly celebration meetings (small church services) and the group divides into two or more small groups. The pastor continues to meet weekly with key leaders in the core group. At the weekly celebrations, all the small groups come together for worship, teaching and children's ministry. Once the core group reaches 60 to 80 committed adults, they are ready for the campus launch, which ideally will begin with 250 to 350 people on day one. At Seacoast, the preferable time from core group to campus is 6 months.

What About Technology?

While working on this chapter, I (Warren) attended the "practice" day of a church opening its second site the following month. It was in a movie theater multiplex in a mall. Several greeters warmly welcomed my wife and me at the entrance of the theater. Signs clearly led us toward theater five (adult worship) and theater four (children's worship). A table with free doughnuts and orange juice caused us to pause and chat with the people staffing it. An abundance of ushers were on hand to chat with us as they helped us find a seat. A series of video images kept our interest as we waited for the service to begin.

The live band began promptly at the announced service time. There were 18 of us in the audience, but the worship leader led with the enthusiasm that would be fitting if every seat had been filled. The worship went for a full half hour, and people continued to trickle in. By 11:30, some 75 worshipers were there, plus the core group of 20 to 30, plus a handful of children for theater four, which they had converted nicely into a children's play area.

At about 11:30, the campus pastor welcomed us, introduced himself, and then introduced the sermon. The message was played by video, filling the screen as a movie would. It was recorded the week before by the lead pastor at the sponsoring church. It worked just fine. The video and voice were a half-second off, a problem I'm certain they'll fix by opening day, but within minutes my wife and I were taking notes on the sermon, laughing at the speaker's occasional joke, and responding as if he was with us in person. Everyone else present was equally engaged.

When I've visited other multi-site churches that use video-cast teaching, I've seen the same level of congregational involvement—if the video is done well. From others I've talked with—even skeptics—the anticipated negative reaction to the video rarely materializes. Geoff Surratt's experience is typical. As he relates in *The Multi-Site Church Revolution*, when the pastoral team at Seacoast first discussed the idea of video preaching at a church service, he thought it was the dumbest idea he had ever heard.

"I don't like to watch preachers on television," says Surratt, "and I think talking heads on television news shows are mind numbing, so why would anyone want to go sit in a school or a theater or even a church building and watch a preacher on a video screen? So my pastor sent me on a field trip to experience video teaching at North Point where Andy Stanley is pastor. On the drive to Atlanta, my mind went over all the reasons it wouldn't work. (Why wait until after I'd experienced it to prepare my critique?) Once there, I crossed my arms and hated it, as planned, until about five minutes into the sermon. 'Wait a minute, what did he just say?' I asked myself as one of his insights connected with me. Soon I didn't really care—and almost forgot—that it was on video. I was connecting to the content; the container didn't really matter. I became a true believer that day in the leverage of using video to teach the good news. This has also been the reaction of thousands of people who have attended our video venues at Seacoast in the years since. People regularly comment to me, 'We didn't think we would like the video, but after a few minutes we didn't really notice that the speaking wasn't live.'"[20]

When newspapers and magazines discuss churches with satellite campuses, they tend to highlight megachurches, one in four of which uses some variation of a multi-site approach. Most megachurches, because of their scale, use a Jumbotron, large projection screens or other digital approaches to teaching.

Is that what everyone does? Is that the only way to make multi-site work? The answer to both questions is no. According to Leadership Network, about a third of multi-site churches use videocast teaching, a third do not, and a third use a combination of the two—videocast at some campuses and in-person teaching at other campuses.[21]

Will It Work for You?

Expanding your church from one location to two or more is a move with a great deal of spiritual potential but also a significant amount of risk. While the key criteria is what God is saying for your church in your community, the following questions are recommended by *The Multi-Site Church Revolution* as strong predictors of the success or failure of a new campus in a new location:

- *How healthy is your church?* Is your church growing? Is it a great gathering place for people to find their way to God, to be discipled and to find a place of ministry? Are the members of your church excited about bringing family and friends? Launching a second site will not bring health to an ailing congregation; and frankly it's generally not a good idea for an unhealthy church to reproduce itself.

- *Is there a driving impetus behind your desire to go multi-site?* Successful multi-site churches typically open a second site because they see no better option to fulfill God's purpose for their church. For some, their building was packed, they had run out of viable service times, and building a larger facility didn't seem to be the answer. For others, there was a sense of mission to go into the next city, the next county or across a cultural chasm they had been unable to cross. Still other churches had a strong desire to take the ministry of their church into the neighborhoods of the members. In each case, though, multi-site was not seen as merely another program or strategy, but rather as a key component to fulfilling their God-inspired vision.

- *Are the key leaders behind the decision?* Going multi-site can stretch the budget, invite criticism from other churches, and make new demands on church leadership. Therefore, it is vital that the key leaders of the church be unified and enthusiastic about the decision to go multi-site to see success. While it is difficult to get 100 percent buy-in when moving in a new direction, if the senior leadership is not sold on the concept of doing church in multiple locations, that should be a major warning light.[22]

Before your church launches a multi-site, the decision makers in the congregation will need to sort through these crucial issues.

The Gifts You Need May Already Be in Your Pews

Jung Hoon Kim came at age 4 from his native Korea to the United States. He became a Christian during his college years and soon wanted to use his musical abilities at church. He found a church in New York City that places a high value on the arts, and he eventually became leader of one of the worship teams there.

When the church began praying about opening a second site (the practice service my wife and I attended), Kim became its campus pastor. This represented a new level of responsibility for him. Instead of leading the worship team, he developed someone else to head the worship team. He also became responsible for developing various outreach initiatives, a children's ministry team and various support teams.

I asked Kim, now age 32, why he accepted the new challenge. "I just like to start things," he said. "We had someone pray to receive Christ, and we still haven't officially launched. I get excited by being on the front edge of something like this."

Too many churches have people like Kim sitting in their pews rather than on the front lines of ministry. If asked, they may step forward. For many churches, multi-site represents a great opportunity to establish a new beachhead in a mission field right at our door.

What Can You Learn from Multi-site Churches?

The multi-site church is not the practice of a handful of innovative churches. Many churches are doing it, and most megachurches are either functioning as multi-site or moving in that direction. It is a big deal—but is it right for your church? Maybe. Maybe not. But there are some things that every church can learn, such as the following:

Churches Can Reach Different People with Different Venues
Church planters have known this for a long time. Churches would often be started to reach different types of people and different locations. When Larry Osborne, one of the early pioneers of the multi-site movement, asked to take me (Ed) to lunch to talk about their strategy, I was skeptical. They worship in 23 worship options in five locations. As a church-planting guy, I just wished they would let those "baby" churches out of the womb and plant some real churches.

Osborne explained that their strategy was not just projecting Osborne's whitebeard face across Southern California. It was to plant campuses that were, to use his terms, "geographically" *and* "demographically" diverse. In other words, not just clones with picture of Osborne projected on the screen. Though most multi-site churches are not as intentional as Northcoast, many have recognized that they can and should do ministry in diverse settings. That's good news.

**Multi-site Churches Are a Natural Extension
of the Megachurch Phenomenon**
I (Ed) asked Andy Stanley in a friendly conversation, "Why don't you just plant new churches? Why project your graven image

across the Southeastern United States?" Stanley answered in two ways. Stanley asked where I see him when I attend Northpoint (I visit there occasionally). I told him I looked at the screen, because it was easier to see. (Yeah, I fell for that one hard.)

Then he asked me about church planting—and humbly indicated that they were planting campuses that already had good teaching and the local leadership could focus on the ministry. If you believe in the validity of the megachurch, it is hard to argue against the multi-site church—in either case you see the pastor on a big screen and other staff are your primary pastors!

The Expectations of "Church" Have Gone Up

Five years ago, most pastors had to compete with Charles Stanley's quality on the radio—now you might have his son Andy at a church down the street. It challenges us to step both our preaching and leadership up to a new level. Certainly, this does not bode well for some, but it is a reality and we need to learn from it.

Multi-site Churches Can Be Simple, and Simple Can Work

Multi-site churches tend to not have individual church "properties" for each "site." They will often have one base campus and the other locations meet in rented facilities. The fact that these "sites" can function so well is because they tend to offer only two ministries: Sunday worship and small groups. They are simple and people respond.

This is a long way from churches that meet Sunday morning, Sunday night and Wednesday night. Multi-site churches (and a growing number of churches in general) just don't consider the programs and facilities of generations past. They are lean and simple and people respond. (Thom Rainer and Eric Geiger talk about this in depth in their excellent new book *Simple Church*.[23])

Multi-site churches will continue to grow in popularity and influence. It combines the best of local fellowship with world-class teaching—two things that are a powerful combination in today's culture.

What We Need to Consider

As with any approach to church life, there are challenges with the paradigm. The multi-site phenomenon is different. Here are a few things for each to consider.

There Are Real Questions to Be Considered About the Attractional Model

In a culture that is increasingly unchurched, the idea of attracting people to churches with great music and dynamic teaching makes assumptions that no longer hold. If they have no religious memory, a better and more convenient site will make little difference.

The multi-site church is working, but will it do so long-term in a truly Christian culture? We do not see many multi-site churches in Europe, perhaps because having a great speaker and powerful music does not appeal to a truly post-Christian culture. As our culture becomes increasingly post-Christian, we have to wonder if the multi-site church will become decreasingly effective.

Someone Has to Answer When It Will Stop

I (Ed) was recently in a meeting with 50 or so well-known evangelical leaders who wanted to plant five million churches worldwide—a worthy goal, indeed. One pastor—of one of the largest churches with the best-known multi-site strategy—suggested the answer: We need video venues in mission stations around the world. He did so with a straight face (though I struggled to keep mine as I considered an African man with a hand-cranked generator under a tree in Kenya watching a white man in a three-piece suit). The reality is that there are cultural differences that must be taken into consideration.

Assumptions About Church in Scripture Cannot Be Found in the Multi-site Church

In Scripture, pastors prayed over the sick (see Jas. 5:14), watched over everyone God had placed in their care (see 1 Pet. 5:2) and broke bread and prayed together (see Acts 2:42). There are certain pastoral acts that could be lost in a multi-site church, and we would do well to use a campus pastor approach (local site leadership) to ensure that these important values are not missed.

Multi-site Churches Can Prevent the Development of More Platform Teachers

If the standard for pastoring is the ability to keep 5,000 people on the edge of their seat for 30 to 45 minutes, many simply will not pursue or use their speaking gifts. Multi-site churches require a speaking ability that most simply do not have, and thus the pool of leadership is reduced. That leads to a great challenge when the compelling communicator projected all over the county falls, dies or leaves.

At Some Point, We Have to Stop Appealing to a Consumer Mentality

One reason that many of these multi-site churches are growing is that they are "better" than the churches already in a community. They offer more quality—and people *are* attracted to such. But at some point, the gospel cannot and must not attract people simply because we do it better. It must ultimately be about Jesus, the gospel and sacrifice—and that does not require a video screen and a national structure.

As a missiologist, I (Ed) always ask if it is reproducible. If something can't reproduce, it has natural limits on its ability to expand and influence. For some models of multi-site churches, multiplication of leaders can be hard. You can always start another site, but what about creating new leaders who develop other leaders? It is comparably easy to start another campus, but it is quite hard to grow another Andy Stanley!

Many Churches that Hold to a "Local Church Autonomy" Theology Have Not Thought Through the Repercussions of the Multi-site Ministry

Simply put, the lead pastor becomes a bishop overseeing a series of churches or campus pastors. For some, that is not a problem.

But for others, they have not even thought through the issues. This model creates a new view of what the church is, and churches need to give that some serious biblical consideration.

Conclusion

We don't want to sound like the person who always criticizes innovation. Our point here is to encourage you to think. All of us are excited about what God is doing through multi-site churches, but, like every innovation, we believe that you need to think it through biblically. We hope that the end result will be more biblical discernment toward every innovation.

CHAPTER 4

ANCIENT-FUTURE CHURCHES

You, LORD, are my God! I will praise you for doing the wonderful things you had planned and promised since ancient times.

ISAIAH 25:1

I (Elmer) was met in the hallway by two young men in their twenties. In the background, I recognized the sound of guitars reverentially playing "Amazing Grace," a hymn written in the 1700s by a slave trader who was dramatically converted to Christianity. As I entered the large classroom where we would be worshiping, I saw many candles. Approximately 60 chairs were arranged in a large circle so that we would face one another.

In my church, the pews and people face the pulpit and the pastor. Before the service begins, people talk to one another across the aisles or pews, but in this church, the music and the candles said, "*Sh-h-h-h.*" The room was quiet, conveying a sense of awe and reflection.

There were four worship stations, one at each corner of the room, but I didn't immediately understand what each was for. In one corner was a table with candles it. In the next corner, I saw three large basins of water, suggesting to me that we might experience a washing of feet. Before I could walk over to observe the other two corners, the leader stood and called our attention to a projection screen on which the words from Revelation 4 were displayed in a PowerPoint presentation. We were invited to read the text in unison.

The leader then led us in prayer, asking us to repeat his words, which we did phrase by phrase: "Lord, we come into Your presence . . . we wait shrouded in the darkness for You to speak to us . . . and just as we can't see everything in our darkened understanding, or know everything in our spiritual world . . . we invite You to come be our Light . . . just as these candles illuminate this room."

Two guitarists came to the middle of the room and began playing "Amazing Grace." It was not played rhythmically or loudly, nor was the hymn strummed with vigor. The room joined in singing "Amazing Grace" at a slower tempo than I usually hear. I found myself meditating on the words as they sang, "I once was blind, but now I see . . ."

"Let's wait on God in prayer," the leader instructed. I began praying silently as did everyone else in the circle. The room was quiet for a few minutes. Then the leader explained that in one corner of the room we could wash one another's feet, and that if God so prompted our hearts, we could ask someone if they would allow us to wash their feet.

Communion elements waited for us in another corner of the room. The table had been covered with a small cloth. Two candles illuminated worshipers as they approached it. There was a small paper plate with broken crackers to represent the broken body of the Lord. Paper cups contained the liquid that would represent the blood of Jesus' death on the cross.

The worship leader sat on one side of the table to face the worshipers who came over. The instructions from Paul concerning the Lord's Table were read. The leader asked the worshipers, "Would you thank God for the body of Jesus that was broken for you?" Worshipers then expressed gratitude for the death of Christ and partook of the elements. Next, the leader asked, "Would you thank God for the blood of Jesus Christ which was spilled for you?" After a prayer of gratitude, worshipers then partook of the cup.

I surmised that the next corner of the room was perhaps for counseling for those who had problems or wanted specific, individual prayer. In actuality, it was for searching, confessing and communion with God. A leader behind the table met the worshipers. Scripture was read and individuals were asked to pray silently to God after first searching their heart for hidden sin and confessing as God showed His light upon it.

There was a mirror on the wall, with the intent that worshipers would look on themselves in a symbolic act that would lead them to look deep within their heart to their inner self as God might see it. The leader was available to pray with the worshipers in any way necessary, or to read Scripture, or simply to be supportive.

The next corner of the room was near a window that shed some light. The leader sat behind a table with Scriptures to read to the worshipers who came to him. This was Bible study. After the Scripture was read, the leader would ask questions such as, "What does that mean to you?" or "What is God saying to you through this passage?" It was an interactive Bible study that applied the Scriptures to the thoughts and lives of the worshipers.

A former student of mine came to me and asked, "May I wash your feet?" My immediate reaction was, "I should wash your feet," but I didn't say that. Instead, I followed him to the corner where the basins of water were waiting. There were chairs on either side of the basin, and when we sat down, my student prayed for me and for him, asking God to continue to use my life as a teacher and to continue to work in his life as a minister.

Then he removed a shoe and sock from my right foot and placed my foot into the warm water. He then took soap and washed my foot, and repeated the process on my other foot. Next, he took a towel and dried both of my feet.

It's very humbling to wash the feet of another person. But for me, it was even more humbling to have my feet washed. It made me feel unworthy. In a situation like that, I believe that most people, including me, would rather serve than be served.

When your feet are washed by another person, it makes you feel one with them. That day, I experienced a bond with my student that I might have never otherwise felt. This outward act produced the inner reality that Jesus intended when He washed the feet of the disciples.

I returned to my seat in the larger circle and continued praying for several minutes. Some in the room were in the circle praying; others had gone to visit the various stations of worship. The Lord was near, and most everyone in the room felt His presence.

After a while, the leader spoke to us. He told about one person in the room who was deeply burdened over a child in his family. The leader asked the brother to come to the center of the room so that everyone could gather around him and pray. Then the leader asked if anyone else had a similar situation of a needy child and, if so, to come and stand with the man in the center of the room. Perhaps 10 or 12 people did so. Then the rest of the worshipers gathered around to lay hands on the others' head or shoulder or to give them "holy hugs" while several led in prayer.

We did another similar round of prayer for someone who was facing problems in her area of ministry. Together we exercised faith, reinforcing Jesus' promise, "When any two of you on earth agree about something you are praying for, my Father in heaven will do it for you. Whenever two or three of you come together in my name, I am there with you" (Matt. 18:19-20).

After the prayers ended, each person returned to his or her seat for further reflection and meditation. People left the gathering as they chose. There was no formal benediction or dismissal.

Connecting with the Past

Interest is growing, especially among younger Christians, in the kind of worship that is both relevant to today and connected with the past. This ancient-future worship ranges from the use of candles to an appreciation of Ash Wednesday and Lent. It may focus on an ancient ritual like baptism or a more general sense of the mysteries of God. It may occur in a historic building with stained glass or a converted warehouse with a digital stained glass image from projection equipment.

Whatever the setting, Christians increasingly desire to participate in worship as an experience, and often they find help in feeling connected with the 2,000-year stream of Church history. They are discovering how to cash in on two millennia of good ideas, many of which draw elements from liturgical worship, though not necessarily in a formal setting.

Ancient-future worship is not, in most cases, a rejection of a particular belief structure. Many churches maintain a high view of Scripture, adhere to the historic doctrines of faith and emphasize a transforming relationship with Jesus Christ. If anything, ancient-future worship rejects modern worship as too narrow. In some places it shows disdain for the "prom song" approach to worship that talks more about good feelings than about God. And it often rejects any sense that Christians have figured out on their own how to "do church."

Dave Goetz, editor of ChurchLeadership.Net, an online publication of Christianity Today, Inc., points out how both pastors and lay leaders hunger more for the supernatural and theological and less for ministry methods. "During the 1980s, church growth techniques were hot," he says, "and during the 90s, leadership skills have been trumpeted . . . but among some pastors, there's a pervasive weariness with ministry technique. People are saying, 'I want to go deeper in ministry and in my spiritual life.'"[1]

Sally Morgenthaler's book *Worship Evangelism* likewise underscores an increasing spiritual thirst as a motivational factor behind this ancient-future approach to worship. "Our failure to impact contemporary culture is not because we have not been relevant enough, but because we have not been real enough,"[2] she says. Carol Childress, researcher for WorldconneX, a global mission network, summarized today's return-to-the-past emphasis as a series of shifts

- From classical to contextual;
- From performance to participation;
- From music *about* God to music *to* God;
- From cerebral to celebration;
- From liturgy to liberty ("planned spontaneity"); and
- From meditation to mission.[3]

In short, recent efforts to be user-friendly while fitting into popular culture by eliminating religious symbols are, for some people, maturing into a longing for a stronger sense of spiritual roots. Churches are putting greater emphasis on the idea of community and are showing how the practices of the Early Church can be a vital spiritual resource for today.

The appeal is both to churchgoers and to today's generation of unchurched people who are largely illiterate of both Scripture and Church history. Instead of being turned off by the rich symbolism of the Christian faith, an increasing number find it to be surprisingly relevant, especially if it engages both their minds and their emotions.

Thus, at Second Baptist Church in Houston, Texas, the worship services led by Ben Young, son of senior pastor Ed Young, often include the Nicene Creed. Worship services at New England Chapel, a new Boston-area congregation of the Christian Reformed Church, uses the high-energy sound of percussion and subwoofers, but it also appreciates the pastor's thoughtful explanation of the mystery of baptism as he sprinkles water on the foreheads of young children brought by their parents. Ginghamsburg Church, a United Methodist congregation in Tipp City, Ohio, launched an Ash Wednesday service several years ago and had to spill over to two such services each Ash Wednesday due to its popularity.

Strong Indigenous Flavor

Unlike the easily predictable, little-varied liturgies of the past, ancient-future worship typically takes an eclectic approach, tailoring worship to each particular context. As in the examples so far in this chapter, no two services or churches are alike in what they do.

This indigenous flair can be seen on the surface with matters as simple as the church name. If they're able to choose or modify their name, such churches steer clear of names with denominations indicated in the titles. They opt instead for monikers like Scum of the Earth (Denver, Colorado), The Bridge (Pontiac, Michigan), Bluer (Minneapolis, Minnesota) or Threads (Kalamazoo, Michigan). Or, more simply, "[NAME] Community Church."

Likewise, the teaching portion of worship often involves an intersection of culture and arts. The idea is to draw people into the message using art as a vehicle. For example, Lake Ridge Church, where I (Ed) serve as co-pastor, would be considered (in my tradition, at least) an ancient-future church. We sing a mix of God-centered hymns and choruses. Some people might call us blended, but we don't; most blended churches we know of sing two hymns in classic style and three choruses from the '70s. We tend to sing more hymns, but they are done in a very contemporary manner. For those who know the genre, we use a lot of Indelible Grace music and love hymns after they have been "Crowderized" to the style of

Dave Crowder. We recite the Nicene Creed, occasionally read responsively, come forward and receive Communion from a common bread loaf and cup and, most of all, reach lost people. We find that it connects with our community in the sterile, vast, suburban wasteland in North Georgia. They are looking for something that is not brand-new but ancient and true—like the gospel and God-centered worship.

The Journey Church in St. Louis, Missouri, is a Southern Baptist church, but you would never know it from its looks. The church recently purchased a large, vacant, Catholic church building. While many low-ritual churches would see its cathedral ceilings, ancient glass and wooden pews to be a hindrance to cultural relevance, Pastor Darrin Patrick views it as an opportunity to connect in the educated, young, trendy community in the city of St. Louis. The church has retrofitted the building with new sound systems, plasma screens and other current technology. The end result is a cutting-edge congregation in an ancient, symbolism-rich church building.

What Can We Learn?

In many ways, learning from ancient-future churches can be like learning from the ancient church. In addition to themes already presented in this chapter, there are several values we can glean from ancient-future churches.

The Gospel Can Be Illustrated Through Images

People have been doing this for 2,000 years. It is easy to imagine a preacher standing in a medieval church. After reading the text about, say, Jesus and Lazarus (and remember, the preacher would be one of the few people who knew how to read), he would point to a stained glass window and say, "That is a picture of when Jesus raised Lazarus from the dead."

Today in most parts of North America, we are not a "pre-literate" culture like those of the medieval era. Yet many would say that we are in a "post-literate" era. People are educated, but they are looking for more than text (ask declining-subscription newspapers if this is true!). More and more people are turning to images for learning, and the church needs to take notice. This trend is not without its challenges, of course, as we are a word-centered faith. But it makes sense for followers of Jesus, who often told gripping stories, to teach by way of visual images, projected images and object show-and-tell lessons.

I (Warren) vividly remember one sermon that used the metaphors of a ladder and the cross. The teaching pastor sat on a stepladder and explained how a "ladder" approach to God always had one more rung and always depended on our human ability to make the climb. He then walked over to the cross and drew a contrast. I knew the right words to describe my faith ("the cross of Christ, of course, 'not of works' as Ephesians 2:9-10 teaches"), but I had never before realized that I actually *lived* by the ladder: trying to please God and others by measuring up on my own strength. God used the visualization to make His Word come alive in my heart.

Most Churches Have Failed to Engage Beyond Our Ears

Ancient-future churches recognize that people hear with more than their ears. I (Ed) remember growing up as a nominal Catholic in a New York City church that had a smell (incense), a look (banners, vestments and stained glass), a sound (bells and music) and a reverent feel (pews and kneelers). There are many times I miss that multi-sensory experience. Many people are seeking something that engages all of the senses.

The Church Did Not Start in 1980 or Even 1780

For some, their understanding of church started with today's "seeker-friendly" church movement of the 1980s. For others, it started in the Second Great Awakening of the 1780s. Ancient-future churches recognize that for two millennia there has been a church worshiping, learning and reaching out. We can learn from and participate in this Christian communion with saints in eras with which we are unfamiliar.

What Are the Dangers?

Even the most ancient of churches had no guarantee of ongoing health. The book of Acts records all kinds of corruption that quickly found a way into the Church. Ananias and Sapphira lied in order to make themselves look good (see Acts 5:1-11). Different ethnic groups (Jewish and Gentile believers) exchanged accusations of being treated as second class Christians (see Acts 6:1-7). Paul and John Mark didn't get along with each other (see Acts 15:37-38). As a result, the Church frequently adjusted its methods in order to follow God more closely—and to avoid unintended side effects.

Over the centuries, glaring errors of faith, emotion and practice crept into the Church, prompting a continual series of revivals, awakenings and reformations. So as we review various practices that have developed historically, here are some matters to discern in order to embrace the richness of the ancient Church while avoiding its errors.

Christian and Non-Christian Religions May Be Married Together with Unhealthy Effect

The desire to glean spirituality from the ancient Church can easily lead to gleaning spirituality from other sources as well. Interestingly, when Paul approached the Athenians in his effort to be culturally relevant, he did four things: (1) He demonstrated that he understood the Athenian position on reality; (2) he acknowledged their underlying spiritual interest; (3) he looked for positive points within their worldview; and (4) he encouraged them to find true fulfillment in Christ.[4] Thus, we have biblical precedent for drawing parallels with non-Christian spirituality, noting carefully that Paul's message remained the same. Whatever spiritual form he used, he made sure to focus on Christ: "I resolved to know nothing while I was with you except Jesus Christ and him crucified" (1 Cor. 2:2, *NIV*).

Our Faith Cannot Neglect the Word

A vital relationship with Jesus Christ can be properly lived out only with the Word of God at its center. Anything that takes the place of the Word is a distraction and not a help. Other things can illustrate the Word, but only the power of God through the Word can change lives. Therefore, the Word must always be central.

There is nothing as powerful as entering a room where a servant of God who has mastered the Word and is filled with the Spirit communicates God's Word in a powerful and practical way. In such a situation, the Word of God attracts the attention of its hearers, seeps into the inner recesses of the heart by conviction, and demands a response.

As good as the group experiences in the ancient-future church are, and as meaningful as meditating and the candlelit atmosphere are, the history of Christianity has hinged on people who sit or stand facing the pulpit where the Word of God commands their attention and is central to everything in worship. Foot washing, communion, problem solving and meditation all have a place in Christian worship (and perhaps have been underemphasized in recent decades), but the purpose must always come back to the centrality of the Word of God and its timeless message of faith in Jesus Christ.

The Gospel Is Not a Smell

This phrase sounds odd, but it is important to remember that the gospel centers on Jesus as presented in Scripture. Thus, the gospel is more than a smell, a picture, a song, a play or anything other than a divine Person described in Scripture. It does not matter if a culture is pre-literate, literate, post-literate or if they prefer the sense of smell to the sense of hearing. The Word of God is the standard for those who want to know and follow Jesus.

Ancient Rituals Often Led to Ancient Errors

The reason the Reformers abandoned icons and ritual prayers is not because those things did not have meaning; it was because they had developed the *wrong* meaning. They de-emphasized a faith relationship with God, the centrality of Scripture and the simplicity of genuine faith. It is odd that many people believe they can adopt various ancient-future practices without dealing with the problems that other Christians have encountered through those same practices. Perhaps images can help us to pray, but will our children say that the images themselves are sacred? Will our grandchildren then pray through them? Finally, will our great-grandchildren pray to them?

Worship Expression Must Not Be Limited to Human Temperament

Proper biblical worship is not measured by form, method, the presence of certain types of musical instruments or the presence of such worship aids as candles, communion cups or a mirror to reflect our meditation. Worship must flow from the surrendered heart that willingly gives God the worship that is due to Him.

Evangelism Must Not Become Weak

In many ancient-future churches, intentional corporate evangelism is weak or nonexistent. Yes, members of the ancient-future church do evangelize through their relationships and will witness through their godly life, but the New Testament demon-

strates corporate church evangelism in an intentional manner
(see Acts 5:48; 10:33; 20:28).

Preaching can be one expression of evangelism, but many
ancient-future churches avoid that function of preaching. To
them, preaching is more than teaching and more than counseling to solve problems. Preaching is using the persuasive communication of the Word of God through the personality of the
preacher to transform the heart of the listener. As Scripture
reminds us, "Woe is me, if I do not preach the Gospel!" (1 Cor.
9:16, *NKJV*) and "For the message of the cross is foolishness to
those who are perishing, but to us who are being saved it is the
power of God" (1 Cor. 1:18, *NKJV*).

Towns and Bird's book *Into the Future* draws these five observations for how to make the most of the 2,000-year heritage of
the Church:

1. Recognize that today's worship motivations often
   stem from a spiritual hunger.
2. Feed that hunger with solid teaching about worship,
   including training about the role of the Holy Spirit.
3. Frame corporate worship in a way that invites engage-
   ment rather than spectatorship.
4. Put just as much effort in planning the rest of the
   worship service as into preparing the sermon.
5. Use the "incarnational principle" as a measuring
   stick for biblical appropriateness.[5]

Ancient, Future *and* Biblical

The church of God was not born yesterday. Ancient-future
churches embrace a church that spans two millennia. They
draw on traditions and practices that God has used in the past,
and they give them new meaning today.

In a world that is increasingly post-Christian, faith symbols are becoming new all over again. For many, even the cross has little meaning. That provides us an opportunity to recast symbols with biblical meaning. This can be meaningful for believers and unbelievers alike.

If those symbols point to Christ and illustrate the Word, they can be tools for God's purposes. Ancient-future churches must hold "the faith that God has once for all given to his people" (Jude 3). If we do so with the same enthusiasm that the ancient church did, we can confidently be ancient, future and biblical all at the same time.

CHAPTER 5

CITY-REACHING CHURCHES

Seek the peace and prosperity of the city to which I have carried you.
JEREMIAH 29:7, *NIV*

When Summit Church celebrated its third birthday in September 2006, it had already done things that most congregations don't attempt in their entire history. It had helped start a total of 104 churches—62 in the city of Vizag, India, others in Africa and Europe, and still others across the United States, including two in its own vicinity of Fort Myers, Florida. It was giving 23 percent of every general offering dollar to world missions, of which approximately 6 to 7 percent went to church planting. It had also established a training center for church planters, put huge energies into raising funds, taken great steps of faith to find and partner with other like-minded churches, and instilled into its people a passion for reaching others for Christ.

This church is serious about its goal to saturate its community—and ultimately the nation and the world—with the gospel.

Summit Church began as a big dream of Nolen Rollins, age 57. The veteran pastor imagined a day when a reproductive, multiplying, church-planting movement of local churches would blanket his town of Fort Myers, Florida and, in fact, all of southwest Florida. He longed for the movement to simultaneously become an instrument of God to transform other major sections of America and the world. In short, he wants to reach his city—and other cities—and he is convinced it will take multiple biblically and culturally healthy churches in each location to do so.

"Life and ministry in Jesus is not about ourselves, but about God's kingdom, and therefore we start churches locally and around the world," says Rollins. "We see our initial Fort Myers campus as our hub campus, and we will also partner with God wherever He is active. We recognize that each church plant will look different."

This attitude has put Rollins on a continual reproduction quest to produce and release spiritual leaders. He has already handed off the role of team leader to Orlando Cabrera and has raised a sizable staff, some of whom are paid and some of whom are volunteers. Rollins, who is gifted in fund-raising, shifted from being point leader to missions pastor and raised more than $12 million from 2002 to 2006 to launch the church and fund its worldwide vision.

"The Bible uses strong words to show that team ministry is important," says Greg Kappas, a staff pastor who drives the church's vision for planting other churches. "Acts 11:25 indicates that Barnabas 'hunted down' Saul, because Barnabas valued doing church as a team. That's our passion because we know we need multiple churches to reach each city."

To that end, the team at Summit Church is continually looking for other churches or clusters of churches who share their city-reaching vision and who are willing to develop circles of accountability. "We partner with those who say, 'We're willing to take ownership of 20,000 to 40,000 people,' roughly a 1- to 5-mile radius around where they meet," says Kappas. "If our geographies overlap, it's fine, preferable even, because each church will reach a slightly different strata of the city—from bikers to athletes to urban professionals to the down-and-out. We need multiple churches to reach each city."

From the outside, Summit Church doesn't look different from most new churches. It meets Sunday mornings, currently for three different service times at the student union ballroom on the campus of Florida Gulf Coast University. It also gathers in small groups during the week. "Community groups are at the very heart of our focus and strategy in reaching our area with the gospel," explains Kappas. According to its mission statement, Summit Church is all about connecting people into loving relationships with Jesus Christ and with others.

The original campus was drawing 900 to 1,000 people weekly by the church's third anniversary. At that same 2006 date, all 104 churches combined represented a weekend worship attendance of some 6,500 people.

Despite these faith-stretching results, the church's leaders feel they have only just begun to meet the challenge God has set before them. "Our greatest challenge is being a very young church with limited budget and too few leaders," says Kappas. That may be so, but Summit Church certainly does not lack vision!

Nolen Rollins and his team are pioneering a city-reaching approach through the planting of new churches and forming alliances with like-minded churches. That's one of many city-reaching models at work today. While churches like the Summit Church group are few in number, others do exist, and their numbers are increasing.

I (Ed) lived in Orlando as teenager. When you live in Orlando, you go to Disney World. A lot. It's the law, I think.

The rides came to feel routine, but not the urban legends. You see, only people who went to high school in Orlando know the true secret: Walt Disney's body is stored cryogenically in EPCOT village; Disneyworld is a sovereign country with its own military; and there is an actual city inside Disney World with its own citizens and elected mayor—all of whom are Disney employees. (Actually, one of these three legends is actually true.)

It is a whole new experience when you drive through Disney World with Al Weiss, head of Disney theme parks' worldwide operations. I had many questions about Disney's secret tunnels, but all Weiss wanted to talk about was church planting. He had a plan—a big one—to reach Orlando for Christ through church planting. Now that plan is bigger—it involves reaching cities all across the world for Christ.

Weiss explains on the Vision USA website, "Since I have moved to the Orlando area, I have watched the population grow from just under 100,000 to over 3.2 million people. As the area has grown, the need for new churches has grown dramatically."[1] Weiss, the supervisor of 100,000 employees worldwide, is listed as one of four Vision USA staff. With Weiss's city-reaching vision, Vision USA was born "to be a multi-denominational movement that would saturate Orlando with new churches. These new churches would cooperate together in reaching their city for Christ."[2]

Steve Johnson, Chan Kilgore and others have banded together with a city-reaching strategy for church planting. Chan Kilgore, pastor of Cross Pointe Church and director for Orlando church planting, says, "When God called us five years ago to plant in Orlando, it wasn't just to plant one church. God had called us to be missionaries to our whole city-region. So from day one, we began to sow into the city. When we connected with Vision USA, it gave us the resources we needed through strategic partnerships with business leaders to begin to saturate our city with church plants." As of January 2007, Vision USA Central Florida (the local expression) has helped launch 11 churches in 2 years with a combined total attendance of close to 2,000 people.

A guy with a vision like Al Weiss is not willing to just stop with Orlando. Now the movement is in 20 cities. Steve Johnson, national director and president, told me why they seek to focus on cities with church planting: "Over the next 20 years, 80 per-cent of the world's population is expected to live in large cities. If we are going to truly make a Kingdom impact, it is going to take place in the city. Our vision has been to saturate those cities with a self-sustaining church-planting ministry that will seek to transform those communities for Christ."

City-reaching strategies can and do make a difference. This mini-movement (no pun intended) is an example of a strategy with a track record and vision. After talking to Al Weiss, I could see it, and so have a lot of other pastors and leaders. Now, if he would just let me see that cryogenic chamber . . .

Can One Church Alone Reach Its City?

The phrase "city-reaching" is a slogan thrown around by many sources and is used in several different ways. Not everyone who advocates city-reaching is referring to the same thing. In 1972, Jerry Falwell and Elmer Towns wrote *Capturing Your Town for Christ* which became a best seller.[3] It proposed that one church could evangelize its town and that every church should have that as its goal.

Then Ed Silvoso wrote *That None Should Perish* in 1977 and *Prayer Evangelism* in 2000, each describing how city churches in Argentina came together to evangelize their town.[4] More recently Frank Damazio, pastor of City Church of greater Portland, Oregon, emphasized in his book *Crossing Rivers, Taking Cities* that the Body of Christ (as the global church) should come together to become the New Testament church to its city and minister to the city as a church should.[5]

Jack Dennison, president of CitiReach International, based in Colorado Springs, Colorado, has been working for years birthing movements of churches that come together in unity to proclaim the gospel to their city.

John Fuder edited a major work, *A Heart for the City,* that was written mostly by individuals associated with the Moody Bible Institute.[6] It is an appeal for Christians to return to renew the city through social concern and a revival of evangelistic outreach—so that inhabitants of the city may become followers of Christ and the church could live out its total ministry. When this happens, the city itself won't fall into decay and inner city blight.

The call for a return to the city seems to be a recent concern for Christians, and evangelicals in particular. In earlier decades, as populations surged in the suburbs, many urban congregations moved there. Other churches trace their beginnings to the suburbs, where church planting is easier because of available space for churches, and the population is relatively stable—at least when compared with the unique problems of the city, and specifically the inner city. Since World War II, the mainline churches have been the primary sources for city-reaching concerns because their churches were primarily located there. However, their central concern has often been social or humanitarian or welfare ministries, such as support for broken or abused families, political advocacy, employment issues for the economically disadvantaged, and so forth. The new approach puts a priority on evangelism.

One Church Evangelizing the City

As described in *Capturing Your Town for Christ,* the first city-reaching method Falwell used in establishing what became Thomas Road Baptist Church, in Lynchburg, Virginia, was to visit every home within 10 miles of the church.[7] He hung a huge city map on the back wall of the bankrupt Donald Duck bottling plant where the church began meeting in the summer of 1956. He drew 10 circles, each one representing a mile and began by visiting every home in the first circle, working 12 hours a day from 9:00 A.M. to 9:00 P.M. His goal was to visit 100 homes a day. Eventually, he visited every home in Lynchburg and then began visiting in the surrounding counties.[8]

Falwell then coined the phrase "saturation evangelism" to describe an approach of "using every available means, to reach every available person, at every available time."[9] In November 1971, Falwell sponsored an evangelistic crusade at the church and saturated the town with the gospel. He tore all 107 pages from the local telephone book and recruited 107 church members to phone every number on their sheet to share the gospel and invite people to church. The high school students tacked a gospel poster on light poles all over the city. The junior high students put a gospel flyer under the windshield wiper of every car they could find. Sixty commercials were run on all 13 radio stations in town and the one television station. An entire page in the local paper was purchased to advertise the gospel on Thursday, Friday and Saturday before the crusade. A church newspaper was mailed to every home followed by a postcard giving directions to the church. Finally, on Saturday morning, 200 volunteers went door to door to share the gospel with every home in the city.

Falwell took his example from Acts 5:28, where the enemies of the Jerusalem church accused them, "You have filled Jerusalem with your doctrine." Falwell said he wanted to fill his Jerusalem with the gospel so that when the Holy Spirit convicted a person of sin and he or she thought of salvation, that individual's first thought would be to come to Thomas Road Baptist Church seeking Jesus Christ.

Next, Falwell applied "super aggressive evangelism," which means being super aggressive in outreach, super aggressive in faith and super aggressive in sharing Christ.[10] Why? Because all are lost and need the gospel (see Rom. 3:23), because Jesus commanded to go preach to all (see Mark 16:15), and because Jesus told His followers they could do greater works than He had done (see John 14:12). As a result, Falwell preached the gospel daily over the radio and was among the first to televise a morning church service. Eventually, he became the first pastor to televise the gospel to the entire United States.

As a result of this city-reaching strategy, Falwell built one of the 10 largest churches in the United States in 1969 and one of the country's first mega-size sanctuaries (3,200 seats).[11] The church's typical weekly attendance today exceeds 10,000, and its Sunday School is more than 8,500.

Many Churches Evangelizing the City

Ed Silvoso is an Argentinean who ministered as an "advance man" for his brother-in-law, evangelist Luis Palau, going into the cities in Central and South America to organize them for a large citywide evangelistic crusade. Silvoso also worked for the Billy Graham Organization, preparing the way for Billy Graham's crusades in South America.

Silvoso grew up in Argentina in an ultra-conservative Plymouth Brethren assembly. He went to the United States and eventually graduated from Multnomah School of the Bible and Western Conservative Baptist Seminary, where he received a strong fundamentalist and dispensational background. God stretched him to become a city-reaching evangelist with a new strategy of reaching cities for Christ.

After spending many years organizing cities for mass evangelism in bullrings and soccer stadiums, as well as advertising the gospel by radio, television and billboards, Silvoso was afflicted with Crohn's disease and had to quit that ministry. He testified, "My 'Head Coach' was doing more than benching me. He was sending me to the locker room." It was in these dark days that Silvoso learned basic principles related to suffering, spiritual warfare and intercession.[12] Through Silvoso's illness, God was going to teach him how to reach entire cities for Christ, not depending on advertising big meetings and big-name evangelists, but by the biblical application of prayer and spiritual commitment. Silvoso determined that he was not going to do it from the top down (the "trickle down strategy"), such as working through denominational leaders, but by working from the bottom up (the "bubble up strategy"), by working with lay people.

In 1987, Dr. David Yonggi Cho of the Full Gospel Church in Seoul, South Korea, asked Silvoso to organize David Cho's visit to Argentina. Following Cho's seminar in the country, Silvoso was led to go to the city of Resistencia, population 400,000, in northern Argentina, a key door for reaching all of northern Argentina. He came up with what is called "Plan Resistencia." Silvoso began by sharing with pastors of the area that he wanted to organize 500 neighborhood prayer cells to intercede for each section of the city, thus emphasizing unity. He told them of plans to visit every home in the city so that every inhabitant would hear from God. The pastors jumped up and enthusiastically applauded Silvoso's dream.

The dream took feet as the pastors began to pray together on a regular basis, exchanging pulpits and sending love gifts to needy congregations. Christians came together to celebrate their newfound unity in Jesus Christ. They took the Lord's Supper together.

Silvoso next organized 635 neighbor prayer cells (called "lighthouses") scattered throughout the city so that there was prayer in every section of the city and every section was prayed for. Then Silvoso organized people in pairs to walk around every block in the city, praying for every home they passed. This has come to be known as "prayer walking" and is defined as "praying onsite with insight."[13] After they had prayed for approximately three months, Silvoso asked each pair to go to each home and explain to the inhabitants that they were prayer-walking and had been praying for them. The walkers asked the people in each home, "How may we pray for you?" The walkers showed the inhabitants notebooks where their names were listed, which included a column for prayer requests. They wrote down whatever the people requested for prayer and instructed them, "When God answers your prayer, make sure you come and tell us so that we may rejoice together."

Little did Silvoso realize it, but this was a radical paradigm shift in the traditional strategy of evangelism. Usually, an evangelist preached on sin to convict the people of sin (making them feel guilty) and to convince them of their need for a Savior. The strategy was to get people "lost" before they would desire salvation. But this new paradigm was to "bless the unsaved" so that "they would know that the reason God is good to them is because He wants them to turn to Him" (see Rom. 2:4).

After six months, to everyone's surprise, the city's churches had grown an astonishing 201 percent![14] Silvoso says that reaching a city for Christ is much like an army capturing a city. He suggests a six-step strategy for city capturing:

1. Look for, and find, people with whom you can form a "faithful remnant" of believers in the city and recognize that they are God's representatives in Satan's dominion.

2. Secure the perimeters of the city. Silvoso says we must recognize that the enemy has infiltrated the city and through sin has established anxiety throughout. The Christians are to begin praying "to destroy arguments and every bit of pride that keeps anyone from knowing God" (see 2 Cor. 10:4-5).

When churches begin to practice unity in prayer, God begins working.

3. Expand God's perimeters in the city. This is when Christians prayer-walk throughout a city, praying for every home and launching a spiritual attack on the forces that hold the city in spiritual darkness.

4. Infiltrate Satan's perimeter by "parachuting behind enemy lines" through a massive "air assault" of specific intercessory prayer to secure a base of operations. This is done by establishing hundreds of prayer cells throughout the city in order to weaken Satan's control over the unsaved and over the city itself.

5. Attack and destroy Satan's perimeters. This is where the church begins to "take over the city by confronting, binding, and casting down spiritual powers that rule the region."[15] The message of the gospel must be proclaimed to every person in the city, and new believers must be discipled through the established "lighthouses."

6. Establish God's new perimeter where Satan once existed. Silvoso calls this "looting the enemy's camp," whereby they entirely dispossess him of his most prized possessions, the souls of men. Silvoso says, "Unless spiritual warfare results in solid, tangible conversions which are incorporated into a growing number of churches, nothing consequential has happened."[16]

Ed Silvoso believes that every church in the city must go back to the same basic foundation of the Great Commission.

He states, "Every promise, every command in the Bible will be misunderstood unless we interpret it in the light of the Lord's command to win the world for Him."[17]

Silvoso also maps out four levels of city-reaching. The first level is when every lost sheep in the city has a pastor who assumes spiritual responsibility for him. This means there must be a measurable evidence of a canopy of prayer over an entire city—every block, every neighborhood and every lost person in the city being prayed for consistently and systematically.

The second level is when every lost sheep in the city knows who his pastor is due to friendly relationships that have been built up with the lost. Christians must go to unsaved people to bless the lost so that the goodness of God leads them to repentance.

In level three, the spiritual climate over the city changes for the better. When the church meets the needs of the lost and godliness has increased throughout the city, people will want to live for God and to perform acts of kindness. Then it becomes even more evident that God is at work in the city.

Level four is when the city has been transformed and evidences of the kingdom of God are seen throughout the city.[18]

This can really happen! When I (Elmer) was in Mar del Plata, Argentina, I saw a room in the secular city hall building that was dedicated to prayer. The mayor had decreed that city hall needed to provide a place for people to come and pray for the city.

Silvoso says, "Gone are the days when an outside evangelist was expected to come and reach the city for us." Whether that outsider was a foreign missionary in a foreign city, or an evangelist at home in America, Silvoso says, "God expects the [resident] church to reach its city, not some outsider." He goes on to say, "Prayer evangelism is the best way to equip the saints to reach their city."[19]

City-Reaching by the Body of Christ

Frank Damazio uses the phrase "city-reaching" to suggest all churches in one area make a concerted effort to reach their city for Jesus Christ. In *Crossing Rivers, Taking Cities*, Damazio says, "The city church is made up of many Christ-led congregations or many local churches. This is a biblical model and one that is easily followed in the New Testament. Every local church must have its own eldership, personality and focus, but in all that we do, we should seek to glorify God and work together as one church."[20] In his concept of city-reaching, Damazio is talking about each church becoming transformed by the power of God, going out to the entire city to reach them for Christ, and, at the same time, maintaining its own unique personality—different from all the other churches.

Damazio describes the personality of a church as, "The unique methods, procedures, philosophy and style of the local church."[21] He says that you must "love your city while loving your church."[22] He goes on to say, "Evangelism is difficult in our 21st Century church because we are not in the city and the city is not in us."[23]

In his book *City Reaching: On the Road to Community Transformation*, Jack Dennison, founding president of CitiReach International, writes, "The city church is under the eldership of regional leaders, calls for the kind of unity the Lord commanded, but has been in short supply." Dennison uses the following illustration: "The Philippine church . . . considers the church to be made up of all the Christian groups in the whole country. When this kind of mentality becomes common in our nation, we will know that we are getting closer to being brought to complete unity so that the world may know that God sent His Son and His Son has sent us (John 17:23)."[24]

Dennison uses his organization to bring churches together in unity to evangelize their city. He lists others who support and promote the idea of city-reaching:

Many others have brilliantly lighted our pathway. I am building, along with other city-reaching theorists and practitioners, upon the foundations these pioneers have laid. Chief among them is Ray Bakke, Harvie Conn, Roger Greenway, Robert Linthicum and Bob Lupton. Organizations have emerged to flesh out and implement the theology and missiology of the city. Notably, these include John Perkins, Christian Community Development Association, Reid Carpenter's Council of Leadership Foundations and Keith Phillips' World Impact, among others. Books such as John Dawson's *Taking Our Cities for God*, Ed Silvoso's *That None Should Perish*, and George Otis, Jr.'s *Informed Intercession* have brought the awareness and language of city reaching into the everyday conversations of Church leaders and laypersons alike.[25]

So What?

One of the most obvious observations about city-reaching is that there is no consensus among Christians as to what it means and how it should be done. In fact, we have very few examples of North American city-reaching churches to include in this volume. It seems that city-reaching is still mostly a concept and not yet enough of a real-church experience. We pray this will change!

City-reaching churches do have one thing in common: They believe they have a call to the whole city—it is part of their "DNA." Pastor Tim Keller, of the 4,000-attendance Redeemer Presbyterian Church in Manhattan, coordinates a church-planting collaborative called Vision NY, which helps hundreds of other church planters seeking to reach New York. I (Ed) have had the privilege to teach this group, and it is clear they join with Tim Keller in his God-called goal to transform the city for the gospel. Tim Keller wants to use church plants to seed the gospel throughout the city.

"City" is a word with many nuances, covering Jerry Falwell's medium-town Lynchburg, Ed Silvoso's metropolis (city plus suburbs), John Fuder's core city, Keller's Manhattan, and more. Think how different New York's Upper Manhattan is from the burned-out sections of the south Bronx. Compare Los Angeles's Wilshire Boulevard, Hollywood and Beverly Hills. When you say *city*, you are covering a whole spectrum, from the most depressed in the city neighborhoods up to the high-rise districts with million dollar condos. As a result, many different city-reaching strategies are needed.

That leads to another issue. Many churches and denominations have headed to suburbia because it is easier to plant churches where the target audience is undergoing social mobility, where there is ground for new buildings, and where there is a homogeneous middle-class value system. Does city-reaching include suburbia?

It's interesting that those who advocate city-reaching strategies almost never mention the house church, which is so popular around the world and has been especially effective in reaching teeming multitudes throughout China. Furthermore, almost no city-reaching advocate mentions using the cell church, which has also been used quite effectively by Dr. David Yonggi Cho in Seoul, South Korea. Seoul is almost devoid of suburbia as Americans know it. Yet Cho has more than 70,000 small cells meeting weekly in living rooms, laundry rooms, recreational rooms and restaurants. These small groups do evangelism, worship and ministry to meet the needs of its cell members.[26] It would seem that any reasonable strategy for city-reaching would include the house church and the cell church. We need to look again at Larry Stockstill's book *The Cell Church*.[27]

The concept of city-reaching is not a new twenty-first-century method of evangelism. It comes out in the pages of the New Testament. When Jesus gave the Great Commission to His disciples (see Acts 1:8), He told them prayer and spiritual power were the ways to accomplish their task. Jesus said, "I will send the Holy Spirit upon you, just as my Father promised . . . [but] stay here in the city until the Holy Spirit comes and fills you with power from heaven" (Luke 24:49, *TLB*). That involved 10 days of intercessory prayer. Then Jesus said, "You will receive power when the Holy Spirit comes on you; and you will be my witnesses in Jerusalem, and in all Judea and Samaria, and to the ends of the earth" (Acts 1:8, *NIV*). Notice the Lord's emphasis on *cities*. The first place He commanded the disciples to go was into Jerusalem, into their city. Too many missionaries go to a foreign field and begin their work in the rural areas, which certainly is often necessary, but they also tend to neglect the places where they would probably be more likely to find the most lost people—in the cities.

Most mission historians believe that the apostle Paul started churches in a major city in each region and then left the region when there was a church established there. He considered a region to be reached when its major city had a church. He knew that the city church would influence the entire region for the gospel and, once established, he could move on to the next place.

For those who think the rural church or the suburban church is the best or ideal place to live, think again. The last two chapters of the book of Revelation describe a city where we shall live eternally: "I, John, saw the Holy City, the new Jerusalem, coming down from God out of heaven" (Rev. 21:2, *TLB*).

Maybe we have not won whole nations to Christ because we have focused mainly on rural areas or suburban areas and have neglected the cities. If your life and ministry is not fully grounded in a correct understanding of the Great Commission, then you cannot fully understand how God would have you minister.

What Can We Learn from City-Reaching Churches?

Some of these city-reaching churches have big names, but all of them have a big vision. There are many ways in which Christians can learn much from them.

Christians Need to See the Cities as Places *They Should Live*
Tim Keller recently wrote some not-so-subtle ideas about city-reaching in *Christianity Today*. He explained:

> More Christians should live long-term in cities... People who live in large urban cultural centers, occupying jobs in the arts, business, academia, publishing, the helping professions, and the media, tend to have a disproportionate impact on how things are done in our culture . . . Christians should be a community radically committed to the good of the city as a whole.[28]

Many Christians see the city as a place of sin and worldliness, which it does tend to be. But they also forget that cities are places of impact and influence. City-reaching churches teach us that too many Christians have neglected the city. It's ironic for us to have a negative view of the word "city" when the story of the gospel ends in a city—and not just any city, but a *holy* one:

> Then I saw New Jerusalem, that holy city, coming down from God in heaven. It was like a bride dressed in her wedding gown and ready to meet her husband. I heard a loud voice shout from the throne: God's home is now with his people. He will live with them, and they will be his own. Yes, God will make his home among his people (Rev. 21:2-3).

More churches are seeing their call to reach their city—and that's a vision that fits well when our Savior wept over the city as "a sheep without a shepherd" (Luke 19:41).

Christians Need to See Cities as Places *They Must Understand*

When Tim Keller came to New York, he was told, "New York City is unmanageable. You must not come here thinking you are going to tame and save it. You must respect it."[29] Every church reaching a city needs to know its community, its history, its people and its challenges.

Christians Need to See Cities as Places *They Should Reach*

Simply put, Christians and their churches need a vision that's bigger than their neighborhood. They need a vision to reach a city, its people and its potential. That also means reaching more than just people who look like us; it means engaging men and women from every tongue, tribe and nation (see www.peoplegroups.info for a helpful tool to identify the "nations" within a city).

Christians Need to See Cities as Places *They Should Transform*

It is not enough to want to convert the city—as important as that is. City-reaching churches know that it is essential to *transform* the cities. To benefit the city is the goal of a city-reaching church.

God's plan is *shalom* for the city. The term is used 36 times in the Hebrew Old Testament and refers "to a state of fulfillment resulting from God's presence and covenant relationship with God's people. It encompasses ideas of completeness, harmony, and well-being."[30] God's plan for the city is a transformed community. He makes that clear when He speaks of Babylon:

> That the LORD All-Powerful, the God of Israel, had said:
> I had you taken from Jerusalem to Babylonia. Now I tell

you to settle there and build houses. Plant gardens and eat what you grow in them. Get married and have children, then help your sons find wives and help your daughters find husbands, so they can have children as well. I want your numbers to grow, not to get smaller. Pray for peace in Babylonia and work hard to make it prosperous. The more successful that nation is, the better off you will be (Jer. 29:4-7).

Being a transforming community of faith is more than just building a big church. It requires being a transformed *and transforming* church—a church that is transformed by the gospel and that seeks to transform its community. That means it impacts its community more than by just *existing* within it.

What Are the Challenges?

The challenges of a city-reaching church are, in many ways, different than the other types of churches we discuss in this book. The issue for a city-reaching church is not so much whether an entire city *should* be reached as it is an issue of vision and call. The challenges relate more to *how* to reach the city. In this regard, there are several principles to consider.

Passion for the City

First, city-reaching churches need to remember that they are not the only ones with a passion for the city. Reaching the city will require working with other believers to accomplish God's purposes. Too many pastors assume that God is not at work until they arrive—an arrogant and simplistic approach. City-reaching churches recognize that they are not "in this alone." Missiologist Robert Linthicum explains, "One must approach the task with the recognition that God is already at work in this community, and your task as a networker is to discover how He is at work."[31]

The caution here is to not partner with a group with which you're not comfortable theologically. This can be a challenge, because whenever evangelicals start a city-reaching strategy, theological fringe groups (sects, cults, and so forth) all want to be a part. Why? Because partnering with you validates them—something they want and need. City-reaching churches need to partner to transform a community with the gospel, but they need to be sure that those with whom they partner believe and live the gospel.

Announcements of Impending Salvation

Second, city-reaching churches need to avoid announcements of impending salvation. Too many city-reaching churches come across as arrogant—as if nobody is doing anything to reach or serve the city, so they are coming to do the job. I (Ed) experienced this myself when I planted my first church in the inner city of Buffalo, New York. I had arrived filled with vision and enthusiasm. I raised funds with my presentation explaining how "no one" was reaching the people in the inner city. Although I genuinely believed it to be true, I soon found it was not—God was already at work in many African American, Hispanic and other churches.

Churches and pastors need to do their research. If city-reaching movements already exist in your area, get to know their leaders relationally, learn their hearts and discern if there is a hidden agenda, political or otherwise.

A Kingdom Focus

Third, city-reaching churches need to be focused on the kingdom of God and not on just one church. The Kingdom is the focus, which means we must check egos and logos at the door.

The temptation will be for each church to want its name to be known more than for the job to get done! Make sure *God* gets all the credit, and that's enough!

Conclusion

City-reaching churches are beginning to make an impact, but we think their impact in North America has not yet been fully experienced. As more churches choose to impact their *entire* community, we believe that their vision will lead to transformed communities and changed lives.

CHAPTER 6

COMMUNITY TRANSFORMATION CHURCHES

Jesus Christ will keep you busy doing good deeds that
bring glory and praise to God.
PHILIPPIANS 1:11

As I (Ed) briefly mentioned near the end of the previous chapter, the first church I started was in the inner city of Buffalo, New York. At the grand age of 21, I moved, along with my new wife, to the inner city and ministered to prostitutes, teachers, drug addicts and the homeless. I remember meeting the mayor, Jimmy Griffin. He was Irish and Catholic, like the family I grew up in. I was planting a Protestant church, yet he was very kind to our new church, helping us set up activities, dealing with permits on our new building and making introductions to key people.

At first, I did not understand why he was so helpful. We would have few votes to offer and many of the people we reached were former Catholics, who would be coming to our church rather than to his. Then one day he told me why: We had cared enough about his declining city to go in there, while everyone else was leaving. As a result, he wanted to help us.

When we went there in 1988, Buffalo had lost almost half of its population from its peak in 1950. My realtor wondered why I was buying a house when everyone else was "evacuating the city." (The $87,000 house I bought at the time sold for $40,000 five years later—*ouch!*) But we knew that God had called us there to plant a church among the urban poor. We preached the gospel, helped the poor start businesses, served people's needs and cared for addicts and prostitutes. Even Mayor Griffin knew that God had used us to make his city different and better. We were never a big church (and this is probably the only time our service there will ever get mentioned in a book) but people perceive Christians differently when they are living like Jesus lived, loving the way Jesus loved, and leaving behind what Jesus left behind.

Back then, people wondered what we were thinking. Today, community transformation churches have often been enthusiastically embraced by Christians of every stripe—and with good reason. They provide a holistic approach to ministry that is often missed by those unconcerned with physical needs.

Bob Roberts, in his recent book *Transformation*, asked a telling question that describes holistic ministry well: "What do you get when a church combines Billy Graham with Mother Teresa?"[1] His intent was not theological, but methodological. Too many churches lack any serious interest or effort in community transformation. In many communities, the church is seen as a parasite and not a contributor. When the mayor of Stafford, Texas, proclaimed in 2006, "Our city has an excessive number of churches," it made national news.[2] However, he simply voiced what many feel: that too many churches exist for their own benefit. They pay no taxes and give nothing of visceral, tangible value back to the community. Imagine if communities *wanted* churches because of the community transformation that they bring!

Good Deeds and the Gospel

The standard response among many Christians is that we are in the gospel-preaching business. We agree. It matters that a church helps people take their brokenness to God. That emphasis in itself is immeasurably valuable in spiritual terms—eternally valuable, in fact.

Yet, Scripture tells a more complete story. You can't read the Old Testament without noting God's concern for the poor and needy, and His rebuke to His people for not caring or not demonstrating His goodness to others. To paraphrase Proverbs 29:7, the wicked don't care about the rights of the poor, but good people do.

The prophet Isaiah speaks of the kind of fast that God desires: "The kind of fast I want is that you stop oppressing those who work for you and treat them fairly and give them what they earn. I want you to share your food with the hungry and bring right into your own homes those who are helpless, poor, and destitute. Clothe those who are cold, and don't hide from relatives who need your help" (Isa. 58:6-7, *TLB*). Jesus likewise emphasizes how God receives glory when we do good to others: "Let your light so shine before men, that they may see your good works and glorify your Father in heaven" (Matt. 5:16, *NKJV*).

What does community transformation like this look like? In their book *Externally Focused Church*, Rick Rusaw and Eric Swanson point out that Leesburg, Florida, is just a speck on the map of central Florida, and yet its First Baptist Church has spawned nearly 70 ministries that intersect the physical, emotional and spiritual needs of the people of that community! Through their men's shelter, women's care center, latchkey ministry, children's home, community medical care center and dozens of other ministries, they regularly lead hundreds of people to Christ and disciple them toward maturity.[3]

Charles Roesel, Senior Pastor of First Baptist Church of Leesburg, says, "For too long we've evaluated a church by how many people stream in the front door on a Sunday." He proposes an alternative: "Evaluate a church by how many people serve the Lord Jesus by serving the hurting all week long."[4] The growth of his church attendance from 200 to 2,000 is no surprise. "As long as a church ministers to hurting people, it will never lack an audience," Roesel points out.[5]

According to the dozens of examples Rusaw and Swanson provide, it doesn't take rocket science for a church to find ways to show the love of God to its city. A very simple example happened in Kansas City at the United Methodist Church of the Resurrection. When the town was going through economic hardships and morale in school districts was sagging, the church prayed for a way to bless the city. A volunteer team at the church had prepared one addressed card for every employee of the Kansas City School District. From the pulpit, Pastor Adam Hamilton challenged each person in attendance to take one of the pre-addressed cards, pray for the person named on it and, as God would lead, write a note of encouragement and thanks to that teacher, administrator, custodian, cafeteria worker, or whomever the recipient might be. The note was to be written in their own handwriting, with their stamp, and with their personal return address on it.

The entire congregation responded enthusiastically—and the response from the teachers and staff was tremendous. They were overwhelmed by the encouragement and offers of support. Many contacted those who wrote them and, as a result, many members of the Church of the Resurrection became involved in tutoring and reading programs in inner-city schools.[6]

As Robert Lewis so pointedly asks throughout his book *The Church of Irresistible Influence*, if your church closed its doors today, would anyone but its own members notice? Would the city be saddened because such a great community transformation partner was gone? Or would it even miss a beat?[7] These are questions that is taking the missional-church discussion to a new level and making it more a question of deed than of words.

As Lewis recounts in his book *Culture Shift*, the congregation he serves, Fellowship Bible Church, in Little Rock,
Arkansas, needed to do far more than express moments of compassion toward its surrounding town. They needed to establish
relationships and to do things the *city* thought were important.
So they conducted a survey and held some focus groups. They
concluded that the community's greatest area of need was its
schools—the inner-city schools in particular:

> We decided to create an event called ShareFest, where
> we would share a helping hand to certain parts of the
> community including a number of specific schools. As
> we approached school officials, they were at first skep-
> tical and cautious. We assured them that our motive
> was not to preach, but to learn how we could help them.
> "Would you make a wish list of things you need for
> your school that perhaps we could help you with?" we
> asked. They did and we proceeded to bless them with
> all kinds of gifts: from new paint to new carpets to new
> playgrounds–all with no strings attached. We simply
> gave and left.[8]

The idea worked so well they did it again the next year. On
the Sunday after they completed their second year, they invited
three inner-city principals to Fellowship Bible Church to speak
in the Sunday worship services. During the interviews, each one
gave glory to God for the church's investment in the community, saying, "We have a new school because of you." Robert Lewis
continues:

> One of our initiatives during Sharefest is to go door to
> door, meeting people in low-income communities and
> asking if we could help with home repairs and needs.

One day as one of our members, Ray Williams, was mowing an elderly widow's yard, a young elementary school student named Michael, who lived there with his grandmother, came up to Ray and said, out of the blue, "Will you be my mentor?"

Ray's immediate thought was, *I don't have time.* Instead he asked, "What do you mean?"

The boy explained that they talk a lot at school about having a mentor, and since he really didn't have a family, he needed a mentor.

"Let me think about it," Ray answered.

God tugged at Ray's heart and he ultimately said "yes." He found out that Michael was a troubled kid. Ray asked the principal if he could start having lunch with Michael and he received a very reluctant okay. Ray started meeting Michael on a regular basis, helping with homework, and in many ways looking out for him as a son.

Ray's entrance into that school through Michael paid off and soon they were asking him, "Can your church send us some more mentors?" We did and even had the privilege of refurbishing that school through Sharefest. All because a white guy named Ray was willing to build a small bridge of love in an inner-city neighborhood.[9]

A Dominant Social Force for Good?

Despite what some may say, Christianity has been and still is the most powerful force for good in Western culture. Churches, for all their faults—both real and imagined—have been a highly positive force in Western society. The command of Jesus' to love our neighbor has inspired a steady outpouring of social and philanthropic work. In fact, historian William G. McLoughlin goes as far as to say that the great spiritual awakenings in

American history have influenced most of our nation's social reforms. He contends that they are "the catalysts of social change."[10]

Numerous studies confirm that the public today, especially media and intellectual leaders, do not see Christianity as a dominant social force. For example, Stephen L. Carter's book *The Culture of Disbelief: How American Law and Politics Trivialize Religious Devotion* describes the marginalization of today's church. According to Carter, a Yale Law School professor who describes himself as a churchgoing Episcopalian, "religion" is no longer invited into public discussion except perhaps as a novelty. The title of his second chapter reveals that when the sacred has been stripped away from public life, we can then only talk of "God as a hobby."[11]

The fact remains, however, that the record of Christian charity is so impressive that even John Dewey, one of the founders of modern humanism, praised believers for their social conscience. And criminologists today, such as political scientist John Dilulio, have studied the data on urban crime and concluded that the best hope for urban youth comes from gospel-centered churches and faith-based ministries.[12]

Christianity has never touched a culture in a significant way without changing it in a positive way. Authentic Christians advocate social justice in their society and practice the social implications of the gospel in their lives. The abolition of slavery, prison reform, the care of widows and orphans, and the development of hospitals and schools are some of the historic cultural and societal reforms that find their roots in the faith of biblical Christianity.

Even today, in an age when it seems Christianity has so little direct influence on contemporary Western culture, deeply committed Christians and Christian organizations are at the forefront of humanitarian programs to feed the poor (famine relief worldwide; breakfast programs in North America), treat the sick (AIDS education in Africa; drug rehabilitation programs in America), and reform society (prison reform, literacy projects, and so forth). Could these be the seeds that will flourish in the next outpouring of the Holy Spirit and give rise to the next cultural transformation in history?

The mere presence of Christians in a community does not transform the culture, however. Cultural transformation only takes place when Christians consistently practice their faith in their personal lives and allow their values to be shaped by biblical principles. When that does not happen, Jesus Himself described those kinds of Christians as being "good for nothing but to be thrown out and trampled underfoot by men" (Matt. 5:13, *NKJV*). Karl Marx called Christianity the opiate of the people because he failed to see Christians allowing their faith to motivate them to address the social problems in London, England. Mahatma Gandhi studied Christianity and the teachings of Jesus at a time when Christians refused to address the issue of Apartheid in South Africa and concluded, "I would be a Christian if it were not for Christians."

How different from the transformational movement described in the New Testament. There, the enemies of Christianity were forced to admit that Paul and Silas had been upsetting things everywhere by proving that Jesus had to suffer and that He rose from the dead. But the Jews were jealous and rounded up some bad characters from the marketplace, formed a mob, started a riot in the city and blamed it on Paul and Silas in order to put an end to what they were doing for Christianity in the community (see Acts 17:4-6).

The source of Christianity's power to change cultures is found in another description of those Early Christians as well: "Now when they saw the boldness of Peter and John, and perceived that they were uneducated and untrained men, they

marveled. And they realized that they had been with Jesus"
(Acts 4:13, *NKJV*). That kind of Christianity has always resulted in positive social change.

What We Can Learn

There are several important truths we can learn from community transformation churches.

Churches Interested in Community Transformation Changed the Roman World

It is a bit of an overstatement to say that the Early Church grew
remarkably in the first century. Although notable in the first
century, the truly remarkable growth did not take place until
the second and third centuries. As sociologist Rodney Stark
detailed in *The Rise of Christianity*, a great plague spread throughout the Middle East in the year 165. As much as one-third of
the population died. In 251, a second major epidemic caused
entire towns to be abandoned. According to Stark, Christianity
spread rapidly because Christians responded differently than
others: They stayed and cared for the sick and dying.[13]

The Poor Are Central to the Message of Scripture

Many evangelicals are just now discovering that the gospel
includes transformation of communities. Rick Warren recently
confessed his own oversight when he wrote:

> Jesus came to preach the gospel to the poor . . . For a
> long time I had blinders on about this. I went to a
> Baptist college and two seminaries and it wasn't until a
> couple of years ago that I asked, "How did I miss 2,000
> verses about the poor?" I just didn't see it.[14]

Scripture provides overwhelming clarity: Part of the role of
Christians in society is to evidence Christ's love though acts of

mercy and to "seek the welfare of the city where I have sent you" (Jer. 29:7, *NASB*).

Things We Should Be Cautious About

There are also some areas where we should be cautious, not about transformation communities but about *balance*.

The Social Gospel Really Is a Concern

The reality is that many churches with a passion for social justice tend to soon lose their passion for those without Christ. Jesus was concerned for both social justice and the lost.

About 100 years ago, a debate was raging across North America and Europe. A movement known as "theological liberalism" emphasized that the Church should have a strong social influence. At the same time, it rejected the idea that people go to heaven or hell when they die based on how they have responded to the message of Jesus Christ. This movement also threw out the idea of supernatural miracles such as Jesus' virgin birth or bodily resurrection from the dead. It also denied that God had supernaturally inspired the writers of the Bible.

Perhaps the most important and influential theologian during that era was Adolph von Harnack (1851-1930). His best-selling book *What Is Christianity?* was highly controversial because of how it redefined the gospel.[15] Then, in 1917, American theologian Walter Rauschenbusch (1861-1918) wrote *A Theology of the Social Gospel* in which he postulated that when Jesus spoke about the kingdom of God, this meant not the community of the redeemed, but the transformation of society on Earth. To him, the gospel meant social reform and political action. This concept became known as the social gospel.[16]

Another movement that was birthed at the beginning of the 1900s had as its slogan: *The evangelization of the world in this generation*. It became the cry of the world's first international interdenominational gathering to promote and strategize missions. But, adversely influenced by the social gospel movement, the focus soon changed. Within a few decades, the group questioned the need for personal witness and instead focused on service. In a few more decades, the term "evangelism" was redefined to mean anything for the betterment of society *except* proclaiming the need to repent of sin and turn to Jesus. The social gospel has, time and again, pushed away the gospel of conversion. It is crucial that we guard against losing the gospel in the name of serving the poor.

The Gospel Is About Liberation, Not Economics

It is important that Jesus started His earthly ministry talking about "jubilee," an economic practice where the poor were restored (see Lev. 25:10; Luke 4:18-19). It was part of His message, but that was not His whole message. Helping set the poor free spiritually in Christ is the beginning of the gospel message. Serving them through acts of mercy is the rest of the message. It is important we keep things in that order.

The Gospel Must Not Be Lost

In their book *Into the Future*, Elmer Towns and Warren Bird offer a checklist of concerns to guard the gospel from being watered down:

1. Are we teaching a practical atheism (compromised theology)? We are if we make little reference to God and show little dependence on the Holy Spirit.

2. Are we controlled more by methodology than by theology (unbiblical principles)? We are if our theological understanding is superficial and our primary interest is in methodology.

3. Are we ignoring the warnings of history (naive view of culture)? We are if we display a minimal sense of historical awareness from similar situations in the past.

4. Are we overly concerned with numbers and bigness (inappropriate methods)? We are if our goal is anything less than being fully committed followers of Jesus Christ, growing toward maturity in the community of a local church.

5. Are we allowing carnal motives to corrupt our testimony for Christ and His kingdom (unholy view of human nature)? We are if we fail to say *no* to ever-present temptations of pride, arrogance, envy and deceit.[17]

Walking Our Talk

What is a *real* Christian like? The answer to that important question—even from those only casually familiar with the Christian faith—usually boils down to one basic concept: A Christian is someone who lives like Jesus would.

In most people's thinking, if we're followers of Jesus Christ, then we help people in need, are honest even when no one's looking, care deeply about the concerns that matter most to God, have left all of our selfish attachments and are following Jesus. In a world that loves to spot hypocrisy in everyone from television evangelists to church-going soccer moms, deeds of compassion make a loud statement about the love and power of God.

How do we reach secular people in today's culture? "The strategic response is to connect Christian social concern with evangelism,"[18] says George Hunter, author of such titles as *How to Reach Secular People, Church for the Unchurched* and *The Celtic Way of Evangelism: How Christianity Can Reach the West . . . Again.*[19]

We are enthusiastic about community transformation churches. These churches see the message of Jesus and combine them with the model of Jesus—to proclaim the gospel and to serve people in the process.

CHAPTER 7

CYBER-ENHANCED CHURCHES

*Intelligent people want to learn, but stupid people
are satisfied with ignorance.*
PROVERBS 15:14, *GNB*

"You can complete your degree entirely online, and the people who truly have committed themselves to it have the possibility of getting an even better experience online than in the class-room," says Dr. Anthony Davidson, professor and assistant dean at New York University Online, which recently launched its first online bachelor's degree programs for adults. "They take classes together and never meet each other, yet they behave like other college students would, asking each other what courses they've signed up for next semester and the like," he explains.

"The technology is such that I can actually have great inter-action with my students," adds Davidson. "There is a white-board available for me to communicate with them; they watch me lecture on live video; I can run PowerPoint presentations; share applications; and break the students into groups in separate chat rooms—everything I'd do in an on-campus classroom."

But can't a student cheat by not showing up? Not accord-ing to other experts. "Pepperdine University's program is built on social-constructivist theory and relies on group proj-ects, journaling and synchronous online participation to eval-uate students rather than traditional tests," says Dr. Paul Sparks, director of the school's online master's program in educational technology. "It's impossible to cheat in such an environment simply because teachers, and other students, can easily hear the 'voices' of their colleagues through the various interactions. You could say our solution to this online learning issue is treating learning as a community activity quite resistant to cheating and fraud."[1]

Churches Do Online Classes as Well

The educational world is not alone in becoming high tech. Churches have become quite savvy in learning to use similar approaches to training. My (Elmer's) closest parallel was a 2004 experience in which I taught an Internet-based class on fasting at the World Prayer Center located at New Life Church in Colorado Springs, Colorado. It was a for-credit course offered through the Wagner Leadership Institute, which for many years has been housed at New Life Church.

The students had been invited by e-mail to take the class and used the Internet to register. They were given the choice between taking a literal chair in person with me in Colorado Springs or to reserve a "cyber chair" in the class via the Internet.

When the course began, I was in a classroom with 14 students. In addition, 14 other students watched and listened through their computers by streaming video. In-class students raised their hands to ask questions. Online students e-mailed their questions. The cameraman in the room intercepted and posted them for all to see. I could read the questions on the teacher's monitor, the in-person students could read them on the class monitor, and the online students saw the questions on their computers. It felt surprisingly natural to conduct a Q&A session through the Internet with students located in Singapore, Hong Kong, Taipei, Seoul and various cities across Canada. One time I answered several questions in a row from a cyber-student who wanted to know what liquids could be consumed during a fast.

During the two days I taught the class, I gave four quizzes and received positive feedback as the students were signing off after the final lecture.

Local and Global Training

The Internet is capable of being used effectively for far more than classroom instruction. Followers of Christ are using the Internet in new and creative ways, often to supplement in-person community, and sometimes in place of in-person gatherings. The common theme in healthy cyber-ministry is that it continues to place high priority on human relationships. However, "virtuality" can never replace face-to-face human interaction.

A case in point is Seacoast Church, based in a suburb of Charleston, South Carolina. This church puts great emphasis on powerful worship and strong teaching in its weekend worship services. But it places equal priority on developing a broad network of laity-led small groups. "If you're not in a small group, you're really not in the church," senior pastor Greg Surratt and other leaders tell the congregation.

Seacoast doesn't want its small-group leaders to fail, so it places a high value on training the leaders to be effective. But surprisingly, when the church offered special classes to meet the needs of small-group leaders, only a small percentage turned up for the in-person meetings.

As the church continued to grow and expand, it faced severe space limitations for its weekend worship. *The Multi-Site Church Revolution*, a book co-authored by Geoff Surratt, brother of Seacoast's senior pastor, chronicled the church's efforts (many of them quite humorous) to find more space.[2] The net outcome was that by 2006, the church was meeting in 10 different locations, with two-thirds of the congregation meeting somewhere other than at the original campus (see chapter 3, "Multi-site Churches").

Sensing God's hand in their multi-campus approach, Seacoast Church is planning to open potentially dozens more locations, each with a campus pastor in the essential role of local point person. Seacoast has found, as have most churches, that their best campus pastors start off as effective small-group leaders. Each of those leaders can become, in turn, a small-group coach, then a pastor to small-group coaches and leaders, and then a full campus pastor.

The church's ongoing growth, augmented by the need for more campus pastors, made the need for training small-group leaders all the more important. So Seacoast put even more energy and attention into its training classes for small-group leaders. But again, they experienced dismal response. They experimented with different dates, different formats, different curriculum and different means of publicizing the opportunity, but still gained only a small increase in response. Additionally, the issue of multiple campuses made it all the more challenging to create in-person meetings.

After two years of extensive development, the church launched a website (www.mynextsteps.org) to offer online small-group training. The response and participation spiked upward.

The first step in this online training course is to take an online diagnostic test called a "Spiritual Health Assessment," which was designed to ascertain where a person is spiritually in his or her personal growth and development as a follower of Christ. After answering 55 multiple-choice questions (which take 5 to 10 minutes in all), each user immediately receives a personalized visual graphic showing progress in each of five areas of training and growth. That person can then click on a purpose area to find resources to help with the next steps—books, articles, messages and Bible studies—many available online.

Next, the online participants choose a track in leadership development. Most start with a basic six-week session on how to become a small-group leader. It includes interactive videos and is designed to be done by a participant or assistant leader in a small group with input and oversight from the leader of the group. Topics range from skill training to theology. All training involves human mentors, with in-person dialog supplementing the online material wherever possible.

"Our training is no longer a story of only 20 people showing up for a class," says Chris Surratt, one of the staff pastors at Seacoast and brother of Greg and Geoff Surratt. "Now well over 100 are benefiting, and that number is growing. Plus the approach works great for our mobile campuses."

Seacoast's experience is not unique. North Point Community Church in Alpharetta, Georgia (discussed in chapter 8), uses the Internet exclusively for its teachers' meetings, doing away with face-to-face encounters except on Sunday mornings when they actually teach. The Internet is used by leaders and teachers in the children's division for content communication, scheduling of events during class and fine-tuning class procedures. One of the main reasons they arrived at Internet teacher training is that people didn't have time for an extra meeting during the week. Demands for attending training sessions or teachers' meetings actually prohibited—rather than helped—teacher recruitment. "Our classes wouldn't be nearly as effective without the Internet," said Kendra Fleming, Director of Children's Ministry at North Point Community Church.

Christ the King Community Church, based just north of Seattle, Washington, has a vision not only of launching hundreds of small groups locally but also of launching worship centers all around the world. One of the frequent sayings of lead pastor Dave Browning aptly summarizes their entire approach to ministry: "Some churches convene by hundreds in hopes of reaching thousands. We convene by tens in hopes of reaching tens of thousands. By gathering 10 at a time we can reach into nearly any pocket or community around the world. We meet in more locations and in smaller locations than almost any other church!"

Indeed they do. In the last decade, the church has expanded from 1 location to 16 in Washington state. Out-of-state congregations are currently in Oregon, Colorado and Hawaii, and international congregations are currently in Panama, Kenya and India.

Given this vision, Christ the King has established a way of training local small-group leaders that also works for small groups based in other states and countries. It involves on-site face-to-face mentoring mixed with Internet-based training through what the church calls Christ the King University (CTKU), available at www.ctkonline.com.

"The mission of CTKU is to catalyze the rapid expansion of Christ's kingdom by preparing leaders for effective outreach," Browning says. "CTKU is an online, multi-media approach to personal development."

Profile of Ginghamsburg Church

A church doesn't need to cover a large geographical area in order to benefit from the Internet. For example, Ginghamsburg Church of Tipp City, Ohio, sees a huge amount of local ministry happen each week through its website. Those who miss the weekend service can watch, hear or read the message online. Or they can join a local online community that offers a discussion forum to help people connect with others who share similar interests. Or they can dialog with others about the day's Transformation Journal—which includes a short teaching, Scripture passage and related questions that the entire church is encouraged to go through together.

The Ginghamsburg Church's website, started by volunteers in 1997, now has more than 4,000 pages. The church website's total ministry involves the following:

- *Care:* Lists of support groups and related information, helping hands bulletin board and job connections.
- *Devotionals:* Available both as e-mail subscriptions and as postings with group discussion. Tailored versions are available for adults, youth and children.
- *Events:* Online calendar, event descriptions and registration.
- *Fellowship:* Many discussion forums, a page for sending encouragement e-cards, and a cell-group sign-up form.
- *Guest hospitality:* Offers virtual facility tours to potential church guests and newcomer FAQs.
- *Memorials:* Photos and videos of deceased loved ones and postings about loved ones.
- *Ministry team support:* Private forums and e-mail lists with password-protected file sharing.
- *Missions:* Information about missionaries and mission trips and photos and mission-trip blogs.
- *News:* Current church news and weekly bulletin.
- *Prayer:* Community prayer exchange, e-mail prayer chains, and light-a-virtual-candle.
- *Resources:* Online store for purchasing items to be mailed or downloaded, and a church business directory.
- *Sermons:* Three versions: video, audio, printed; delivered via web pages, podcast, vodcast and RSS.
- *Service:* Servant role catalog and commitment form.
- *Stewardship:* Ability to make financial donations.

The list above is generic only; the website is not laid out that way. It is currently divided as follows:

- Worship Together
- Explore Ginghamsburg
- Visit Our Ministries
- Connect in Community
- Grow in Christ
- Serve Others
- Get Assistance
- Church Resources

Interestingly, the church's web ministry began very simply. Mark Stephenson, a church member, started it in 1996. "When I began, I had not built a website before and knew little about how it might be used at a church," he recalls. "I started the ministry because I felt in my heart that God wanted me to do this and that the web was going to be an incredibly powerful tool for ministry. Plus, I love computers. What could be more fun than doing computer stuff for the Kingdom?"

Working evenings and weekends as an unpaid servant, Mark spent much of the next year learning how to build a website. "I found a church brochure and typed it into my computer," he reports. "I used one of those old hand-operated scanners to scan in the church logo from the brochure. I then spent hours trying to fix it so that it did not look like I scanned it in. Somehow I was able to create the first pages of the website by typing the HTML in a text editor and mostly messing up a lot."

As the ministry grew, many other volunteers joined Mark. They brought additional skills, passions and available time. They created online communities. They recorded church sermons on VHS tape, digitized them and put them online in streaming video and also in text format. "Before I knew it, we had about

30 unpaid servants and our website had over 1,000 pages," he says. "According to website statistics, people were coming to the website from around the world from over 30 different countries."[3]

Today Mark Stephenson is fulltime on church staff as Director of CyberMinistry and Technology, and he leads a worldwide ministry called "Web-Empowered Church" (see http://webEmpoweredChurch.com) that is developing free web software and training for Christian church and ministry websites. He is also author of *Web-Empower Your Church: Unleashing the Power of Internet Ministry*.[4] He has watched the church's cyberministry develop to the point that national media, such as the *Wall Street Journal* and *Dallas Morning News*, have featured it.

Mark's guiding vision is for the church's website to enhance everything the church does, even its most basic, relational goals such as creating community. "One thing we learned is that online community is a whole lot like face-to-face community. Visitors are just people communicating via a little different mechanism,"[5] he says. Any church, small or large, can use the Internet to support ministry, he believes. "Online community can happen when there is an environment that provides healthy social interaction, exchange of opinions, requests and responses, and useful information."[6]

Totally Online Church?

A handful of much-publicized "churches" are completely Internet based. Perhaps the best known is Church of Fools, originating from Liverpool, England, which opened in May 2004 as a three-month experiment to reach people who don't go near brick-and-mortar churches. Visually designed in a Romanesque style, Church of Fools offered a regular Sunday service, impromptu weekday services, private prayer, occasional counseling and freewheeling group discussions via text. The unusual cyber-church features three-dimensional cartoon surrogates controlled by individual computer users that act like sinners, saints and skeptics.

The church was an outgrowth of Ship of Fools (www.shipof fools.com), a humorous and sometimes irreverently challenging web magazine and online community that began several years ago for post-modern Christians to explore new ways of looking at church without a top-down institutional structure.

Opening day was a bit chaotic, as someone claiming to be Satan briefly grabbed control of the cyber pulpit. Other ornery participants worked in teams to block the church "door," keeping out more serious visitors. Order was imposed by barring sanctuary access, limiting how far visitors' typed comments could be "heard," and boosting the number of volunteer wardens who could use "smite" buttons to eject unrepentant online disrupters.

"What we're doing is similar to churches in difficult urban situations," cofounder Steve Goddard told an interviewer. "We don't want to eject people just because they're not behaving in the way churches traditionally expect. Our aim is to welcome people who don't normally go to church, so 'difficult' people are, by definition, who we're aiming for."

Most visitors entered the church as eavesdropping observers, each represented by a ghostlike avatar that's invisible to others. Up to 500 at a time could wander the church, walk down to a discussion lounge, give a blessing or make 11 other gestures privately. Some visitors become one of 25 to 30 solid avatars. These figures walk, kneel, sit and make public gestures, such as throwing their arms up in a hallelujah exclamation. They also could use typed comments to pray, shout out, whisper confidentially to another "solid" or conduct dialogue with groups of them.

About 60,000 people visited the site the first two days, and then, predictably, attendance dropped off. But for the three-month life of the church, a steady stream of people tried it.

A more serious, ongoing cyber-church is Alpha Church (www.alphachurch.org), which has about 6,000 regular online participants. Alpha Church describes itself as a full, online Christian global church in which people can worship at any time, take Holy Communion, receive baptism (with the help of a friend), and chat with other people who are growing in their faith and understanding of Jesus Christ.

"Bobby" is a full member of Alpha Church. He attends his church every week, sometimes several times during the week. Bobby was the first to be baptized at Alpha Church. As a young man working in a suburb of Atlanta, he had spoken on many occasions with the Alpha Church pastor, a former United Methodist pastor named Patricia Walker. He had done all she'd asked him to do, and he was ready. He had two witnesses by his side. He had invited his family and his friends to the big event. He even invited all his coworkers. All the necessary trappings for the event were on his office desk: a Bible, a towel, a basin of water and the telephone. The big moment came.

As family and coworkers crowded into his suburban office, Bobby telephoned Pastor Walker, put her on speakerphone, and proceeded with the ancient rite of baptism. "In the name of the Father, the Son and the Holy Spirit," came the voice over the phone as the two witnesses poured water over Bobby's head.

Can a community exist that consists only of patterned ones and zeros traveling thousands of miles through copper wires and fiber optic filament? For some today, the answer is a qualified yes. For most, the answer is an unreserved no.

When one looks at innovation through the lens of Scripture, most would consider these "churches" to be more like outreaches. However, the Alpha Church and others do not. They consider themselves to be functioning biblical churches, much to the chagrin of many Christians (more on that later).

Church Outreach Through the Internet

Back in 2004, a survey of more than 2,000 adults by the Pew Internet and American Life Project measured the different ways that Internet users go online for spiritual purposes. The findings included the following:

- 38 percent have sent and received e-mails with spiritual content.
- 32 percent have gone online to read news accounts of religious events.
- 21 percent have sought information about how to celebrate religious holidays.
- 17 percent have looked for information about where they could attend religious services.
- 7 percent have made or responded to online prayer requests.
- 7 percent have made donations to religious organizations or charities.[7]

Interestingly, research on Internet usage among Protestant churches in the United States confirms there is a growing technology gap between larger and smaller churches. A 2005 study found that 27 percent of churches still have no technological connectivity at all—no staff e-mail, no website and no Internet connection. Larger churches, however, provide much more content for visitors to their websites. Researcher Ron Sellers, president of Ellison Research, says, "Their sites are . . . much more interactive, with ways to contact staff, learn about upcoming events, watch streaming audio or video, and submit prayer requests."[8]

Statistics about Internet usage are usually outdated as soon as they're reported, but the general picture since 2005 is that more people use the Internet than attend church. The Barna

Research Group calculated that 56 percent of American adults attend church during a typical month, but an even higher percent access the Internet during that month.[9] However, only a portion of those Internet users currently go to faith-related websites. According to the Pew Internet and American Life Project, 64 percent of Internet users in the United States perform religious and spiritual activities online—a group whose size continues to increase each year.[10]

The Barna Research Group predicts that by the end of the decade, upwards of 100 million Americans will rely on the Internet to deliver some aspect of their religious experience to them and 50 million will seek to have their spiritual experience solely through the Internet rather than at a brick-and-mortar church. A Reuters report disputes the conclusion that millions will eventually abandon their physical church to join online spiritual communities, saying that most religion surfers combine their online activities with their off-line religious functions.[11]

"Using a computer for online religious activity could become the dominant form of religion and religious activity in this century," says Brenda Brasher, author of *Give Me That Online Religion*.[12] While researching her book, Brasher discovered more than one million religious websites, encompassing every major religious tradition in the world.

"The Internet is not moving people away from their congregations and their faiths. It's helping them move closer," concludes Lee Rainie, director of the Pew Internet project.[13]

Podcasting and Blogging for Jesus

Mark Batterson, pastor of National Community Church in Washington, D.C., likes to have fun when people ask him how many people visited his church during the last month. In 2006 he was saying 12,771. When his listeners are taken aback, he then eggs them on further. "Truth be told, they didn't really visit us. National Community Church visited them."

The people Batterson is describing didn't physically attend a weekend worship service. "Many aren't ready to walk into a church service yet," he says. "Plus, others live halfway around the world."

Is there a catch to this story? "All of them invited our church into their iPods," he explains. "In a sense, they invited me to go jogging with them, to commute to work with them, or to hang out with them." All they had to do was clock onto the www.the aterchurch.com podcast.

The church was already recording the weekly messages on CD, so all they had to do was start uploading them to the MP3 format required for a downloadable podcast. They launched in July 2005 with only a few people pulling the podcasts. Then the *New York Times* did an article on religion and podcasting called "TiVo for Your Soul." It featured National Community Church. That story was followed with primetime reports by both CBS and FOX news for the D.C. market. "Six months later, we're impacting more people via our podcast than we are with our weekend services," Batterson says.

This outreach venue is new for Batterson and his team. "Podcasting 101 wasn't offered when I was in seminary," he says. "Neither was Blogging 101. But the digital revolution has presented us with an unprecedented opportunity. It's redefining the way I think about evangelism and discipleship."

Batterson draws a lesson from history, noting that when John Wesley was ordained in 1728, the standard assumption is that his preaching would take place behind a pulpit inside the four walls of a church sanctuary. Outdoor preaching was considered to be improper.

But there were too many people Wesley wanted to reach who wouldn't or couldn't come to church. So he broke the mold.

"He was not trying to be different for different's sake," comments Batterson. "His unorthodox methodology of 'field preaching' and 'circuit riding' prompted disenfranchisement and death threats." So why did Wesley take his preaching offsite? "In his own words: 'I look upon the world as my parish,'" says Batterson.

"Like Johann Gutenberg did when he used his new printing press to get more Bibles into more hands, why not redeem the iPod into a tool for evangelism and discipleship?" asks Batterson. "The message is sacred; the medium isn't. Who says preachers have to preach from behind a pulpit and parishioners have to listen while seated on wooden pews?"

Batterson receives e-mails that confirm his decision to use cyberspace to enhance his local church. Here's one e-mail that reached him:

Dear Pastor Mark,

I read about your church in the *New York Times* article. It was through that article that I started subscribing to your podcast. I'm writing from Singapore, and I just wanted to thank Theaterchurch.com for expanding their outreach outside the U.S.

Your last series really spoke to me. After listening, I really heard and felt God telling me to return to my burning bush experience. I needed to re-anchor in the things that God had done in my life when I was at college in the U.S. eleven years ago.

As I listened to the messages over my Powerbook, God's presence was SO strong. He enveloped every corner of my room. That evening, God met me and gave me back my fervor.

It's exciting to hear what God is doing with Theaterchurch.com 10,000 miles away from where I am physically. I live halfway around the world, yet it doesn't sound like it's that far away![14]

"Religious believers want more 'God on their iPod,' and churches are rapidly finding that through podcasting, church members can take the Sunday sermon with them throughout the week," comments Lee Rainie, president of Christian.com and owner of www.GodCast1000.com, the largest podcasting directory on the Internet dedicated solely to Christian podcasts—including video podcasting. "While only a few megachurches can afford to preach their message to the world through TV and radio broadcasting, almost any church can have a podcast that goes around the world."[15] Likewise an article in the *St. Petersburg Times* says, "webcasts are perhaps the biggest thing since televangelism to reach people around the world."[16]

For example, Harvest Christian Fellowship in Riverside, California, made it possible for people to watch two- to three-minute video sermons by their pastor, Greg Laurie, on their cell phones for a modest monthly subscription price.[17] As another example, pastor Mark Driscoll of Mars Hill Church preaches to a large crowd (5,000 each week) in Seattle, one of the most unchurched cities in North America, and reaches many more through his podcasts (which are offered free). Some 230,000 people download his MP3 messages each month, the second-most frequent download on I-tunes the week of this writing.

Huge numbers of people today—believers and seekers alike—are looking to the Internet for spiritual resources. In the extreme, a few churches are experimenting with the idea of being entirely Internet based. More likely are churches that have used the Internet to effectively enhance every aspect of discipleship and community building. Pioneers like Mark Batterson are using the Internet to help the church go forward in its mission. "I'll be the first person to say that podcasting is a poor substitute for church. But it's a great supplement," he concludes.[18]

In 2006, LifeChurch, a congregation based in Edmond, Oklahoma, with nine different locations across Oklahoma, Arizona, Tennessee and Texas, set up www.mysecret.tv as a forum for people to confess anonymously on the Internet. The website represents the first time the church has had an interactive website tied to its sermons. Craig Groeschel, the church's lead pastor, said that after 16 years in the ministry, he knew that the smiles and eager handshakes that greet him each week often mask a lot of pain. But he told the *New York Times* that the accounts of anguish and guilt that have poured into www.mysecret.tv have stunned him. "I can't tell you how many hundreds of times people have told me that 'I'm going to tell you something, Pastor, I've never told anyone before,'" Groeschel said, as reported in the *Times*. "I realized that people are carrying around dark secrets, and the Web site is giving them a first place for confession."[19]

LifeChurch has also created an Internet campus. No, it's not like watching a televangelist on TV, where viewers are completely disconnected with one another. While viewers can experience the service anonymously, LifeChurch.tv encourages people to register and login, and then hang out in the virtual lobby after the worship experience to chat with other worshipers as well as the campus pastor. Just like their physical campuses, the Internet campus has small groups, called Life Groups, that people are encouraged to join (and that are listed online). Many groups actually meet together physically during the week in places like St. Louis, Missouri, and Charlotte, North Carolina.

Using your God-given gifts to serve others is an important aspect of life in a local church, and LifeChurch.tv's Internet campus provides numerous opportunities to do so. People can start their own Life Group, help answer technical questions, or even go on a virtual missions trip to the popular social networking website, MySpace. One week, for example, a bunch of folks from the Internet campus gathered in the chat lobby to pray and to talk about how to share the gospel in MySpace. Then everyone logged into their MySpace accounts and began having spiritual conversations with their MySpace friends and inviting them to one of Life Church's Internet campus life experiences. At the end of the micro mission, they met back in the chat lobby to discuss what God did during that time and to thank Him for His work.[20]

What Can We Learn from Cyber-Enhanced Churches?

Churches should definitely use the Internet. Duh. That should be about as much news to you as the fact that churches should answer the phone. But they don't (in both cases, actually). According to Barna, 55 percent of churches polled don't even answer the phone![21] So the fact that many churches do not use the Internet shouldn't come as a shock.

If churches are to reach connected people, they need to be connected churches. For some reason, Christians have been slow to adopt the Internet as a means of communication. Some are still wondering if it will catch on, like indoor plumbing did. Yet today as individuals we process e-mail all day, read the *Drudge Report*, listen to streaming video from CNN and pay our bills online. We do much of our interaction right now over the Internet—except when it comes to church.

We believe churches can and should embrace the Internet in every way it can without losing the essence of church. This will not always be easy. As Marshall McLuhen proposed decades ago, "The medium is the message." In other words, how something is communicated will in many ways impact and even alter the message. Yet, there are and should be ways to use such technology. Here are a few.

The Internet Can Be Used to Connect

Many churches have realized that the Internet need not be a tool of isolation but can be a tool for connection. Who would have thought that those scary people finding dates on the Internet would become mainstream—but they are. They connect people with similar core interests (or something similar, according to Neil Clark Warren's secret formula) and introduce them to each other. Churches, particularly larger ones, can connect people with similar needs, burdens and concerns easily and quickly.

It is not just large churches that can use such cyber enhancements to connect. Churches small and large can connect members though community bulletin boards and prayer chains. Many churches offer private web pages and forums for churches to share and fellowship together. Some organizations, such as Church Community Builder, are built around the premise that the Internet should be used to build community (hence the name) rather than decrease it.

The Internet Can Be Used to Inform

The Internet is information. That's really all there is to it. Bits of zeros and ones put together to form letters, pictures and other media that combine to create information. That information can and should be a tool to inform God's people.

Currently now on my (Ed's) iPod, I have downloaded five Masters level seminary courses that I listen to each morning, music that I listen to throughout the day, a morning devotion, and several sermons from pastors I admire. I get almost all of my information now from podcasts. Print alone no longer cuts it (our publisher, Regal Books, long ago branched into video and other non-print formats). People look to the Internet to inform, and they read books like this one to tell them to do that!

The Internet Can Be Used to Disciple

Discipleship best happens in community. But information can make discipleship more effective. Information does not necessarily lead to discipleship and life transformation, but it can be a help in the process. When a person can learn about the Scriptures and their application, this can and should be a good thing.

What We Need to Consider

This is a tough one, so let's start with the easiest part. Although Internet "churches" may get a lot of attention, we simply cannot find a biblical basis for a church without real-life human community. If you can't meet with one another (see Heb. 10:25), accept one another (see Rom. 15:7), bear with one another (see Eph. 4:2), submit to one another (see Eph. 5:21) and be removed from one another (see 1 Cor. 5:9), then that is not church. The New Testament contains 59 different "one another" commands.[22] In order to be the church, you need to be able to personally engage with *one another*.

For example, how can a church pray together if it exists only in cyberspace? Sure, IM (instant messaging) might work in some cases, but praying that way is rather difficult, especially if that's your only option. And how can we cry with those who are hurting and minister to those who are sick? Jesus *touched* people. People *touched* Jesus—and from that personal, physical touch, power drained from Him, presumably *to them*! Furthermore, there are certain biblical practices that take place in groups such as corporate singing, baptism and the Lord's Supper. Scripture even commands the *public* reading of God's Word, not the private reading of it (see 1 Tim. 4:13).

We simply cannot see how a church can fully be a true church if it exists solely as a cyber-church. However, even when a church regularly gathers together, there still are challenges to consider. Most have to do with community, but not all—though all of the challenges do pertain to how the medium impacts the message.

First, cyber-enhanced churches tend to be focused mainly on information. If information led to transformation, then American Christians, especially certain evangelicals, would be some of the most godly people in the world! We already have Christian radio teachers, books, televangelists, CDs and DVDs. Now, we can add Internet tools as Internet forums, podcasts, list servers, RSS feeds and a host of other information delivery services. More information doesn't necessarily mean more holiness!

Second, cyber-enhanced churches can evidence less community. Many people will argue otherwise. They will say, "You can be honest in cyber world" or "People build relationships online." All are true, but the reason many defend these kinds of things is simple: It is obvious that you cannot build the same relationship online that you can in person. Can the online experience enhance relationships? Yes, but it should only enhance, not replace.

Third, cyber-churches require less commitment. The nature and attraction of the Internet is that it is anonymous. It is something you can visit and leave without fanfare or notice. The Church is not supposed to be that way. It is to be a covenant community filled with people who "sharpen" each other as they "rub off" on one another and keep each other accountable.

The Future

A decade from now, we believe that an ever-increasing number of healthy and growing churches will be cyber-enhanced. Churches will find technology to be a great tool to help them advance the cause of the gospel. This might include elements such as the following (all of which exist today):

- People enter the church and sign in to receive their automatically generated nametags (or likewise as they drop off their children).

- When they sign in, they do not use a printed pass-down-the-pew friendship pad; rather, they sign in electronically. Those who are absent will be noticed (based on not signing in, for example) with notifications e-mailed to small-group leaders and pastors.

- Small-group members share concerns, prayer requests and information in their online group community forum.

- Members take spiritual formation instruments online, determine areas they need to develop, and then download modules that give more training about needed areas.

- Members' spiritual gifts are recorded and matched with ministry needs, helping them decide where to get involved.

- Many tithers will give through online automatic deposits.

- Church members will read church community blogs via RSS feeds.

- Podcasts and videocasts of sermons and small-group lessons will be available each week.

Technology is a tool. Churches have always been slow to embrace tools, and cyber tools are no exception. Yet, when churches use Internet technology to build community and provide information, these tools can advance biblical relationships for God's glory.

CHAPTER 8

NICKELODEON-STYLE CHILDREN-FOCUSED CHURCHES

But Jesus said, "Let the children come to me, and don't try to stop them! People who are like these children belong to God's kingdom." After Jesus had placed his hands on the children, he left.
MATTHEW 19:14-15

I (Elmer) am a member of Thomas Road Baptist Church in Lynchburg, Virginia. In recent years the church built a huge four-level climbing tree—twice the size of a McDonald's playground—to attract children before and after Sunday School, and even during the workweek. Every day at noon, dozens of children climb, swing, hang from, and crawl through the seemingly endless tunnels in Kid's Cove while parents eat lunch at the Lion and the Lamb—the church's lunch bar in the huge Main Street (foyer).

I'd love to see the reaction of Robert Raikes—founder of the Sunday School movement—to our climbing tree and the way it symbolizes our approach to children's Sunday School. Would he have a heart attack, based on the shock of visiting an innovated Sunday School like ours? I think not, because Raikes was himself considered to be crazy for some of the methods he used to promote Sunday School in the 1780s. He offered a gold dollar for memorizing all of Proverbs. He gave gifts of books, when at the time only the rich owned books. And he literally hobbled the mischievous boys (those with Attention Deficit Disorder?) with pieces of firewood to keep them from running away from class!

Children's ministry has come a long way in its more than 200 years, and my church is not alone in its Nickelodeon-style approach. This chapter looks underneath eye-catchers like our climbing tree and their counterparts in other churches, and it explains the new face of Sunday School (actually, alternate names are now more popular). It shows how churches of all sizes can impact impressionable young lives with the relevance of the gospel.

North Point: Pioneer in Children's Ministry

The children's ministry of North Point Community Church in northern Georgia planned UpStreet, a 70-minute Nickelodeon-type Sunday School program for 2,000 children, followed by KidStuf, a 45-minute children's church conglomeration that is led by two mismatched hosts, several wacky actors, cool captivating videos and compelling storytellers so that kids would attend and learn the Bible in a fast, noisy, multimedia programmed, kid-focused, parent-centered, nurture-centered extravaganza each Sunday morning. Following the rule of "fun, fun, fun," the church attempts to teach in a profound way the one truth—what they call "the bottom line"—each Sunday.

According to Kendra Fleming, Director of Children's Ministry at North Point Community Church, there are five things that every kid really needs to know. First, there really is a big God whom kids can trust no matter what happens. To get this truth across, they throw a really big party every Sunday to celebrate who God is and what He has done.

The second thing every kid needs is someone else who believes what he or she believes. As a result, UpStreet is programmed so that kids spend quality time with their friends in small groups talking about their faith. Kendra says, "We do children's ministry for kids through small groups." Then she emphasized, "It's very important that we create an environment to engage the kids at every level of their experience." Therefore, in each room there is a circle rug (approximately five feet in diameter) placed on the carpeting where kids sit on the floor in groups for Sunday morning Bible study. Kendra told us several times, "Life-change happens best in small groups."

The third thing every kid needs is another voice that says the same thing his or her parents are saying. In their small groups, leaders are serious about having fun with the kids yet are passionate about teaching them too. So they drive home one point—the "bottom line"—every week in UpStreet and in KidStuf. Their brochure says, "We don't have time to teach everything. And we know we shouldn't just teach anything. That's why we 'teach less for more.'" As a result, they say that every kid has to connect with the same leader, and the same friends, during the same hour every Sunday on UpStreet. They connect to get one point across each week—that "bottom line" is on the wall when they come in, on the lips of the teachers, and communicated to the parents before they leave.

The fourth thing every kid needs is nosy parents who make it their business to know where their kids are spiritually. As a result, they insist that the parents come with their kids to KidStuf so that they will know the "bottom line" and be able to apply it in their family Bible time. Because what happens at home is more important than what happens at church, they have a "no drop-off" policy at KidStuf, which means that kids are not allowed in if their parents don't come. Parents and children are separate for UpStreet, but KidStuf is a family learning event.

The fifth thing that every kid needs is uncommon sense to help him or her make wise choices in life. That's why they make sure the Bible is never boring and kids walk away with one "bottom line" truth to remember each week. Life is made up of difficult choices; they want kids to make smart choices so that they can become what God has created them to be.

The leadership believes that they only have a short window of time before a kid becomes a teenager (only 364 weekends). They say that every kid must realize three things: (1) They need to make wise choices; (2) they can trust God no matter what; and (3) they should treat others the way they want to be treated. Therefore, every week they try to get across one basic point that will lead to wise choices. They want every phrase, every story and every song to somehow highlight one of those three choices.

Kendra said, "We always write out the bottom line on a chalkboard for everyone to see, i.e., what we're going to teach each day." She adds, "We believe the kids learn one thing best. We want them to know one thing from each lesson, so we use every available experience to drive home that lesson."

Each small group in UpStreet has approximately 8 to 10 kids, with an adult to lead the Bible discussion for the day. Kendra says, "Kids connect with leaders, so we build relationships to teach the Bible."

In the old days, they used furniture such as tables and chairs for each group, but for a number of practical reasons, they found the furniture unwieldy and that it got in the way of relationships. So Kendra says, "Sitting on the floor is more relational."

After the kids finish with UpStreet and the parents finish with adult church, they tell the parents, "Make sure you don't miss KidStuf." Why? Because KidStuf is not just for kids; it's where the parents learn the main focus that the kids have learned that day. "UpStreet makes the 'bottom line' stick in the kids' minds, and KidStuf really drives it home."

The children's ministry at North Point makes a big deal about attendance—every week. They say that what happens at the child's home is more important than what happens at the church. But they just as quickly say that it's worse for the kid and parents to skip KidStuf than it is for the kids to skip school. They promise to the parents, "We promise we will make sure you will get plenty of 'stuff' to take home with you to make your job as a parent easier."

While the kids are in UpStreet and the adults are in their worship hour, the leadership divides the 70 minutes of UpStreet into the following:

- 10.6 minutes getting ready to listen
- 12.4 minutes listening
- 15.1 minutes singing
- 6.3 minutes praying
- 24.9 minutes hanging out with their group and talking about everything they've learned

The leadership says, "We're never sure what happens to the other .7 minutes, but we're sure it's a meaningful time."

Kendra says they don't follow a Sesame Street approach (which is cognitive approach to education) or a Disney approach (which is an entertainment approach) but a Nickelodeon approach because it's fun that leads to learning for the kids, helping them to accomplish God's will for their lives.

Staying Connected

The children's ministry has other ways for parents to stay connected and to know what their kids are learning. The church has established a website (www.parentconnection.org) that gives an audio download of what the kids are learning each Sunday so that parents can plug that into their discussion with their kids.

The program *JumpStart* is a unique 30-minute presentation where parents and kids learn what it means to have a personal relationship with Jesus Christ. In the old days, this would have been called an evangelistic presentation or a church membership class for children. *JumpStart* is designed to help parents guide their kids through the most important decision they will ever make: salvation!

Several times a year, the leadership has a family *Birthday Celebration* in which they spotlight kids and teenagers who have made a decision to accept Christ. Because they have come to trust their really big God, the leadership thinks they ought to throw a really big party, just as they have birthday parties at home. So friends and families gather to see kids get baptized and to celebrate the event with a time of worship.

Twice a year, the leadership plans *Kids Venture* in which group leaders and kids have fun outside Sunday morning. This is an opportunity where parents get a chance to connect with their children's leaders. The church also provides *familytime kits* to provide parents with tools to teach their kids about character and faith. This synchronizes the same lessons that are being taught each week in UpStreet and KidStuf. Family time kits have conversation starters for meal times and Bible stories for bedtime to help lead their kids in their faith.

Each summer, kids who come to UpStreet also are invited to a unique program called *Summer Craze*. Since KidStuf isn't held during the summer vacation, a special team of college interns work hard to create extra drama, music and activities that are featured during the regular UpStreet hour.

A Multi-sensory Environment

Florence Baptist Temple in South Carolina is a church of more than 2,000 worshipers with approximately 1,500 children and adults in Sunday School. The pre-school department (ages 2 to 5) is a showcase of 18 theme rooms, each one decorated with city streets, hills, gardens, houses to play in, roofs to climb on, boats to sit in and rocks to climb over. It's like walking through a Christian Disneyworld.

Mrs. Liz Lewis, pre-school director, noted that the church spent thousands of dollars transforming classrooms in their new building into learning areas so that the lives of children could be transformed. Mrs. Lewis noted, "You can build new buildings, with new equipment and beautiful pictures on the wall, but you're not going to change their lives without Bible teaching and the power of a personal knowledge of Jesus Christ as Savior."

Room decorations are created so that the children will look at the Bible through the things that surround their daily life and the lives of those in the Bible. Mrs. Lewis says, "The room is only an attraction to capture their attention. It's here that they experience the Word of God, live with other Christians, and experience the truths of Bible stories." She explained, "Learning is the result of all we do, that is, teacher training, safety precaution, hygiene concerns, a close relationship with their parents."

Amy Giles, children's director for the church, indicated that younger mothers are the most anxious about their children. Parents bring their children with the idea they will cry and rebel but are usually shocked to find their children running to climb onto the boat at *Captain's Galley* or climbing in the tree house at *Teeter Totterville*. Even then, some parents come sneaking back down the hallway to peek around corners to see if their children are content. They are surprised at how the room consumes the child and becomes a teaching partner with the instructors.

On April 16, 2006, the church had 195 children in attendance in 18 rooms, 36 teachers for children aged 2 and 3, and 15 teachers for children aged 4 and 5. Here is a brief description of some of the rooms at the church:

1. *Captain's Galley* is a dock bordered by tin-roof hous-es. One wall is covered with boards to look like the inside of a house on the waterfront.

2. *Teeter Totterville* is a large tree house with a small roof and porch where children can play. It has a number of trees around the edges, plus a sandbox.

3. *Main Street, USA,* has houses with wood-shake shin-gles, white curbs, street lights, a fire station and matching wallpaper.

4. *Carousel Corner* has half of a merry-go-round with a brightly colored carousel tent and matching wallpaper.

5. *Sunshine Express* appears to be an old railway station with a water tower, caboose, ticket window and a bench where customers can sit while waiting for the train.

6. *Friendship Village* has a small church, horse stable, house and animals, such as horses, dogs and cats.

A Brief History of Teaching Children the Bible on Sunday

Sunday School has gone through major changes in the last 200 years in the way it teaches the Bible. Now that our children have learned in a Sesame Street world, it's only natural for the methodology and approach of Sesame Street, Nickelodeon and Disney to influence the way we teach them on Sunday. Are there some dangers? Sure, and we will discuss them below. But there are also some opportunities.

In the original days of Robert Raikes, pupils read Bible sto-ries out loud and then teachers questioned them about what they read. The next phase was teacher instruction, in which teachers explained and applied the Bible to the students. The modern phase is a Sesame Street or Nickelodeon focus, which involves using multi-sensory communication of a Bible lesson. Students learn in a multi-receptive experience, with state-of-the-art sets, costumes and full use of electronic information technology.

Teachers embody multi-sensory teaching by dressing in costumes of the biblical period, constructing rooms that represent biblical situations such as a Palestine town built in classrooms the size of play houses, or teaching students in a lakeside scene with bushes, Disneyland rocks, carpet grass, rugs painted with pictorial lakes and rearview screens depicting Bible scenes. Students respond in multi-sensory experiences by dressing the role, taking part in action stories, and so forth.

The first way the Bible was taught to children on Sunday was when students read out of Bible storybooks (small booklets about 100-plus pages that were approximately the size of an address book or a checkbook). In this Lancasterian method of teaching, teachers would "hear the lesson" when students stood to read part of the lesson from the book and the teacher would then correct pronunciation and help with words that were difficult. At the end of the reading, the teacher would ask the pupil two or three questions, which were usually printed in the booklets. The pupil had to remember the reading in order to answer the teacher.

I (Elmer) have a copy of the first book printed by the American Sunday School Union in 1815 hanging on the wall in my study. In addition, I have approximately 300 other small Sunday School books used by early historic Sunday Schools. They are a fascinating walk through the history of Sunday School.

Around 1900, when the spread of liberal theology affected Sunday School materials, independent Sunday School publishing houses began producing both a teacher's manual and a pupil's manual. They introduced a teacher's manual to help teachers learn the text so that they could explain it to the pupils. Pupils no longer read lengthy passages out of a Bible storybook, but rather listened as their teachers explained the Bible. As a result, in this second phase the lecture or explanation method became the driving force of Sunday School.

Beginning approximately 100 years later, the Nickelodeon Sunday School slowly appeared on the scene from several different sources. It focuses the entire curriculum on multi-sensory experiences, meaning that sensory experiences are used to communicate the Bible to young people. Pupils learn viscerally by their physical sensory experiences. They learn more than Bible content: They learn Christian joy by laughing, they learn Christian compassion by helping another, they learn Christian sacrifice by giving, and they learn Christian gratitude by praising God. They learn Bible experiences that translate into life experiences. In essence, students learn more than Bible content: They acquire attitudes, values and built-in applications.

Rooms are being transformed into biblical scenes. For example, one classroom is a Palestinian village containing flat-roofed houses, synagogues and other things that would be found in a Palestinian street and/or marketplace. Students walk the Palestinian street, enter Palestinian houses and even climb onto the roof of a Palestinian home. The children experience freedom, ingenuity and (by observation) even learn a little bit about construction and carpentry.

Another room has sloped landscaping that depicts a Palestinian hillside, with green Astroturf carpet laid on the slanting hillside to depict grass. There are fake bushes and even fake rocks. The children sit on a reclining hillside and hear stories, just as the multitudes sat outside listening to Jesus.

This multi-sensory Sunday School is a product of the Sesame Street generation. You will remember the puppets popped up from a garbage can, others came out of windows, and still others appeared in all different places of the set. What children expect on television, they can now enjoy in Sunday School.

Transition in the '70s

When I (Elmer) began writing my book *The 10 Largest Sunday Schools and What Made Them Grow*, I noticed a stark contrast between the Sunday Schools of large Southern Baptist churches and the Sunday Schools of Independent Baptist churches.[1] Southern Baptists had followed the teachings of A.V. Washburn, who stated as his first Sunday School law, "Enrollment and attendance increase in proportion to visitation at a ratio of 10 to 1."[2] As a result, Southern Baptist pupils met in a large assembly area for the opening exercises, then they usually divided up into smaller classes in rooms traditionally 10 feet by 10 feet, with the ideal being 1 teacher and 10 pupils in each class.

The small Southern Baptist classes were designed to have a close relationship between teacher and pupil, help students become more involved in class learning, and help the teacher apply the lesson down to the level of the student, since these were age-graded classes, whereby students enjoyed experiences with those of the same age. In contrast, I found the Sunday Schools in large independent churches using a "master-teacher" strategy due to an abundance of pupils who come because of their bus ministries. Bus workers went house to house on Saturday inviting children to ride their bus to Sunday School the following Sunday morning. Bus workers were very energetic and successful in filling buses with children who were brought to Sunday School.

Many Independent Baptist churches didn't have enough teachers to fill classes with only 10 pupils per room. As a result, they pragmatically evolved into a master-teacher concept of teaching. In this concept, the best teachers were placed in front of children, sometimes 50 pupils—and I've seen classes with upwards of 200 in one room being taught by one teacher (obviously, that teacher was extremely gifted).

The master-teacher approach became effective by using as many teaching tools as possible, capturing as many learning opportunities as possible. Master-teachers used video projection, i.e., films, filmstrips, overheads and rear-screen projection, to get their point across. Master-teachers used a platform area for puppets, just like a Sesame Street television stage setting. Master-teachers began building music and audio environment into their teaching situation to motivate learning. They used costumes and short drama activities to communicate to students the stories of the New Testament. Also, they used props such as David's slingshot, a shepherd's staff, a plastic snake, a stone used to cast at the sinful woman, and anything else that came to their imagination.

I (Elmer) have been in classrooms where master-teachers have taught in rowboats to teach how disciples reacted to a storm. I have also seen them teach straddled to a live donkey to teach the triumphant entry on Palm Sunday and use a bowl of figs to teach Christ's cursing the fig tree or a bowl of olives when lessons were about olive trees. In addition to this, I've seen vines, stalks of wheat and banners used to portray the message of the day.

What's the Appeal?

So why does this method work, and why should it appeal to us?

One reason is because it attracts parents, who come because their children want to come. Of us three authors, I (Ed) am the one who currently lives most in this world. I have three daughters (pray for me), two who are preschoolers. They love

North Point's children's program—and I am bitter because they do. You see, I am also planting a church in a high school just up the road from Andy Stanley World. The children's program for our new church is pretty simple—a couple of teachers, a few rugs and some activities. We can't compete with the animatronics at North Point. (And they really are doing a great job, all kidding aside.)

When my wife and I take our daughters there, we never hear the end of it. "When can we go back? That was cool. When can we see Captain Dave? How come I can't be captain, Dad?" Simply put, children love it; there is a real appeal. I imagine that lost people might feel that same appeal, even as smaller churches take a similar approach with a more scaled-down version.

Some who read this might object, appealing to biblical "sobriety" as if the goal is to make children sit still. There is not much use in trying to convince them—they will always see seriousness as spirituality. Yet children also need to know that God is a God of joy.

When parents pick up their children from Sunday School, they tend to ask two predicable questions. First, they ask, "Did you have fun?" If you don't get an affirmative answer, then the next question seems to be less important: "What did you learn?" For children's ministry, those are two important questions that we all need to ask. Can they have a good time (as God created children to do) and can they be taught (as God commanded us to do)? So, what are the upsides and the down?

What Can We Learn from Children's Ministry Portal Churches?

There are many strengths of the Nickelodeon Sunday School. The first is its appeal to an experience-driven generation of children whose parents spend billions on interactive games, attend schools that are highly experiential, and learn from many computer-generated programs that are multi-sensory in their approach. It's possible that a highly motivated contemporary child will be turned off by the traditional drab Sunday School, but the Nickelodeon Sunday School will motivate the child to learn. Educational theorists discovered 30 years ago that children learn better if they are not faced forward in a sterile environment. Some churches are catching on.

Second, there is an advantage in creating learning experiences in Sunday School the way children experience life. Just as people in the Bible experienced the message of God, children today can live and love God from the bottom of their heart. Many adults go through Walk Through the Bible Classes so that they can "see" the full story of Scripture. Learning environments like these can accomplish the same purpose.

The third advantage is the extremely important benefit of removing barriers to the learning process. Whereas the traditional Sunday School must deal with children in culture shock as they are time-warped back to the flannel boards of the 1950s, those who attend a Nickelodeon Sunday School find themselves naturally learning without effort and without being coaxed to pay attention.

Perhaps the greatest advantage of the Nickelodeon Sunday School is its evangelistic appeal. Because salvation appeals to the intellect, emotion and will of the convert, so the Nickelodeon Sunday School informs the child's mind with the gospel message, motivates the child's emotions to respond, and persuades his or her will to decide for Jesus Christ. When children want to come to church at the age they are most likely to respond to the gospel, it is good news indeed.

At the Center for Missional Research that I (Ed) lead, we recently did a comprehensive study on churches with high rates of children baptisms (in our faith tradition, a child is baptized after he or she makes a profession of faith in Christ). We wanted to know why some churches reach children and some don't. (The entire study, including PowerPoints, is free online at www.missionalresearch.info.) We surveyed more than 300 churches as follows:

Size 1: **46** (0 to 169 resident members)
Size 2: **46** (0 to 169 resident members)
Size 3: **98** (325 to 622 resident members)
Size 4: **101** (623+ resident members)

Total: 304

We found some key things that all churches of all sizes had in common. First, they had supportive senior pastors. Research missiologist Philip Connor wrote, "Of most crucial importance is that churches with successful children's evangelism describe their senior pastor to be *very supportive* of children's ministry. In fact, over 90 percent of churches describe the senior pastor's support to be at this level, regardless of church size."[3] Pastors like Andy Stanley and Bill Monroe have invested the time and resources to make such children's ministry possible. For very large churches, they follow much the same pattern that Kendra Fleming does:

> The very large church's evangelism philosophy is very much built on an intentional step by step process designed to spiritually grow children. Not only did 45 percent of very large churches state this as their evangelism philosophy, but a further 37 percent describe their church's evangelism philosophy among children to be a set of age appropriate programs/activities that coincide with pre-planned adult programs.[4]

Research and observation both show that these kinds of children's ministries make a difference. They challenge children by

engaging and teaching them. They reach parents by making children their allies in reaching their parents. They are the ultimate
at attraction (which can be both a blessing and a bane).

Where I (Ed) live in North Georgia, parents are obsessed
with their children. Children can become idols. They build their
lives around them—and North Point is appealing to that need.
Discerning, meeting and presenting the gospel within cultural
realities have been a mission strategy for 2,000 years. Are there
dangers to churches appealing to cultural needs? Sure, but it is
also a mission opportunity.

Using felt needs to reach people has always been decried by
some, and we need to carefully evaluate those criticisms. How
we appeal to someone—churched or unchurched—will ultimately affect how we retain him or her. A church that appeals
to culture should have a spiritual formation strategy to lead
people to an understanding of Christ and His mission (and,
lest you wonder, North Point works hard to move beyond their
children's program).

What Do We Need to Consider?

In addition to its strengths, there are also a number of challenges of the Nickelodeon Sunday School to consider. The first
is the overwhelming appeal to the experience of the child while
minimizing the structural or content (i.e., doctrinal) nature of
Christianity. There is a tough balance here: On the one hand is
the church lady, lecturing against the danger of having fun;
on the other is the church that is so focused on the fun they
forget the faith.

While experience is an outstanding motivation for the
Nickelodeon generation, there are many truths that must relate
the mind to the Word of God that are not experience-generated.
For instance, it's difficult to communicate the Trinity through

total experiential motivation—the child must know the Trinity and believe in the Father, Son and Holy Spirit, or else he or she hasn't experienced biblical Christianity.

There's another factor that also can't be taught by experience: Sunday School must teach the total content of Scriptures from Genesis 1:1 to Revelation 22:21. Because the Nickelodeon Sunday School appeals to that which works in experiences, there are obviously many sections of the Bible that would be considered dull history or boring doctrine. Remember, "Everything in the Scriptures is God's Word. All of it is useful for teaching and helping people and for correcting them and showing them how to live" (2 Tim. 3:16). Did you see that word "all"? All means *all*. We have not fulfilled all of the commandments until we teach all of the content of the Word of God in Sunday School. The Jebusites may not be as exciting as Bob the Tomato, but knowledge of the Scripture is the goal, not just entertainment of the children.

A third challenge of the Nickelodeon Sunday School is its inability to give attention to the fine points of biblical revelation. While minutia may be glossed over in the broad experiential sweep of things, remember, "God is in the details." And it is through the accumulation of many details that broad principles of Scripture are established. Isaiah asked the question, "How can you possibly understand or teach the LORD's message?" (Isa. 28:9). He answers his question that those who are taught should be like "those just weaned from milk and those just drawn from the breast" (Isa. 28:9, *NKJV*). He assumes they should not be spiritual babies (see 1 Pet. 2:2). Isaiah stresses that our education must place small things together for deeper comprehension: "You don't even listen—all you hear is senseless sound after senseless sound" (Isa. 28:10). The effective Sunday School needs teachers to build the small points of theology one upon another. This suggests there is a place for an indoctrination methodology along with an experiential curriculum. We need both.

The gospel is a story: It starts in a garden and it ends in a city. The drama of redemption unfolds act by act throughout Scripture. The challenge can be that these ministries tell stories—and we have to be careful that these stories do not become replacements of *the* story, the unfolding drama of redemption.

There's another challenge of the Nickelodeon Sunday School, and it has to do with size. Because many children are taught in large arenas, personal relationship between teacher and pupil is minimized. Yet, isn't relationship the heart and core of teaching? While Nickelodeon Sunday School depends on experiences to communicate Bible knowledge, in traditional Sunday School the teacher relates to the pupil, loves the pupil and follows up to make sure the pupil is growing. The teacher asks questions to make sure that the Bible is clarified in the pupil's mind. And while Jesus was lecturing (not producing experiences), didn't He ask many questions to make sure people understood what He was saying?

Churches have to work hard to be sure that a Nickelodeon environment fosters a teacher-student relationship in which learning takes place. In the Center for Missional Research study mentioned earlier, we explained:

> Another element discovered among effective churches is high quality programming utilizing creative and dynamic activities; yet as great and essential as these factors are, they never seem to be enough. Churches having a life-changing impact with their children are the ones that connect children to one another and have adult leaders (and/or mature older students) who regularly interact with and care for them. Despite all the pizzazz and glitz of incredible programs, mentoring

seems to be the key to sustained, effective evangelism among children.[5]

One last observation about the challenges of the Nickelodeon Sunday School: When teachers are wearing costumes and are acting in the role of those in the Bible, obviously the dramatic presentation makes its point. But can students identify with the everyday life of the teacher when they perceive them as actors rather than mentors? Since the life of the teacher is still the life of teaching, those who teach as mothers communicate their lifestyle to the pupils. And those fathers who are businessmen communicate the power of the gospel that is translated into the world in which the man is employed.

Challenges

Are there challenges with children's ministry that are sensory and experiential? Probably. Is God using such ministries? We believe He is. Churches are stepping up to new levels of ministry that engage children with the gospel. God is blessing such churches.

So what are the challenges? We have listed many of them above, but there is also a philosophical issue. Will this approach ultimately impact "lostness," or simply raise an impossible bar for other churches to reach? When a church is built around attraction, it reaches people by attracting them. In other words, something has to be appealing to the community, and it's that appeal that brings people to church. Such is the case with the Nickelodeon Sunday School—it is very attractive to parents.

However, the question remains: How many people are just looking for an attractive children's ministry to get them to visit a church? More important, what kind of person is attracted to such churches? We think this "pool" of those who are attracted to churches with great programs is primarily made up of Christians in smaller churches and a shrinking number of the unchurched. Simply put, a growing number of unchurched people are not attracted to exciting stories of dynamic children's programs—it just does not interest them. They are no more likely to be attracted to the church than we are to the local casino. If we already decided that we are not interested in the casino, the fact that it does things better to attract us simply won't work.

The children's ministry does reach Christians seeking a church and, to some degree, the interested unchurched. However, our culture seems to be increasingly secular, which makes us question why more churches are focusing on the interested unchurched segments of society. Generally, people who are open to being reached by a "better version" of church have already responded. What is needed now is a new way to reach beyond the low-hanging fruit of those with a religious memory who hope their children will have a religious upbringing.

In many cultures, that time is not yet here. In many places these great churches are reaching high numbers of people, but we notice that most of these churches with such children's programs are in areas with a stronger church presence—such as the American South, Texas and Southern California. As our culture becomes more lost, we would expect this method to be less prominent. Still, thank God for churches seizing the divine moment through the Nickelodeon Sunday School today.

CHAPTER 9

INTENTIONALLY MULTICULTURAL CHURCHES

*Faith in Christ Jesus is what makes each of you equal
with each other, whether you are a Jew or a Greek, a slave or
a free person, a man or a woman. So if you belong to Christ,
you are now part of Abraham's family.*
GALATIANS 3:28-29

Redmond, a suburb 15 miles east of Seattle, Washington, is best known as the home of several major corporations: Microsoft, Nintendo, AT&T Wireless and Eddie Bauer, among others.

According to the 2000 census, Redmond's 45,256 residents parallel most other American towns in which one ethnic group is dominant. In Redmond's case, the racial makeup is 79.3 percent White, 13.02 percent Asian, 5.6 percent Hispanic, 1.5 percent African American, 0.5 percent Native American and 0.2 percent Pacific Islander, with 2.5 percent from other races and 3.1 percent from two or more races.[1] The racial makeup of nearby Kirkland (population 45,045) is 85.3 percent White, 7.8 percent Asian, 4.1 percent Hispanic, 1.2 percent African American, 0.5 percent Native American and 0.2 percent Pacific Islander, with 1.7 percent from other races and 2.9 percent from two or more races.[2]

Going to church on Sunday morning in the Redmond-Kirkland area is much like worshiping in any other town in the country: Most congregations are solidly of one race. This happens regardless of church size. For example, in Redmond, the biggest attendance church in the state is predominantly White; most smaller churches are likewise identifiable by one principal race. However, Antioch Bible Church, also located in the Redmond-Kirkland corridor, is notable for breaking that norm. Their website and literature emphasize a multicultural theme, affirming that Antioch is a church:

- for all people, of all cultures, races, backgrounds
- where diversity of worship styles is the norm
- where God's Word, the Bible, is the authority
- where every member is a minister
- which aims to transform the entire community
- where people are first, programs are second and facilities are third
- in which people's preconceived ideas of what a church is all about may be challenged!

Ken Hutcherson, a former professional football player with the Seattle Seahawks, San Diego Chargers and Dallas Cowboys, has been a pastor since 1984. He is African American and is leading the congregation "to create an environment where multiethnic/cross-cultural churches are normal instead of the exception," according to the church's website.

Not only has Antioch Bible Church become a dynamic multiethnic, cross-cultural church averaging more than 2,000 in weekly worship, but another 7,000 people in weekly worship attend the 35 daughter, granddaughter, associational and vision partner churches of Antioch/Antioch Global Network. Most of them are multiracial as well. Antioch Bible Church represents a wave of churches whose innovation is to lead the way in modeling racial reconciliation and building skills of cross-cultural understanding, appreciation and communication among God's people.[3]

Hutcherson is not alone in his dream. God seems to be raising up others with a similar passion. In Columbia, Maryland,
Moody Bible Institute graduate David Anderson started a
church in 1992 that has become a celebration of all colors and
cultures doing life together and worshiping God together.
Today, Bridgeway Community Church is fulfilling its vision "to
become a multicultural army of fully devoted followers of Christ,
moving forward in unity and love, to reach our community, our
culture, and our world for Jesus Christ." The congregation is
about 55 percent African American, 30 percent White and 15 percent Asian and other races.[4] Anderson, in his book *Multicultural
Ministry: Finding Your Church's Unique Rhythm*, says:

> Evidence of this country's rich racial mix is all around
> us in our schools, our stores, our neighborhoods, our
> recreational facilities—everywhere except our churches.
> Heaven may include every culture, tongue and tribe,
> but in the United States, Sunday morning remains one
> of the last bastions of ethnic separatism. It's time to
> stop merely talking about multicultural worship and
> start living it.[5]

Multiethnic Is Easier than Multicultural

Merely announcing that you want to be multiethnic doesn't guarantee that it will happen. In researching this chapter, I (Warren)
went with my wife to a church in our area that advertises itself as
"multiethnic." The pastor, an African American, has a powerful
testimony of having been the victim of racial prejudice during his
teen years. He has a strong desire to lead the way in helping people—especially Christians —to overcome racial stereotypes.

But to our surprise, the congregation was almost entirely
African American, as was the staff. Most aspects of the worship

style also fit comfortably within African American tradition, yet the congregation was meeting in a town that was overwhelmingly white! Our conclusion is that a church must do far more than state its intentions in order to successfully become multiethnic. The idea of being monocultural has a heavy gravitational pull, at least in contemporary America, and ethnic diversity does not come naturally in most places.

A Christian sociologist named George A. Yancey analyzed data from a landmark Lilly Endowment study of multiracial churches across the United States and wrote a book with the subtitle *Principles of Successful Multiracial Churches*. He found that seven general principles are present when a church becomes multiracial:

1. It must have a worship style inclusive of multiple cultures.
2. It must have ethnically diverse leadership.
3. It must have an overarching goal to become multiracial.
4. It must intentionally want to become multiracial.
5. It must have leadership with appropriate personal skills.
6. It must be in a location that can draw multiple races.
7. It must demonstrate an adaptability to overcome various challenges that arise.[6]

Yancey defines what he means by multiracial: "A church in which no one racial group makes up more than 80 percent of the attendees of at least one of the major worship services."[7] Based on that definition, only 8 percent of all American churches are multiracial.

Even fewer churches, however, are multicultural. The term "multiracial" indicates the presence of multiple races. The term "multicultural" emphasizes contrasting racial groups bringing distinct cultures into the congregation, such as through multiple choirs with different styles, rotated preachers, intentional multicultural staff, classes in cross-cultural ministry, bilingual worship, and multi-congregational facility usage.

In another church visit in preparation for this chapter, I (Warren) went to a church in New York City that presented itself as one-third White, one-third Black and one-third Hispanic. Indeed that was the case, as it seemed that three distinct groups were in the church, with no plan or intention of leaving their respective cultural comfort zones! It was like three churches meeting in the same location. Each group hung out with its own, and from what I could tell, each reached out only to those of its own ethnic background. The pastor and his wife were both from Boston, and their distinctive Bostonian accents made them stand out almost as if they represented a fourth culture. The pastor seemed oblivious to the cultural divide evident in the congregation. Instead, he spoke only of their forward progress, commenting to me in his thick New England accent, "My wife and I had a *haaad* time communicating until we went to accent reduction class!"

Other churches have found a more successful breakthrough of cultures. You can't worship at the Brooklyn Tabernacle—known for its Grammy-award winning, multiracial choir and its pastor's books about the church's spiritual renewal—without sensing several cultures in each service.[8] On the West Coast, Church On The Way in Van Nuys, California, where Jack Hayford was senior pastor for many years (and where Jim Tolle is senior pastor today), is a model of multi-congregational facility usage as a way of exhibiting multicultural ministry. The church's facilities are used by Arabic-speaking, Iranian, Bulgarian and Filipino congregations. On any given weekend, there are four English-language services on one campus and five Spanish-language services on the other campus. Pastor Jim Tolle, having been a child of missionary parents and an adult missionary himself in several Latin American countries, is bilingual and also bicultural, and he goes back and forth speaking in most of the services. On many weeks, the Spanish-language congregation has a higher attendance than the English-language congregation!

Church On The Way, like many intentionally multicultural churches, incorporates race issues into its statement of core values: "Racial Harmony in God's Kingdom (see 1 Cor. 12:13; Gal. 3:27-29; Eph. 2:11-22; Col. 3:10-11). Under God our Creator, ethnic diversity is respected; and under Christ our Redeemer, all humanity is invited to answer the Bible's call to the values and virtues of the Kingdom of God."[9]

Churches of all Sizes and Life Stages

Recent research on megachurches uncovered that they are generally well ahead of the rest of the church population in being multiracial and multicultural—often intentionally so.[10]

Another group leading the way in interacting with people from every tribe and tongue is church planters. Typical is Mark DeYmaz, who in 2002 launched Mosaic Church of Central Arkansas, which he describes as "an awesome blend of numerous ethnicities and cultures." He purposed, however, not to launch the church as a solo church planter. He waited until he had a leadership team with at least three different ethnicities represented and the core group modeled what they hoped the church would become in terms of ethnic and cultural diversity.

As the book *Starting a New Church* by Dale Galloway with Warren Bird points out, one of Mark DeYmaz's favorite conversations starts like this: "Hey, I heard you're starting a multiethnic church in Little Rock, Arkansas. Why on earth would you do that?"[11] In response, DeYmaz might point out that while there are some 600 churches in Pulaski County, "You can count on one hand the number with any significant percentage of ethnic diversity, and virtually none with integrated leadership." Or he might share his experience with a large, affluent white church that filled dozens of positions of responsible leadership over eight years, but *not one* with a person of color. He asks rhetorically, "Why is it that the 'best person for the job' always looks like you?"

More significantly, DeYmaz will likely share the biblical mandate for church unity and what he ultimately believes to be the primary biblical model for corporate evangelism and church planting/development. Beginning with Christ's prayer for unity in John 17, he walks the listener through Christ's command to "therefore go and make disciples of all nations" (Matt. 28:18) and then takes them into the book of Acts to ask why one has to read all the way to chapter 8 before finding anyone willing to leave Jerusalem for the sake of the gospel.

DeYmaz says, "In His prayer, Christ not only described His mission of evangelism (see John 17:1-4) and prayed for the apostles that they might perpetuate that mission (see John 17:5-19), but He determined for us who would come after them ('for everyone else who will have faith because of what my followers will say about me . . . then this world's people will know that you sent me. They will know that you love my followers as much as you love me' [John 17:20,23]). The greatest tool we have for evangelism is unity!"

The church at Antioch-Syria in Acts 11 then becomes for this pastor the link between Christ's heart for the lost, His prayer for those who would believe (see John 17:20), and the full expression of unity to be found in and through an ethnically and economically diverse local church. "The church at Antioch," DeYmaz notes, "was established and led by men of diverse cultures (see Acts 11:20; 13:1) in a cosmopolitan environment

bringing both Jews and Greeks together in Christ to worship
God as one." Martin Luther King, Jr., among others, lamented
that the most segregated hour in America is Sunday morning in
churches. Fortunately, that situation is changing.

How about your congregation? Would today's equivalent
of Moses, who was a tri-cultural person—a Hebrew-Egyptian-
Midianite—feel welcome in your church? How about Mordecai
and Esther, who were Persian Israelites, or the apostle Paul,
who was both Jewish and a Roman citizen? As Orlando Crespo,
InterVarsity Christian Fellowship's director of ministry with
Hispanic students, points out, "For each of them, their ethnic
identity was central to God's plan for the deliverance of his people. If any of them had chosen to simply assimilate to the dominant culture, they would have missed God's deepest purposes
for them."[12]

Not a High Success Factor

American Christians have become enamored in recent years
with the idea of multicultural churches. Most that try, however, do not succeed. Church is hard enough without throwing in
the challenge of multicultural relationships. Those that do welcome many races have learned some things along the way that
we need to remember . . .

Multicultural Churches Are Not the Same
as Multiracial Churches

Most of the churches identified as multicultural do not evidence multiple cultures; instead, they are attended by people
who are different races. For example, one prominent church is
often called multicultural, but the reality is a little different.
Asians, Hispanics, African Americans, and Anglos in the area
are all young professionals. They work together, listen to the
same music, go to the same restaurants and are actually part of

the same culture—regardless of their skin color. Being multicultural is harder. It can mean engaging in Asian styles of relationships, African American approaches to worship, Hispanic approaches to teaching, Anglo approaches to conflict, or a mix and match. That takes more work. Though some Christians value a multicultural church, most nonbelievers do not share the same passion.

Reaching the Unchurched Is Harder in a Multicultural Context

It is not just reaching across the Christian/non-Christian cultural barrier, but there are now cultural barriers within the leadership team. This creates some challenging interactions. The gospel is transcultural, but communication is not. Hundreds of books have been written over the centuries to help missionaries reach across cultures for the sake of the gospel. My (Ed's) father always told me something growing up that relates to multicultural churches: "If it was easy, everyone would be doing it." That states well the situation of the multicultural church.

Multiculturalism Is Really About Community

Most cultures (particularly outside the United States) place great value on community. Jesus taught that our faith would be evidenced by our love for one another (see John 13:34-35; 1 John 4:7-8). This is best evidenced when a team is modeling Christlike community in a multicultural setting. Multicultural churches can be a powerful apologetic for the gospel as people see us loving across cultural barriers. Multicultural churches live out a principle so simple we should learn it in second grade Sunday School: "A new command I give you: Love one another. As I have loved you, so you must love one another. By this all men will know that you are my disciples, if you love one another" (John 13:34-35, *NIV*).

Learning Each Other's Culture Takes Time and Effort

Multicultural churches have to function as multicultural teams. In addition to learning and reaching the community, the team has to take the additional time to understand and relate to each other. That takes a commitment that most church lack. (It is much easier to swap pulpits with a black church once a year and consider ourselves culturally savvy!)

Concerns

I (Ed) can remember at least 10 times when someone has rebuked me after I spoke about church planting. I am often asked, "Why can't church plants be more multicultural?" I tell them that I would like to see more of it, but church plants usually reach one predominant ethnic group. They then usually press, stating that we should be multicultural. Obviously, I agree!

Usually, I end the discussion with one question of response: "How has your church made the transition to a multicultural community?" There is always some excuse, and then the questions grind to a stop.

There are some obvious challenges to multicultural churches. Most of them can be overcome, but knowing them helps the process. These challenges include the following.

Most Americans Have Little Cross-cultural Awareness

When in close contact with those of another culture, people often experience culture shock. Most Christians are unable to bridge the bicultural divide. Sadly, most don't want to. Most Anglos don't go to an African American church, because they don't relate well to African American culture or they prefer their own culture more. Further, it is not their preference to worship in the same manner. They generally prefer worship and preaching in a comfortable cultural form.

Cross-cultural Conflicts Are Inevitable

These conflicts do not necessarily have to breach trust. Multicultural churches must be proactive in dealing with conflict. When dealing with conflict, the Anglos on the team may expect a clear expression of ideas and identification of points of conflict, while the Asians may value the feelings and reputation of those involved, not wanting anyone to lose face. For some Asians, a more circular approach is needed to avoid embarrassing anyone. Americans tend to view this as duplicitous and unhelpful. (Even the solutions to conflict are sometimes fraught with conflict!)

Leadership Is a Flashpoint

Outside of some general biblical teaching, culture determines how much and what style of leadership is practiced in each cultural setting. There are some biblical requirements about leadership standards, practices and ethics, but how leadership is exercised varies from culture to culture. It is essential to find a leadership style that works well for all of the cultures involved.

Multiculturalism Is Not Fully Achieved in Worship

Multicultural churches do more than worship together. A church truly becomes multicultural when its people spend time together outside of the worship service. I once observed a multicultural team meet to plan a strategy. Many have noted that charismatic churches have tended to be more integrated than non-charismatic. We think that is correct, but our observation has been that many such churches fail to move beyond the worship service. People of all types are attracted by the worship, but they are often not connected in life—or they may have worked hard for cultural *tolerance* but were not able to experience *camaraderie*.

Worth the Work

Multiculturalism is hard but is filled with promise. Multicultural churches are not a panacea. For churches willing to dedicate themselves to true multiculturalism, there is no greater witness than God's people from every "tribe, language, nation and race" (see Rev. 5:9) reaching out to add others to the mosaic that is the kingdom of God.

Our hope is that more churches will become like heaven: filled with men and women from every tongue tribe or nation. The song around heaven's throne reflects a multicultural people:

> You are worthy to take the scroll
> and to open its seals,
> because you were slain,
> and with your blood you purchased men for God
> from every tribe and language and people and nation.
> You have made them to be a kingdom and priests to
> serve our God,
> and they will reign on the earth (Rev. 5:9-10, *NIV*).

If we will be singing praise for eternity alongside with the multicultural host, then perhaps we should get used to that before we get there.

CHAPTER 10

DECISION-JOURNEY CHURCHES

Since we live by the Spirit, let us keep in step with the Spirit.
GALATIANS 5:25, *NIV*

In November 1978, I (Elmer) visited every refugee camp along
the Mekong River in Thailand, hoping to deliver food, blankets,
Bibles and Christmas toys to the children of the thousands of
refugees coming out of Laos, Cambodia and Vietnam.

America had recently retreated from its initiative in Vietnam,
and when the American military protective shield was removed,
those who were loyal to American democracy or Christianity
were slaughtered by the Communists. Thousands fled into
Thailand, where the government set up 13 large refugee camps.
Many nations joined in humanitarian efforts to help preserve the
lives of the refugees.

I arrived a day earlier than the team of 22 other people from
Liberty University. I hired an interpreter for the day and began
walking through this refugee camp of 12,000 people. It looked
more like a German concentration camp from World War II
than a community where free people were living.

Inside the camp, I found a number of Christian church
buildings, each reflecting the different cultures of the various
ethnic groups in the camp. Each facility was vastly different, representing a different way of life and a different way of worship.
A tribe from the low-lying jungle area in Laos built a church of
bamboo on stilts even though the ground in the refugee camp

was hard and dry. Hundreds of crosses were woven into the bamboo structure to represent their Christian faith. Another church represented a mountain tribe from Laos. They had cut down huge trees, dragged them into the refugee compound to use as benches, and made this church away from home look just like it did back in the mountains.

Christians are in a clear minority in this section of the world, and their places of worship are recognizable even if they're as different as slender bamboo and mighty logs.

As I interviewed dozens of Christians, one of the first questions I asked was, "When did you become a Christian?" The people were puzzled with my question. Originally I thought the problem was with my interpreter, who was a Buddhist. All my questions met the same confusion in literally hundreds of queries. I varied my questions, such as, "When did you accept Christ?" and "When did you pray to receive Christ?" or "How old were you when you got saved?"

It turned out that I was the one confused, not them.

When I looked at their faith in Christ through the eyes of their own culture, rather than through the eyes of my American culture, I began to realize the bias I was bringing with my questions. Back in the United States, Christianity is the dominant faith. Many people think of their country as a Christian nation, and they even think of themselves as Christians because they live in a culture that they perceive as heavily shaped by Christian values.

As a result, in American evangelism we emphasize a crisis decision in order to help people distinguish a living faith from a cultural Christianity. One view involves a faith relationship with Jesus Christ and the other labels you a Christian solely because of the place you were born or the good works you've done.

The believers I spoke with in Indochina didn't see salvation in the context I had experienced growing up in America. Rather, for them to become a Christian, they rejected Buddha as a god and began saying, "Jesus is Lord." Their Christianity was based more on embracing a new worldview, rather than an emotional crisis. To them the word *believer* meant understanding who Jesus was, appreciating what He did on the cross and putting their trust in Him. To them, belief was a lifestyle response, rather than a point-of-crisis decision.

That first-day experience of interviewing Christians changed my perspective when I preached for the next two weeks in all the refugee camps. I told the crowds that Buddha is not god. "You must say that Jesus is Lord and follow Him, walking daily with Him," I appealed.

Why So Many Nominal Church Members?

My cross-cultural experience so many years ago in that refugee camp in Thailand addresses a nagging conundrum that per-plexes many American church leaders today: *Why are there so many church members who claim to be Christians and yet rarely attend church or get involved in ministry?* To answer this question, some say, "The church didn't properly teach them what it means to accept Christ." Others say, "They're simply following the crowd— living a minimal, nominal-commitment, consumer-driven standard of American approach to their faith." Still others say, "Maybe they're backslidden or they weren't saved in the first place; their names were just added to a church roll."

There is a small but growing group of church leaders who say the American church's view of conversion is wrong or sig-nificantly imbalanced. They maintain that the church has emphasized salvation in an unhealthy way—as an isolated event in which once a person is saved, he or she is set for eternity and the race is over. They observe that decision-based Christianity has produced many conversions but few disciples who are living changed lives. We call these groups "decision-journey churches." They put far less emphasis on a one-time decision and far more on the journey connected to a person's decision to follow Christ.

These growing numbers of church leaders look differently at the doorway to salvation than do the majority of evangelical churches. These new churches are called "decision-journey" or "faith-journey" churches because they teach a different model of walking through the door of salvation to become a follower of Christ. They have not changed the doorkeeper—He's still the Jesus Christ who said, "I am the door. If anyone enters by Me, he will be saved, and will go in and out and find pasture" (John 10:9, *NKJV*). These surfacing churches still believe that Jesus is "the way, the truth and the life" (John 14:6), but they believe the method by which a person believes and acquires salvation is different from normal expectations in America. Therefore, the ministers of these groups are offering salvation with different metaphors than how American churches have expressed it in the past.

The decision-journey type of church is rooted in theology, such as the doctrine of salvation and how a person becomes a Christian. Most of the other church types in this book are rooted in methodology. While the decision-journey churches are motivated by theology, their programs and ministry methodology are more influenced by their view of conversion.

Christ-followers Are on a Faith Journey

Dave Ferguson, lead pastor of Community Christian Church, a multi-site congregation in Chicago, Illinois, came to the conclusion, "We're not going to call anyone a *Christian* because of the abuses of that name in America." (This is a bit ironic in light of the word "Christian" in the name of the church!) Rather, Ferguson prefers a term that conveys an ongoing process: *Christ-follower*.

Just imagine describing all the members of your church as Christ-followers.

Ferguson began the church in 1988 with his brother Jon and three friends from college. The men were all in their early twenties, and the "glue" that held the young church together was their passion to help people find their way back to God. That is a phrase that dominates Ferguson's description of his church, and it is a statement that appears in most of the church's publications: "Helping people find their way back to God."

To Ferguson, the prodigal son's return to the father (see Luke 15) is a microcosm of everyone's journey to God. Starting with Adam and Eve, who abandoned the dream that God gave them in the Garden of Eden, every person is lost and now must find their way back to God.

Therefore, Ferguson does not use the word "members" to describe the people who make their spiritual home at Community Christian Church. In fact, the church doesn't even have membership as we know it, so there is no such thing as a membership count and no comparisons with the number of members in other churches. Rather, Ferguson says that "*belonging* begins before *believing*." His strategy is to get people to become a part of the fellowship, where they will eventually become believers—or, as he calls them, Christ-followers.

What does it mean to *belong*? Ferguson speaks about three Cs as a person's path to God. First, there is *celebrate*, which is worship; it is relationship between the person and God. Second is *connect*, in which a person makes a commitment to do life with others through small groups; it is he or she and others. Third is *contribute*, with a focus on the person and the world. Through the third C, individuals become involved in difference-making ministry to others.

Community Christian Church has eight locations in greater Chicago, with 22 celebration (worship) services each weekend.

More than 5,000 people attend on any given weekend. Slightly more than half of the celebration services feature in-person teaching; the others run videos of Ferguson or other teaching pastors doing the teaching.

Ferguson indicates that people at Community Christian Church become a part of the process without ever being asked to join the church. They most often begin the journey by simply experiencing the first C (celebrate). The journey continues as they experience the second C (connect); it is then that most people make a commitment to become a Christ-follower. Soon after that, people move to the third C (contribute).

When asked if, biblically speaking, a specific point in time exists when a person makes a decision to receive Christ, Ferguson answers, "There is a point in time, but people are not always aware of it." As a result, the church does not ask people to join the church, nor do they ask people to become involved in a membership class. Rather, the teaching motivates them to take one step at a time as they respond to God's call to be a Christ-follower.

Ferguson recalls a time he was leading a small-group Bible study that looked at John 3:3: "You must be born from above." One of the participants spoke up, "That's what happened to me—being born again—isn't it?" She couldn't pinpoint a time when she became a Christ-follower, but she knew at that moment she was following Him.

Ferguson uses the illustration to teach other small-group leaders that they should "treat everyone like they are a Christian until they realize they are not." Ferguson wants new attendees to belong so that they'll believe. He wants small-group leaders to incorporate people into a group, treat them as one of the group, and get them into the Word of God so that they find their true spiritual condition and become a Christ-follower.[1]

A Journey Involving Constant Decision Points

Community Christian Church is not the only congregation that emphasizes the idea of the daily walk with Jesus as being a journey more than an initial step. A Google search of churches named "The Journey," "Journey Church" and the like identifies a surprising number of mostly new churches with "Journey" in the name.

I (Warren) have been attending The Journey Church in New York City, which Nelson Searcy started in 2001. Everything about the church is designed to help people take the next step in their journey of a faith relationship with Jesus Christ. Every conversation and communication, whether verbal or written, seems geared to help people take yet another incremental step forward in faith. They have a big heart for people who are not yet believers, but they likewise want growing Christians to grow more. The median age at The Journey is in the 20s, and pastors Nelson Searcy and Kerrick Thomas, both in their 30s, relate well to a generation that is constantly surrounded by a cafeteria of choices.

Sermons don't ever conclude with the general statement heard in many churches: "Well, that's something important to think about" or "May God bless His Word and apply it to our hearts" or "We're out of time, so I'll pick up here next week." Nor do they end with a single-pointed call to pray the sinner's prayer of salvation: "I want to invite you now to receive the Lord Jesus Christ as your Savior . . ."

Instead, each sermon offers multiple choices: "Some of you haven't yet trusted Jesus Christ to forgive your sins. Others of you may want to make a commitment to read this entire section of Scripture during the week. Perhaps others of you may want to make this the week that you join a home-based growth group." E-mails and letters likewise do far more than inform; they ask, "Are you looking to get connected? Here are some ideas." Options range from being on a service team that helps people in need, showing God's love in practical ways to the community, to participating in a "play group"—a one-time event of attending a play there in Manhattan and then going out to coffee shop to talk about it afterward.

Nelson Searcy came to faith during his college years. He respects the journey that many people take before they decide to walk with Christ. He also realizes the many decisions that people take to become mature in their spiritual relationships. "We want people to make a decision to receive Jesus Christ, but we also want to help them take the steps necessary to reach that point, and then to take the lifelong journey of steps of walking with Christ after that point," says Nelson.[2]

Historically, What Is *Conversion* in America?

The Protestant Reformation was a theological revolution against certain abuses of the Roman Catholic Church. It was grounded in a biblical understanding of justification by faith. Reformers Martin Luther, John Calvin and others made a strong commitment to correctly know and apply the Word of God.

As a result of this legacy, people who become Christians in Protestant churches have tended to develop a strong rational-based faith. They may acknowledge that saving faith encompasses the total personality, as the intellect understands God's plan of salvation, the emotion loves and hates sin and the will chooses to obey Christ. Yet most Protestants develop a strongly dominant knowledge-based faith, tending to ignore the role of emotions in personal salvation.

Protestants who first came to America—such as the early settlers in Massachusetts and Virginia—certainly emphasized the core doctrines of Christianity such as Jesus Christ dying on the cross for the forgiveness of sins and that those who believe in Him will obtain eternal life. However, teaching about the role of one's *experience* in conversion was mostly absent among early American Christian leaders. Even in the First Great Awakening, very little was said about the individual's response of emotions and will to God's offer of eternal life.

Thing changed during the Second Great Awakening when emotions become a driving force in conversion. The Cane Ridge Revival in Kentucky, which began in 1801, seemed to mark the difference. The revival occurred in the wilderness at a meeting where more than 14,000 people gathered to hear all-day preaching, singing and testifying. Near the front of the crowd, where preaching took place, workers had built "pens." These were small enclosures where people came forward to privately pray, cry out and seek salvation from God. Conversion was not characterized as intellectual belief alone, but an overwhelming emotional experience where a person would "pray through" or "hang on until they got it" or "find their peace." The idea was for individuals to continually seek the Lord to be saved.

The spread of Methodism is one evidence of the great influence of this revival. At the beginning of the American Revolutionary War in 1776 there were 243 Methodist churches in America. Thirty years later, there were a quarter million Methodists in 5,000 churches throughout this young country.

One of the products of the Second Great Awakening was Peter Cartwright, who became a famous evangelist and pastor and planted hundreds of Methodist churches. He searched three long months for God. The conviction of sin was so great that he couldn't go about his normal activities. He went forward in many of the Cane Ridge-style meetings to pray for hours on end, but he could not find God. When Cartwright finally prayed his way through, he had an emotional response:

> Divine light flashed all around me; unspeakable joy sprang up into my soul. I rose to my feet, opened my eyes,

and it really seemed as if I were in heaven . . . I have never for one moment doubted that the Lord did, then and there, forgive my sins and give me religion.[3]

Charles Finney, an atheist lawyer, also had a dramatic religious conversion. On October 10, 1821, he went into the woods on the top of a hill near his law office in Adams, New York, 100 miles east of Rochester. He prayed all morning and at noon returned to his law office a transformed man.

Finney began preaching, but his legal training influenced his preaching so that his sermons were rational presentations of the gospel. A remarkable revival occurred in Rochester, New York, in 1830 when he introduced what he called "new measures."[4] (Today, we might say "new methods in ministry" to mean the same idea.) As Finney was preaching, people rushed forward to pray, yell out, or mourn for salvation. To Finney's logical mind, this deterred the presentation of the gospel, so he instructed his people to listen carefully to his sermon, and then at the end they could come forward to seek salvation. Finney had the back of the first three pews removed so that three benches remained. He called them a "mourner's bench," where people could mourn for salvation. This practice instituted what became known across Christendom as the "gospel invitation" where preachers publicly invited people to come to the mourner's bench after the sermon and intercede for their souls.

Later in some churches, the elders refused to remove the backs of the pews, so he placed chairs at the front of the church and called them "anxious seats." Even later he began preaching in some churches where communion was taken at a church altar (a high church), so the gospel invitation was thus called an "altar call." People were invited to come, kneel at the church altar and "pray through" until they got salvation.

The Chicago Fire Changed It All

Dwight L. Moody, an evangelist known across America and Europe, was building a great church in the city of Chicago during the 1860s. He, like Finney and others, instructed hearers to listen carefully to the sermons and then to go home and plead fervently for salvation. In October 1871, Moody was preaching a six-week series of messages on embracing the life of Christ from the cradle to the Cross. On Sunday evening, October 8, he completed the fifth sermon in his series, preaching on the text, "What then shall I do with Jesus which is called Christ?" At the conclusion of his message, he announced, "I wish you would take this text home with you and turn it over in your minds during the week, and next Sabbath we will come to Calvary and the Cross, and we will decide what to do with Jesus of Nazareth."[5]

That evening the great Chicago fire broke out and thousands in the city died. Many who had heard Moody preach were in eternity by dawn.

This dramatic reality completely changed Moody's preaching for the rest of his life. "I have never dared to give an audience a week to think of their salvation since," Moody later explained. Moody concluded, "I have asked God many times to forgive me for telling people that night to take a week to think it over, and if he spares my life, I will never do it again."[6]

The Chicago fire changed the method of evangelism used across America for the next 100 years. Prior to that time, evangelists typically challenged listeners to pray through or to agonize over their sin. Salvation was thought of as an emotional process. After the Chicago fire, Moody gave an invitation after each sermon. He preached one particular sermon on "Instantaneous Salvation" to explain how people could be saved immediately by accepting Christ.[7] This sermon emphasized the choice of the will in conversion, not an emphasis on intellect or emotion. Other evangelists followed Moody's example for more than a century, including a young preacher named Billy Graham, who epitomized the new position with his use of the title *The Hour of Decision, Decision* magazine and other uses of the term "decision."[8]

To many, salvation was a decision (an exercise of the will) to follow God, with less or no emphasis on emotional expression and only minimal understanding of the content of the gospel required.

The Abuses of Instantaneous Conversion

When I (Elmer) was doing research in 1969 for *The 10 Largest Sunday Schools,* America's largest-attendance church was Akron Baptist Temple in Akron, Ohio.[9] Pastor Dallas Billington never had formal theological training, yet he mastered the Scriptures. He also knew people and how to communicate well. One of his phrases has stuck in my mind ever since: "Never pick green fruit." In the sermon I heard, he described the devastation when wheat was picked too soon and which then rotted in the bins and became useless. Billington likened it to the negative results of forcing people to make a prayer too soon, "Come into my heart, Lord Jesus," when they didn't know who Jesus was, or they didn't understand the impact of sin, or didn't even realize they were lost.

Billington said that when people are forced to make a salvation prayer too soon, they only repeat empty words and are therefore not truly born again. He claimed that when preachers used a call to salvation only as a formula, their converts didn't possess eternal life. They entered the church and were baptized, and many times they were persuaded that their soul was secure, but they were actually lost forever. Billington believed that American church rolls were filled with names of people who claimed to be Christian but were never saved.[10]

In my (Ed's) research role at the North American Mission Board, it is striking when I realize how many decisions are rededication decisions. A little more than a decade ago, our research team did a study of baptisms (in our faith tradition, baptism is to follow conversion). Yet, 40 percent of those being baptized indicated they were actually making a rededication from an earlier decision. It seems that in baptistic traditions, there are so many calls to commitment that many are being baptized over and over. When decisions are the focus, decisions come and baptisms follow—often over and over. But what about life transformation? When does that finally take root?

Counterpoint

You might ask, "Wasn't the Philippian jailer converted right on the spot? Didn't Paul and his assistants offer him instantaneous salvation at a crisis point?" "After he had led them out of the jail, he asked, 'What must I do to be saved?' They replied, 'Have faith in the Lord Jesus and you will be saved! This is also true for everyone who lives in your home'" (Acts 16:30-31).

How about some of the other crisis conversions in the New Testament, such as that of the apostle Paul, the woman at the well, Cornelius and the thief on the cross? Certainly there were times when Jesus and others would affirm, "Today you and your family have been saved" (Luke 19:9).

Then there is the apostle known as doubting Thomas. For a time, Thomas believed and then wavered. Would he prefer the word "journey" to describe the months surrounding his conversion? He followed Jesus for several years and said he was ready to go to his death for Jesus (see John 11:16), yet he also confessed his uncertainties to Jesus when he said, "Lord, we do not know where you are going" (John 14:5). When told that Jesus had come back from the dead, Thomas even refused to believe unless he could see and touch some tangible evidence (see John 20:25). Eight days later, when Jesus appeared to him, Thomas confessed, "My Lord and my God" (John 20:28). (Church historians speculate that the apostle Thomas later carried the gospel to India and there gave his life on behalf of his Savior.)

Journey churches are for today's doubting Thomases and many others who relate better to the idea that when God makes their broken life whole, it might not be instantaneous and could involve a long process of development.

Is It Enough?

For a long time, the pattern of confrontational evangelism, emotional reaction and life transformation has been the norm. There is nothing wrong with the pattern—if it still happens. Certainly it does occur in some places and among some people.

Now that we live in a new culture—one that is post- and pre-Christian at the same time—churches need to understand that most people do not have the necessary knowledge or experience to trust Christ after a gospel confrontation. We live in a different situation, and that situation requires different methods and means of communication and ministry. There must be some knowledge of the gospel in order to respond to it. Yet many people just assume that if they preach loud enough, people will understand. Like many Americans overseas, they raise their voices but not their communication. Communicating without understanding only leads to misunderstanding.

Decision-journey churches recognize that most people in North America already are followers of another "religion"—the religion of American spirituality—and that they therefore may currently believe that there is a God, that he or she loves everyone, that all people go to heaven unless they are really bad like Hitler, and that spiritual life is important for personal peace.

Thus, when these people hear about Jesus, the gospel and turning away from sin, they filter it through their existing religion—unless they are given time in community to understand the real meaning of the gospel.

We have already moved into a post-everything age: post-Christian, postmodern, post-truth. Part of today's communication need may be to allow lost people to live in Christian community in real time, not in some reflection of a past reality. All the talk of what Christians *are* breaks down when people see what real Christians *do*. The unchurched and unconvinced are allowed to make their journey and live in real time among real believers. Accordingly, they make their decisions about becoming a Christ-follower in journey as well.

What Can We Learn from Decision-Journey Churches?

There is much to learn from decision-journey churches. Most growing churches have recognized that the time to consider the reality of the gospel has lengthened for many people. In times and cultures of the past, people would fall under the conviction of the Spirit simply by falling under the shadow of a man like Charles Finney. Do such things still happen? Sure. However, they are much more likely to happen when someone already knows that there is a God, that He sent His Son named Jesus, and that his or her sin needs forgiveness.

Elmer Towns and Ed Stetzer include the evangelism journey in their book *Perimeters of Light: Biblical Boundaries for the Emerging Church*, where they explain the value of seeing evangelism as a journey.[11] As the following chart indicates, decision-journey churches invite people into the community (the space between the funnel lines) so that they might continue to move toward Christ and His church. Eventually, they make a commitment to

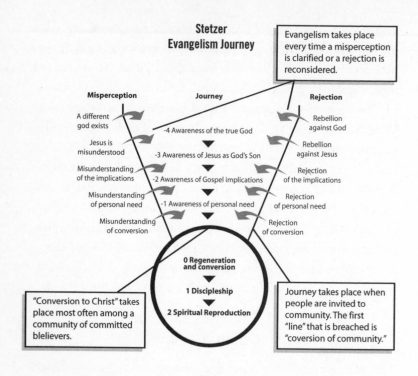

Stetzer Evangelism Journey

Evangelism takes place every time a misperception is clarified or a rejection is reconsidered.

Misperception	Journey	Rejection
A different god exists	-4 Awareness of the true God	Rebellion against God
Jesus is misunderstood	-3 Awareness of Jesus as God's Son	Rebellion against Jesus
Misunderstanding of the implications	-2 Awareness of Gospel implications	Rejection of the implications
Misunderstanding of personal need	-1 Awareness of personal need	Rejection of personal need
Misunderstanding of conversion		Rejection of conversion

0 Regeneration and conversion

1 Discipleship

2 Spiritual Reproduction

"Conversion to Christ" takes place most often among a community of committed blelievers.

Journey takes place when people are invited to community. The first "line" that is breached is "coversion of community."

Christ—whether or not they clearly identify the date and time—and move into the family of God.

Decision-journey churches teach us important truths about counting the cost. Jesus told believers they must consider the cost before following Him (see Luke 9:23; 14:28). It seems that churches expect people to consider the cost in the 30 or 45 minutes of a sermon—just in time to walk down the aisle. If it worked that way in a more Christian culture, so be it. But, today, people start off farther away from the gospel, and that walk down the aisle may take a few years. Andy Stanley put it this way: "Nobody goes from atheism to faith during a sermon. . . . Salvation is not a process, but coming to faith is."[12] If God has not called your church to become a pure decision-journey church, then perhaps He has challenged you to consider a new openness to seeing evangelism as a journey—one best made with friends in community.

Beyond the obvious "people need more time to consider Christ," we would suggest several other lessons that can be learned from the decision-journey church.

- *It is natural, biblical and appropriate for people to consider the cost before committing to Christ.* Too many Christians have reduced the gospel to a certain prayer to pray and a card to fill out. It is unimaginable that the Early Christians lived in this manner. Instead, they became followers of "the way" (see Acts 9:2) by joining with other people on that same path. In Luke 14, when large crowds were following Jesus, He turned to them and told them that it was not easy and they needed to count the cost before deciding to follow Him. Perhaps if our churches gave people more time to consider the cost, they might make more serious disciples when they begin to follow Christ.

- *For too long, Christians have been responding to shouts of "fire!" rather than to the sovereignty of God.* Many of us have determined that the gospel is a "one shot" proposition, that if people do not "get it" right now, they will be lost eternally—even if they have another 50 years of life ahead of them on Earth! God is Creator and Ruler of the universe; He knows our future. Our task is to be faithful each day to live in His ways and to tell the gospel to the lost and trust God with the results and the timing. Pushing for a premature decision from a position of fear is not what Jesus taught. His focus was on the power of the Spirit: "No one can come to

me, unless the Father who sent me makes them want
to come" (John 6:44).

- *There must be a safe place in Christian community for
  unbelievers to consider the cost.* Most churches have two
  categories: members and prospects. That creates boundaries instead of bridges. Churches would do well to recognize that there is more than one type of Christian
  community. One is a *covenant community*, a group of
  Christians who have made a clear commitment to
  Christ and to each other. The other is *Christian community*, where believers and non-believers alike are seeking
  to move closer to God. All churches need to find ways
  for men and women to be part of a Christian community even before they become Christ-followers.

- *Becoming a Christ-follower takes time.* The time between
  considering the gospel and making a commitment to
  Christ often takes longer today. That's all right. Well
  thought-out commitments often make better commitments. We have all witnessed many instantaneous
  conversions that did not seem to stick in the weeks or
  months that followed. However, those who take time
  to process through the truth claims of Christ are better prepared to make a "dangerous decision" (following Christ) while in a safe place (among God's people).

What We Need to Consider

We believe God is working in powerful ways at churches where
unbelievers are welcomed and challenged. Confrontational evangelism seems much less effective today than it may have been in
decades past. The vast majority of lost people are not miserably

waiting for someone they don't know to explain spiritual laws. They need time and true friends and authentic relationships as the context in which to help them consider those same spiritual laws.

There are also challenges to be considered. Decision-journey churches invite people into Christian community before they are Christians, and that has some challenges. Over the course of time, some churches want to welcome everyone, but they soon find that those they welcomed also wanted to be *affirmed*. Theologically, that can be tricky!

Decision-journey churches need to know that while there is a place for unbelievers in community with Christians, there is also an accountability that Christians have for each other. For example, 1 Corinthians 5:9-13 speaks of those "in," "out," and "immoral":

> In my other letter I told you not to have anything to do with immoral people. But I wasn't talking about the people of this world. You would have to leave this world to get away from everyone who is immoral or greedy or who cheats or worships idols. I was talking about your own people who are immoral or greedy or worship idols or curse others or get drunk or cheat. Don't even eat with them! Why should I judge outsiders? Aren't we supposed to judge only church members? God judges everyone else. The Scriptures say, "Chase away any of your own people who are evil."

In North America, we think of church as a building. Thus, unchurched people can be in the church (as *in* a building) when they do not know Christ. We even encourage Christians to invite their unsaved friends to church. However, the New Testament paints a different picture: Unbelievers did come in contact and even live in *community* with believers, but the *church* was a different thing. That's why 1 Corinthians goes into so much detail—people in the church *do* judge each other in the best sense of the word. Christians in churches commit to live like Christians and to hold each other accountable to do that very thing. Non-Christians are not expected to live like Christians because they are not yet part of that commitment and community.

Church, or those that were "called out" (from the Greek word *ecclesia*), is those who have committed their lives to Christ and to each other. Thus, in the biblical sense, church is a committed community of Christians bound together by a series of decisions and practices. Yet, in a cultural sense, church is a meeting and a community that Christians and non-Christians alike can and should be a part of.

Decision-journey churches often struggle with how to make the distinction of what the Bible teaches. For some, that means an abandonment of the concept of church membership. That's not a problem per se. Membership is a term and concept that has come to mean participation in an organization. Membership has its privileges, but it also has its problems.

The Bible teaches that some are in a different kind of community—one that is shared among committed Christians. Some decision-journey classes are recognizing that need and are using the term "partnership" instead of "membership." Christians can and should be in partnership with each other in a special way—all while in community with believers and unbelievers alike.

Some decision-journey churches have struggled with the tendency to become wide but not deep. Because they are focused on bringing committed and uncommitted alike into community, they sometimes tend to focus on what all have in common. Thus, they end up with the lowest common denominator—teaching so basic that everyone can understand but one that never leads to deeper biblical teaching. Many decision-journey churches have recognized that they need progressively deeper opportunities for growth in maturity.

Christians and Unbelievers Together

God is using decision-journey churches. These churches are encouraging their people to invest and invite in their unchurched friends. By inviting people into their Christian community, they are inviting them to see Christ lived out.

Being a decision-journey church is challenging to those who are a part of the journey because they invite unbelievers into their life and space. Instead of challenging the lost to consider a tract, they themselves becoming living epistles—and let's be honest, sometimes we are not the best examples. So, decision-journey churches challenge believers to live Christlike lives so that people in their community will be attracted to their Christ.

Decision-journey churches have learned a powerful lesson: Christians need to be in community with unbelievers. All churches need to recognize that unbelievers and believers alike will be a part of their community—and discerning churches will see that as an opportunity rather than a problem.

CHAPTER 11

ATTRACTIONAL CHURCHES

*Go home to your family and tell them how much the Lord has
done for you and how good he has been to you.*

MARK 5:19

The Gospels are packed with stories of people who point others to Jesus. The verse above is about a man with evil spirits. His life was such a mess that "night and day he was in the graveyard or on the hills, yelling and cutting himself with stones" (Mark 5:5). After Jesus healed him, "the man begged to go with" Jesus (v. 18), but Jesus said no. Instead the man was to go home and tell his friends and family about God's goodness to him.

Likewise how many sermons have we heard praising the disciple Andrew? After learning about Jesus, "the first thing Andrew did was to find his brother [Peter] and tell him, 'We have found the Messiah!'" (John 1:41).

How about the Samaritan woman, who met Jesus at the community well? After her encounter with him, "The woman left her water jar and ran back into town. She said to the people, 'Come and see a man who told me everything I have ever done! Could he be the Messiah?' Everyone in town went out to see Jesus" (John 4:28-30).

Even in Jesus' parables, He seems to affirm the idea of finding friends and family and bringing them to Himself. And if the invited guests won't come, according to one parable, Jesus says to "go out along the back roads and fence rows and make people come in, so that my house will be full" (Luke 14:23).

After Jesus rose from the dead and went back up to heaven, the Early Church followed that same pattern. Since they couldn't bring people to a literal Jesus, they brought inquirers to the Body of Christ—the Church. On Pentecost, "a crowd gathered" (Acts 2:6) to discover what was happening. As news about the Early Church spread, "a lot of people living in the towns near Jerusalem brought those who were sick or troubled by evil spirits, and they were all healed" (Acts 5:16). When Peter and John healed a lame man in Jesus' name, a crowd gathered (see Acts 13:11-12).

Fast forward almost 2,000 years and the Church is still proclaiming the good news about Jesus and representing Him as the Body of Christ. The biggest difference between then and today is that most churches now have buildings for their meetings, which typically gather at pre-scheduled times for their various services and programs.

The innovation for today is the motivation churches tap into as they invite people to come. "The woman at the well was literally thirsty," we argue, "so Jesus met her felt need, and then he used the experience as a bridge to address her spiritual need." Likewise, Peter was interested in fishing, so Jesus said "I will teach you how to bring in people instead of fish" (Matt. 4:19-20). On other occasions, Jesus even taught Peter a thing or two about fishing (see Luke 5:4; John 21:8-11).

Extending that logic, churches ask, "What legitimate need can we help meet, as a way of winning a hearing for the gospel?" This type of church that uses this approach is sometimes called an "attractional" church.

Attractional Churches Reach People for Christ

If I (Warren) ever join a recovery group, it will be for people with an addiction for visiting different churches. I love learning how

God is at work in so many different kinds of churches. Each different church seems to have a different story, and so often the building they've constructed and use up to seven days a week is linked to that story.

Take Lima Community Church, for example. This Nazarene congregation is located in a very challenging area of Lima, Ohio. As recounted in *Moving from Maintenance to Ministry* by Dale Galloway and Warren Bird, the church, starting in 1941, has had a long history of strong, stable leadership.[1] Over the years the church became known as a community willing to do whatever it takes to reach those who are hurting. "The church was and is a very accepting, loving environment," says Vince Nelson, executive pastor. "People are attracted to it when they come to it."

An estimated 87 percent of the county is unchurched. More important, "the brokenness of this community is staggering," says Nelson, including broken families and a divorce rate 14 percent higher than the national average, and higher-than-average financial struggles.

In response, Senior Pastor Dan Huckins has led the congregation into a new emphasis of reaching the missing, starting with the children. "Today the church's growth engine is in children and family ministries," Huckins says. Thus in the last few years, the children's and youth ministries have developed a huge draw.

"If you haven't seen the creative decorations, you won't believe your eyes," says Cindy Porter, children's director. "Our desire is to create an 'I want to be there' atmosphere," Porter says.

Youth ministries have likewise become a community-wide draw. The youth team gets to work in one of the top youth-center facilities in the state, a 32,000-square-foot building. Young people not only have access to a great gym for volleyball, basketball and other sports, but they also have skateboard ramps, a climbing wall and a game room with X-box consoles.

For example, a recent event with a crowd of 450 youth drew one-third of them as new kids to the church. Upward Basketball, another strong ministry, has doubled from one year to the next and regularly draws large crowds of young people.

As with the children's ministry, paid staff roles are minimal. There is a heavy volunteer base. The heart of the church today is the people who have stepped up and taken ownership. Volunteer involvement has enabled the student ministry to turn the page, from the thriving Sunday-night Axis ministry for junior and senior high, to an in-town, student-involved ministry that goes to the poorest area of town, to Wednesday night, youth-based small groups by adults.

The growth momentum has recently taken the church past 2,000 in attendance, making it one of the larger congregations in its denomination. To Dan Huckins, the future of the church is in no way limited to the size of small-town Ohio. "Over the years, a lot of churches ask 'why?' But this one keeps asking 'why not?'" he says. "The church has always had good pastoral leadership, but it's also been placed in a community with a lot of hurting people."

As people's lives are spiritually healed, they are more able to culturally impact the greater community as well.

"To the degree you find out how to plug into the brokenness of your community—that will take the limits off your growth," Dan says. "We figure there are 94,000 people in our area who are missing from being involved in a good local church. We're willing to change and respond to people in need. We want to be a church that goes after the missing."

For Lima Community Church, attractional evangelism seems to work well. Their credo is to care deeply about people, reach out to them, invite them into your life and bring them to church—which is not only an exciting group of people but is also a place, something of a destination, featuring everything from high-tech worship to X-box consoles for teens.

Ministry Has Focused on Baby Boomers

Today's headlines present a steady diet of stories about the first wave of the Baby Boomer generation turning 60. Technically, Boomers are those born between 1946 and 1964. The book you're reading was first published in 2007, which at that time placed Boomers between 43 and 61 years old. (Of the writers of this book, Elmer is part of the Builder Generation, Warren is a Baby Boomer and Ed is part of that emerging generation that eschews labels as irrelevant and unhelpful.)

Back in the 1980s, when large numbers of Boomers were starting to raise their families, churches all over were trying to figure out how to reach them. One such pioneer was Doug Murren, who led Eastside Foursquare Church in Kirkland, Washington, from 10 people to more than 4,000 in weekly attendance, with 17,000 decisions for Christ over a 15-year period. Our publisher, Regal Books, asked Murren, a nationally acclaimed innovator and pioneer in ministry to Baby Boomers, to publish what he had learned. The Charles E. Fuller Institute of Evangelism and Church Growth had him tour the country doing seminars for pastors based on that book, which was titled *Baby Boomerang,* an image that suggests the Boomer generation is coming back to church, much like a well-thrown boomerang loops back around and returns home. His subtitle is even more telling: *Catching the Boomer Generation as They Return to Church.*[2]

The book, which was very popular with pastors and church leaders, emphasized the idea of training the people of your church to be "bringers and includers." The job of God's people, it emphasized, is to find a relational bridge with neighbors and friends. While you can bring them to church anytime, the church will especially help by (every month or so) making the worship services and children's programming particularly geared to newcomers. It worked well in thousands of churches besides Eastsquare.

Murren's approach also matched the leading church growth research of the day: Win Arn, among others, discovered that in a typical church, most people had come not at the personal invitation of the pastor, nor due primarily to advertising, but on the arm of a friend. Some 85 percent of the people in any given church say they came that way.

Interestingly, as Murren looked back on the peak of the Baby Boomer era, he said he would carry the lay responsibility even further, hinting that maybe he wouldn't focus quite as much on a staff-driven event (bringing your friend to church) as he would on a relational community event (bringing your friend to your small group).

In *Leadershift*, a sequel to *Baby Boomerang*, Murren wrote:

As I look back on my 15 years at Eastside . . . If I had it to do all over again, I would try for the congregation to be 80 percent more lay driven but with only 30 percent as many staff. In fact, one of the big mistakes I made was being too staff focused. Eastside grew 80 percent to 100 percent many years, causing constant change and upheaval. Staff turnover is unsettling when a church is built on the premise that paid staff are central to its existence. . . .

Perhaps my deepest regret surrounds something I first saw in 1984, but didn't act upon seriously enough for almost a decade. I got a glimpse at the power of small group community for evangelism, discipleship, and leadership development. It could have been part of the core fibers of the congregation, but unfortunately we didn't move that way. We did make the move in 1993, and the church had 450 groups when I left in 1996. If I could relive yesterday, I'd build those groups even more around interactive study together for discipling purposes. I'd be careful not to allow the sermon to be too much of the primary tool for discipleship. . . .

I'm thankful to God for all the things Eastside has done well, and continues to do. We learned how to target lost people. We developed an understanding of Baby Boomers. We showed that worship can be evangelistic. We saw how laypeople bringing their friends to church can become the strategic doorway for new birth.[3]

Murren's *Baby Boomerang* offered a very popular attractional model, but he was certainly not the only one or first one to do it. Christians everywhere have tried to figure out how best to show the Baby Boomer generation the relevance of the timeless gospel.

One of the most popular products distributed by the Virginia-based Church Growth Institute (www.churchgrowth. org) is a kit called *Friend Day* by Elmer Towns. Almost 50,000 churches have used a *Friend Day* campaign. It is a step-by-step template for creating a high-attendance day at church by being very intentional about praying for, inviting and then bringing a friend to a certain special day at church. The designated day has an extra attractional touch—a guest musician, a celebrity testimony, a children's emphasis, a church fair or similar activities. The build-up includes statements by pastors and influential leaders about who they've invited to church, and strong encouragement for everyone else to do likewise.[4]

The approach worked well in churches of all sizes and denominations. Like Home Depot's slogan today, "You can do it, and we can help," God's people by the hundreds of thousands stepped out in faith ("you can do it"), initiated a prayerful invitation to a friend, and then brought that friend to church, where the gospel was presented and a wow-factor hopefully impressed them to come again ("we can help").

Attractional Is Not New

Has the Church only recently become attractional? In chapter 8, we mentioned that Robert Raikes (1735-1811), founder of the Sunday School movement in England, gave a gold coin for perfect attendance. Early pioneers of Sunday Schools in America gave blue and red tickets. When young "scholars" accumulated the right number of tickets, they got a free book. More recent Sunday School contests have awarded not only pins, key chains and Bibles but also free trips to Hawaii.

Even Hollywood has been tapped for decades to attract people to church. Henrietta Mears, at the First Presbyterian Church in Hollywood, California, brought the famous horse Trigger and its rider Roy Rogers to church to attract visitors. And haven't churches used guest speakers, including sports stars, television celebrities, former U.S. presidents and musicians like Elvis Presley? (Some churches promised Elvis sightings even after he died!) The attractional church is not new but fits into a continuous historical stream. Even so, just because others have done it, and done it for a long time, doesn't make it right.

Downsides of Attractional

An attractional church, as presented in this chapter, is one that is built around the concept of "come and see." There are emphases, programs, or activities that attract people to visit the church to "see." The hook used to attract people ranges from size to quality to worship to teaching to children.

For many, attractional is losing its luster, and attractional churches are starting to lose their popularity. Why? Because it assumes a level of interest that only a churched culture cares about.

You might immediately object, since attractional is normal in almost every kind of church today. If not intentionally promoted by the leadership, it is certainly lived out in the lives of its members. People bring their friends when they are excited about the church—they find it attractive and are convinced that others will as well.

Jack Hyles led First Baptist Church of Hammond, Indiana, in holding the record for many years as the country's largest Sunday School (starting in 1971). It has been pastored since 2001 by Hyles's son-in-law, Jack Schaap. The church describes itself as independent and fundamentalist, and its website and literature warmly welcome people to "join us for our regular schedule of services."[5]

John MacArthur's church, Grace Community Church, hardly a bastion of the church growth movement, proclaims and promotes on its website that it seeks to "teach people about Christ and their need for salvation."[6]

The church Brian McLaren started, Cedar Ridge Community Church, promises dynamic community that sure sounds attractive to us when it says that it "exists to help people have life to the full. We welcome people into a dynamic Christian community where they can connect—with God, with one another and with opportunities to make a difference in our changing world."[7]

First Baptist Church of Hammond makes its targeted invitation rather clear when they write, "First Baptist Church has the kind of music you'd expect to hear in an old-fashioned, Bible-preaching, soul-singing, fundamental Baptist church. Come and see."[8]

When Fundamentalist Schaap, Calvinist MacArthur and Emergent McLaren all use attractional language, it should cause us to think through our objection. Is it so wrong to seek to attract people in a culture where we still have a religious memory, albeit a fading one? Is it wrong to ask them to "come and see"?

Clearly, most churches and Christians today think attrac-
tionally, whether they are intentional about it or not. Even
those who would avoid the term and the approach were often
impacted by attractional ministry. For example, Chuck Smith
would probably indicate that they built much of the Calvary
Chapel ministry on expository Bible teaching and praise worship music. Few churches do it better. However, the first
Calvary Chapel was already doing such teaching and worship
when their world changed. David Di Sabatino, probably the
leading scholar on the Jesus People Movement, wrote in his
doctoral thesis:

> The alignment of the internationally known Calvary
> Chapel church with the Jesus People Movement is cen-
> tered around the work of two contrasting images. Calvary
> Chapel was founded on the alliance of pastor-teacher,
> Chuck Smith Jr. and hippie evangelist Lonnie Frisbee.[9]

Soon, the small church that Smith pastored was attracting
attention, attracting the news (*Life* magazine, *Time* and others),
and was an attractional church. When Lonnie Frisbee showed
up, the attraction factor grew. For example, quoting the *Orange
County Weekly* (from Orange County, California), "Young people around the land heard about 'the hippie preacher in Costa
Mesa' who was goofy, brusque and looked as if he's just walked
out of the Bible."[10]

Simply put, churches often grow by attraction. That may
bother a lot of people, but it doesn't make it any less true. One
thing that all of the above examples have in common is that they
are led by dynamic communicators—and people would rather
listen to good communicators than bad—even when they are
preaching the same gospel.

So, let's confess it: Attractional works. It doesn't mean it is perfect and without repercussions. And, for those of you who have a bit of an edge on the subject, let's also confess this: We are attractional. The issue is how much and with how much discernment.

Using "felt needs" to reach people has always been decried by some, and we need to carefully evaluate those criticisms. How we appeal to someone—churched or unchurched—will ultimately affect how we retain them. And a church that "appeals" to culture should have a spiritual formation strategy to lead people to an understanding of Christ and His mission (and, lest you wonder, pastors spend hours in prayer and discussion, working hard to move attendees beyond having their felt needs met and into serious discipleship).

Attractional churches are built around the idea of what Vineyard Cincinnati founder Steve Sjogren calls "come and see." They have successfully tapped into many sociological realities. Yet the gospel first and foremost should be "go and tell," which Sjogren has modeled through his widely popular emphasis on servant evangelism.[11]

For decades, we've focused heavily on "fixing up the barn" so that the wheat will harvest itself. We have big, clean and appealing barns now, but the culture is less impacted by the gospel than it was before we spruced up the buildings and spiced up all the churches in the '80s.

However, valuing Go and Tell as the only approach seems to reflect a misunderstanding of who Jesus is and what He called us to do. Jesus is more than a humble Galilean peasant who lived in community with a counterculture motif. He's also the exalted King and worthy of all praise—even the praise of millions. The Gospels tell us He spoke to multitudes of people (thousands) on numerous occasions. Scripture teaches us to use both Go and Tell and Come and See ministry approaches. You probably use the same approach—"please tell your friend about Jesus and bring her to church."

Things We Can Learn

There are several things that we can learn from the model of attractional churches, as follows.

Lost People Think Like Lost People

It's simply not possible to lead an attractional church without appealing to people—and lost people are often "appealed to" by attractional churches. We live in a consumer-oriented society, and appealing to consumers is both a part and a result of being an attractional church.

So the question is not whether consumerism exists or whether churches appeal to consumers. Instead, the question we should be asking is, What will churches do with consumers (the unchurched) when the Bible calls us to a life of sacrifice and service? Attractional churches with conviction will lead the uncommitted consumer to become a committed disciple.

Jesus Attracted People at Times

When Jesus healed and did other miracles, He attracted a crowd. They saw needs being met and they responded accordingly. Then, Jesus challenged them to become true followers. Vineyard leader John Wimber built a whole movement on the idea of Power Evangelism—people will see the miracles and come to learn more. He cited Jesus as the best example. It would seem that attracting people is not without biblical precedent.

Churches Do Grow When They Do Things with Excellence

There is no denying it. Churches more frequently grow when they have emphasized quality, excellence and other factors that attract people. It is not good or bad; it is just true.

So, the method changes but the message does not? Well, maybe. The question is how to do so without confusing the medium (attractional ministry) with the message (the gospel). Are there opportunities? Certainly. Are there concerns? You bet.

Things We Need to Consider

You may have noticed our caution to approach this subject. Why? Because like so many others, our immediate thought is the excesses rather than the opportunities. Like any innovation, there are concerns. Here are a few we consider important:

Attractional Churches Need to Work Hard to Get Their People into the Community

Ultimately, only the leaders of a church can develop and maintain an outward-focused environment and ministry. People must see evidence that the source of the attractional ministry (usually a dynamic teaching pastor) is personally engaging in incarnational ministry. For example, such a pastor might meet weekly with three unchurched friends at a local coffee shop.

If attractional churches do not get their people on mission, their future is in doubt. Another attractional church will soon spring up, siphoning off the consumers into a new and better (or cooler, or more kid friendly, or more charismatic) church experience. With a church full of people who only know how to invite their friends to see the show, soon the church will begin to decline. Like a bear fed by the tourists, it does not have the will or the ability to reach the lost through its church community. The attraction can soon become its downfall.

Attractional Churches May Fight Over Attendees

I (Ed) often speak of the "charismatic church of last resort" when I consult with those in the charismatic movement. Please don't misunderstand. Though we are not charismatic, our point is not to criticize. It could be the "bible church of last resort" or many others. Let me explain.

A friend of mine planted a charismatic church in a community where I pastored. It exploded in growth. Hundreds came. The worship was free and the church was filled with outpourings of the Spirit. Many of those who attended expressed their enthusiasm that they were no longer "stifled" in their worship. The charismatic megachurch in town would not let them bring their tambourines or dance, and my friend's church would. People were attracted to the church because it was the freest, most charismatic church in town—for a while.

In a few years, another church decided to get even freer in the Spirit! Soon, many of the people who were worshiping at my friend's church left for the next "move" of the Spirit. They were attracted to more worship, more freedom, more enthusiasm, more *more*! And that's the downside: Attractional works only until someone does it better. When that occurs, you need to be sure that you do not get angry at the people who leave—you taught them to think that way when you attracted them in the first place!

Attractional ministry can ultimately lead to dueling attractions. Who can do it better? Who can have the bigger children's program? More charismatic worship? Better music? The irony is that churches will pour immense energy into such approaches—while a smaller and smaller part of the community is even willing to consider the church in the first place. Alan Hirsch's newest book, *The Forgotten Ways: Reactivating the Missional Church*, comments:

[We] can intuit that in American the current "market appeal" of the contemporary church growth model might be up to 35 percent (as opposed to 12 percent in

Australia). But even if it is at this level of appeal, it is decreasing. It's time for a radical rethink taking into account both the strategic and missional implications.[12]

Attractional Churches Can Trivialize the Gospel

Trivialization is probably in the eye of the beholder, but the gospel cannot be reduced to Christian pop culture or a gimmick. It is interesting, though, that some will be fine with certain innovations if they are done as outreaches but not as church. For example, some Christians have started outreaches to attract the pro-wrestling crowd. A recent *ABC News* report from Canton, Georgia, said the following about this:

> [Bob] Fields says almost 900 others have been converted, though he admits the violence may not be for everyone and hears his share of criticism. "We just tell them, this is not something that everybody is going to enjoy," Fields said. "We're trying to appeal to that wrestling crowd, and we're trying to get the wrestling crowd that typically doesn't go to church, doesn't really abide by any faith or have any beliefs in Christianity."[13]

Another story from *ABC News* talked about *Fear Factor*-type ministry, where young people participate in bizarre feats to reach people:

> "Fear Factor" is a reality TV show in which contestants compete by participating in dangerous activities or by eating stomach-turning foods for cash prizes. "Through this ministry, kids are surrendering their lives to Jesus and developing a deeper relationship with Jesus," Anthony Martin said. "The method of the ministry that we use to bring people is going to change, but the message is going to stay consistent."[14]

If we had churches for wrestlers and gross-food eaters, that might seem more problematic than outreach events for the same. But when the focus is on the attraction or the innovation, it is often impossible to be focused on God, His Word and His worship. For some, the weightlifting Power Team might be okay for evangelism, but a church focused on bodybuilders would seem to be focused on the wrong type of strength.

Attractional Churches Can Segregate God's People by Preference

Every attractional church we have seen is filled with a similar kind of people. Why? Because like-minded people are attracted to the same thing. There is a danger that such churches can promote division in the Body ("We have better [fill in the blank] than you do!").

Hard Questions

However, hard questions still remain: Does attractional ministry impact the real message that people hear? Does consumerism guide the process of growth in attractional churches more than the Spirit? Is the effectiveness of attractional churches a cultural phenomenon? Will the attractional church remain prominent in a culture that increasingly has no Christian memory we can appeal to?

Attractional churches are probably the most common of the growing churches today. They are also the most criticized. Whether we like it or not, living the gospel and being the Church is a challenge in every culture—and churches of all types should work toward being both. Attractional churches need to remember two key things if they want to be discerning and biblical: (1) Who they are often produces a level of commitment they may not want; and (2) how they grew often produces a view of outreach they shouldn't solely rely on.

Can attractional evangelism be done in a way that honors God? Sure. Many churches that use words like "dynamic," "exciting," and "need-meeting" are biblically faithful, leading people to be on mission in culture and to transform communities. It just takes an awareness of the opportunities and challenges in order to hold a biblical balance. Perhaps it also takes recognition that attractional models work best in certain contexts, and that once that easy fruit is gone, we will need to plant new seeds and harvest in new fields.

WHAT DO THESE CHURCH TYPES TEACH US?

When Elmer Towns and Warren Bird asked me (Ed) to become the third author for their book on innovation, I was intrigued and worried. I was intrigued because I think innovation is a challenge in many places today. Some have innovated too far, but most have not innovated at all. Yet there is little in print that deals with innovation with an open, but discerning, attitude.

I was worried because I have become convinced that two of the biggest issues for evangelicals in the next 10 years will be ecclesiology and missiology. Ecclesiology ("study of church") helps us to understand what a church is and how it should function. Missiology ("study of mission") helps us to see what methods and ministries will be most effective at reaching our community. This book deals with both in a way that is affirming and discerning—and that is a difficult balance, fraught with potential for misunderstanding.

Church Innovation Matters

What needs to change in the North American Church? Everyone has an immediate, personal suggestion: We need to have culturally relevant worship, elder rule, house churches, verse-by-verse expository preaching, multi-sites, and so forth. The reason why people are so quick with an answer is that we all realize the North American Church is in trouble. We differ in what we need to do—and how much innovation it involves.

What is "innovation"? According to the *Encarta Dictionary*, "innovation" is:

1. origination; the act or process of inventing or introducing something new; or

2. something newly invented or a new way of doing things—such as using *Encarta* rather than *Webster's* to supply definitions.

It is significant to note that all present traditions were once innovations; someone or a group had introduced something new or invented a new way of doing things. When the Early Church began to meet on Sundays, it was an innovation. When the Early Church started meeting in buildings in the late second century, it was an innovation. When worshipers sat down for portions of the worship service, it was an innovation. Jump ahead a few centuries to when people brought indoor plumbing to their church facilities, it was an innovation.

Yet, in a way unlike we have seen in many centuries, innovation has been the "watchword" for 50 years. Churches have innovated again and again. The headline churches in Elmer Towns's 1990 book *Ten Innovative Churches* included churches that seem quite tame today (such as Skyline Wesleyan in San Diego, California, or First Baptist in Jacksonville, Florida), and the innovations they pioneered are "ho hum" today because virtually everyone is doing them now. While the innovations of 1990 seem tame to Scum of the Earth Church, organic house churches and cyber-enhanced churches in this book (among others), they will probably seem tame when you read the edition that comes out in 2020!

Yet all of our innovations, whether bold or common, haven't done much good in terms of addressing the Church's deeper issues. After 50 years of sprucing up our churches and spicing up our worship, the culture is less reached and those who go to churches are less committed. There is *something wrong*—and innovation has not "yet" answered the deeper issues. And yet . . . church innovation still matters.

Some assume that because methodological innovation is not working, there is something wrong with the gospel and the Scriptures. Thus, they innovate their theology. The logic goes like this: If we just changed our view of the atonement, sexuality or Scripture, that would "fix" the problem of the Church. Beyond the obvious difficulty that such a solution is theologically problematic, there is another problem: It doesn't work! It's been tried many times before. The Modernists of the early twentieth century tried to accommodate Christianity to modern science; they ended up scientifically correct but spiritually bankrupt. In the 1960s, some of the mainline denominations tried to think outside the box in the name of relevance. Sadly, many ended up irrelevant because they had no message other than the often fuzzy message of culture—*do good, try hard, be "spiritual."* After they innovated away the Scriptures, even the unchurched were no longer interested.

Innovation as a Way to Be More Relevant

Instead, some are seeing innovation as a contextualization strategy. They have determined that the "how" of ministry is in many ways determined by the "who, when and where" of culture. Yet, they are still recognizing that innovation is not *the gospel*—the gospel exists, God owns it, and we are to contend for it. Our task is to proclaim that gospel, and churches can and should continuously innovate to make that happen.

A helpful contrast might be found in Jude 3 and in 1 Corinthians 9:22-23:

- Jude 3: "My dear friends, I really wanted to write you about God's saving power at work in our lives. But instead, I must write and ask you to defend the faith that God has once for all given to his people."

- 1 Corinthians 9:22-23: "When I am with people whose faith is weak, I live as they do to win them. I do everything I can to win everyone I possibly can. I do all this for the good news, because I want to share in its blessings."

Jude 3 tells us to *contend*. First Corinthians tells us to *contextualize*. They both matter. The focus here is on *what to contend for* and *what to contextualize* in the innovated church. Are there some things for which we are to contend with the church? Yes. There are theological, moral, spiritual and communal issues for which we are to contend. Are there some things to contextualize and innovate in the church? Yes. The challenge is to know which is which. Our challenge to you is to sort that out for your particular context.

Does the Church Matter?

As we think about innovation, some may ask, "Does the church still matter?" It is a fair question considering the state of the church today. After World War II, many European Christians were rightfully disgusted with the church. It had failed in its mission, compromised with Nazism, and capitulated to the forces of nationalism, rather than contending for the gospel. Some people see parallel problems with the established church today, in how we've largely capitulated to everything from materialism to consumerism. Brian McLaren, in an influential article, asks, "What if saving the church is a self-defeating mission?"[1]

The reality is that some are rejecting the church as God's missionary instrument. They are seeing the *missio dei* ("mission of God") as something that encompasses much more than the *missio ecclesia* ("mission of the church"). They are partly right. Although the church is not the *center* of God's plan, it is *central* to the plan of God. Ephesians 3:10 states, "Then God would *use the church* to show the powers and authorities in the spiritual world that he has many different kinds of wisdom" (emphasis added).

So the short answer is yes, the church matters.[2]

Whenever Christian people decide that the church does not matter, they end up following the world's agenda and the church is soon marginalized to irrelevance. However, whenever the Christian people decide that the world does not matter, they end up in sectarian irrelevance. Both are dead ends of Kingdom growth. Instead, the church must be viewed as both essential for the gospel but also essential to the world.

The church matters to the mission of God, in every era and in every culture. In theological terms, though the *missio dei* is larger than the church, the *missio ecclesia* is to fulfill the mission of God in the world with the help of the Holy Spirit. The mission of the church is to fulfill the mission of God. The church is His hands and feet and lips in the world. Ultimately, we must not degenerate into a false sense of the church as "institution." When the church continues to perceive itself properly and operate as the "people of God," then the evangelistic mandate is kept alive through the *missio dei*. However, if the infectious attitude of the world that regards the church only as a religious or political establishment begins to hold sway among Christians, then the temptation faced is that survival of a local congregation or denomination is the ultimate goal.

The church matters. Scripture teaches that it does. As Jesus ascended into heaven, He challenged His disciples to witness for Him all over the world (see Acts 1:8). He had previously declared, "I will build my church" (Matt. 16:18). Surely, we should join

with Christ in this. On a mountaintop in Galilee, Jesus commanded His apostles to make disciples of all the "nations" (literally, ethnic groups) of the world and to "teach them to do
everything" (Matt. 28:19-20). Again, the apostles obeyed Jesus'
command by planting churches through which the nations
could be evangelized and taught. The letters to the seven churches in Revelation 2–3 reveal Christ's concern for the churches in
Asia Minor and His desire to see them believe and behave
appropriately. Jesus evidenced His passion and the purpose of
the church on multiple occasions.

Paul had much to say about the church. In Ephesians 5:23, he
stated that Jesus is the head and Savior of the church. Then in
Ephesians 5:25, he declared that "Christ loved the church and gave
his life for it." As *Christians* ("little Christs"), we surely should emu-
late Jesus in His love for the church. In Acts 20:28, Paul exhorted
the elders of the church at Ephesus to be "like shepherds to God's
church." He meant they should care for and guard the church. In
1 Corinthians 14, Paul encouraged the leaders in Corinth to edify,
build up and strengthen the church through worship. Again and
again, Paul wrote of his prayers for the church.

Mind the Box
Again, we must both contend (see Jude 3) and contextualize
(see 1 Cor. 9:22-23). Essential values, when they are not con-
tented for, become compromised in inappropriate innovation.
When they are contextualized, the innovation is not only
appropriate, it is also expected.

If we did not innovate, we would still be meeting in synagogues on Saturday. Innovation is needed, but biblical discernment must come first. If not, we can innovate away what church
is. Churches often wish to do ministry out of the box. That can
be a good thing, depending on how you define the "box." If by
box we mean traditions (often past innovations) that have lost

their meaning in contemporary culture, we can and should innovate so that the gospel can be more clearly presented. If, however, the box is the biblical church and its essentials, our innovation is compromise, not contextualization.

What Does This Mean to Me as a Church Leader or Participant?

We have looked at 11 models of innovation to revitalize a church and help it reach lost people for Jesus Christ. Each chapter has described a number of methods and principles. As you consider the overall message of this book to you as a church leader, remember first that there is a difference between methods and principles. A lot of the innovations described in this book are nothing more than methods: the cowboy church . . . the surfer church . . . the recovery church . . . the Nickelodeon children's ministry program. Those are all methods that are probably different than anything the church has used before in its ministry.

Also, remember that a method that works in one culture may flop in another. Because cultures are different, it takes different methods to reach people in different cultures. The same thing can be said about time: Methods change over time. What worked 200 years ago, such as the circuit-riding Methodist preacher who focused on church planting, often doesn't work today. Therefore, we need to remember the following:

- An effective method is always the application of a principle to culture, so look behind every method to see if it's based on a biblical principle.

- The methods (innovations) mentioned in this book may not be effective one, two or three decades from now.

- These methods may not work outside the United States in a different culture.

- These methods may not work in every place inside the United States, because the American society has so many cultures that tradition may work in one place and not work in another.

Most of these innovations were birthed out of failure and frustration and usually applied where a church was not growing or was dead. Because the former church was not doing what it should do, someone had asked the question, "What if . . ." and then prayerfully came up with a new innovation to preach the gospel and win people to Christ. Notice, we never condone the changing of the message, only the changing of the method.

These new innovations usually rely on one or more people who see a need not being met. For example, they see a group of people that need the gospel, such as alienated homosexuals, so they create a ministry through a recovery church to build a bridge of healing in the name of Jesus Christ. Such ministries don't evolve of themselves, nor do they evolve out of need or out of the fact that they're being done elsewhere. Rather, innovations usually come from a visionary leader who takes the initiative, invents new methods and then takes the risk to reach a new group of people that were previously unreached or alienated from the church.

Another dynamic to keep in mind is that innovation usually doesn't come out of group consensus. Usually the large body of Christianity does not vote to change itself. If anything, larger Christianity writes creeds, adopts models of ministry and approves written standards of performance, all designed to *keep from changing*. It's usually the "rebels" or the entrepreneurial leaders with a burden from God who begin doing what no one else is thinking or dreaming. They see a need, devise a plan to meet the need and launch out because God has led them to do what seems to be the impossible. And when they succeed, many others follow their example and get on board the innovative train to help fellow innovative leaders accomplish the goal that they now share.

That's another way of saying that innovations are usually not very comfortable. So when you begin to talk to your church about these innovations, some people may not be comfortable with them. Be prepared for questions or oppositions or even hostility. Most people want to remain in a comfortable church, with a comfortable ministry, getting comfortable results. But remember, Jesus didn't die for us to be comfortable. He died for the sins of the world; therefore, we must reach out to lost people with new and innovative methods.

What, then, do we do with comfortable people? We take them where they've never been, to do something they've never done, to accomplish something for God which has never been accomplished.

Generational Differences

Let's discuss briefly the issue of innovations between parents and their children. In the last 50 years in America, it seems like every generation was different than the previous one. As an example, the Builder Generation that came out of the Great Depression was different from their parents. They survived financial disasters, they became success driven, they learned a thousand different ways to make money, they built families, businesses, and some even built industrial empires. Their culture drove them to overcome adversities to be survivors. That was the Builder Generation.

- The Builder Generation—1926-1946
- The Boomer Generation—1946-1964

- Emerging Postmodern Generations—1964-1988
- The Generation Next (and various splinter groups)—
  1988-2006

So what do we learn about the different generations of America? It seems that each generation produced a different culture, developed different value systems and, as a result, is perceived differently from their parents. What's wrong with this? In their churches, Christians have too often chosen their church traditions over their children.

The last five generations have hung onto their church traditions and would not change their methods. Their children grew up wanting to express their Christianity through their cultural values, and their parents said no! Generation wars broke out over church innovations.

The Builders loved the music of American revivalism of the last century and the great hymns of Europe sung to piano and organ. But their children wanted a little "beat" with their music on an acoustical guitar, some drums and perhaps a little flute. When the Boomers grew up listening to the Mouseketeers, Peter, Paul and Mary and the Beatles, no one ever thought they'd want praise groups—singing groups—like they had as kids. Their parents grew up listening to solos, gospel quartets and choirs. So Boomers like praise worship teams, not choirs. They like praise music led by groups, and so worship wars broke out between the Builders and the Boomers.

When Generation X came along (originally called Baby Busters), the difference between them and their Boomer parents was the amount of volume through the amplifiers. Emerging generations also tend to be pushed away from anything in church that comes across as "slick"—so professional and polished that it loses authenticity.

What about subsequent generations? Terms become less helpful as the culture fractures into multiple expressions. Emerging generations worship through many of the innovations described in this very book. Such generational change can inevitably produce conflict.

If you want to see strong emotions over innovations, just look to music. Every generation thinks the way to do music is that which they sang during their puberty years when they were forming their self-perception as they left childhood and pushed their way into the adult world. Don't we all sing for the rest of our life the type of music we sang in our teens? Yet every generation condemns the innovative music of the next generation.

The reality is that your children will go to an "innovated" church—the only question is, Will it be yours? Why? Because the way you do things today will, in many ways, seem quaint in 20 years. New churches will do things in new ways. Your church will either change or decline—and your children will be the ones who are most strongly impacted.

Too Much Innovation?

So what can you learn from this book? Always keep your focus on the gospel message. Don't change it, and don't let anyone else change it for you. But when they sing the gospel message by a different instrument, if you don't like it, at least pray for those who sing it, and grow in Christ because of it.

Another thing you can learn from this book is passion: Those who pay the price of innovation usually do so because of a great passion for lost people. And isn't that the lost chord of traditional Christianity? Where does the established church first lose its vibrancy? Usually we don't lose our passion for prayer or for Bible study or even for fellowshipping with other Christians. Usually the first thing to go is passion for lost people. So what drives the best of innovations? *A passion for lost people!*

Therefore, examine carefully the innovations in this book to see if they ignite a passion in your heart to motivate you to do what you should be doing: carrying out the Great Commission in your neighborhood! Don't just clone someone else's church; find God's unique call and niche for yours.

One more thing: Never innovate your church just for the sake of innovation. If you read what's in this book and you think it's good, don't try it in your church just for the sake of trying something different or new. Make sure that the innovations we describe will work in your church and in your culture before you dive into water that that may be too deep for you to swim. The following are some questions to ask yourself:

- An innovation may be exciting, but is it scriptural?
- An innovation may be good, but is it right for how God wired *me*?
- An innovation might work, but will it work in *my* church?
- An innovation could win people to Christ, but will it win the people in *my* community to Jesus Christ?
- I may like this innovation, but will people at my church follow me as I try the innovation?
- This innovation may seem workable, but can we make it work in *our* particular situation?
- This innovation might be necessary, but can we afford it?

The last question is perhaps the toughest:

- What will happen to the church if I'm not there to carry out an innovation to its ultimate conclusion? (Remember, they may replace you while the innovation is underway or before it can happen.)

John Naisbitt said in his explosive book *Megatrends*, "We're living in a 'yeasty' age; this is a time between two ages. The fading industrial era is coming to an end, and we're moving into a coming information-process era."[3] What does that mean? You will have more information and more ideas to try more innovations than you've ever thought of before. Learn how to evaluate the strengths and weaknesses of innovations and then how to implement your innovations—and be sure that you have a good idea of the ups and downs and the strengths and weaknesses of your innovation before you begin. If you think that an innovation will only bring in the good times, you're wrong. Be honest about your innovations and happy that you're living in this "yeasty" age. We live in a time filled with opportunities to do more for God than we've ever done before.

Eleven Truths to Learn

From the *ancient-future* church, we can learn that historical worship practices and creeds can contribute vibrancy in a post-Christian world, and that these methods may have a place in some modern churches.

The *organic house* church teaches us to look again at the simplicity of Christianity as the church assembles for basic worship, teaching and fellowship, without programs, buildings, expensive musical instruments, budgets and elaborate infrastructure.

Our faith is stretched by the *city-reaching* church that feels an obligation to present the gospel to everyone in its "Jerusalem" because the Great Commission begins, "You will tell everyone about me in Jerusalem" (Acts 1:8).

The *community transformation* church reminds us that the powerful work of God through local churches should positively influence their surrounding communities with life-changing attitudes, good works and life-uplifting programs.

The *cyber-enhanced* church will use every available aspect of informational technology to reach the lost with the gospel, strengthen believers, carry out the aims of a church to its members and help it reach lost people at every available time and place.

The *Nickelodeon-style children-focused* church tells us to reach and teach our modern Sesame Street generation through a multi-sensory presentation on the part of teachers because children have been conditioned to learn through total involvement of all their sensory receptors.

The *intentionally multicultural* church purposes and carries out the intent of Scripture that "faith in Christ Jesus is what makes each of you equal with each other, whether you are a Jew or a Greek, a slave or a free person, a man or a woman" (Gal. 3:28).

The *decision-journey* church teaches us that a Christian "conversion" is simply an outward profession by some who do actually possess Jesus Christ and that churches should more accurately offer salvation in biblical terms so that prospects for salvation will not be prematurely judged as having salvation, when in fact they are not saved.

The *multi-site* church demonstrates that more communities and people can be reached for Christ by one church that centralizes its resources of church planting (i.e., finances, staff supervision, trained personnel and adequate resources) while encouraging an intentional, planned expansion of worship locations.

The *recovery* church believes, "If the Son gives you freedom, you are free!" (John 8:36), so it offers biblical help and healing and support to those hurting and addicted through counseling, teaching, fellowship and the availability of all resources of the church and its members.

The *attractional* church uses every possible means (that are not unbiblical) to attract every possible person, to take advantage of their ministry (both for salvation and Christian growth) so that they may adequately evangelize their community for Christ.

Implications

What does this book mean to you and your church? It's an overview of what's happening in the larger church world. We don't suggest that you should plan to model your church after any or all of these churches. While some churches may be revitalized by following one of these models, your church may stagnate, or even split, because some of these models are too foreign for the people in your church.

We want you to be encouraged as you read how God is working in other churches. Perhaps you shouldn't be like any of them. We think it's alright for you to be different from them as they are from you. But we also want you to learn from these churches. They are probably different in makeup from your church and they may do things differently. They can teach you something that may sharpen your church's focus, or they may inspire you to add an additional outlet to your church's programs.

If you learn anything from these 11 innovations, then we've accomplished our goal. Our aim is to revitalize and revive the whole church of Jesus Christ. Obviously, some churches are so far beyond this book in spirituality that we won't help them. But perhaps we can serve the Holy Spirit in bringing the new life of revival to your church. Remember what we said earlier: Revival is God pouring out His presence on His people. We want these innovations to help revive churches everywhere so that God's presence will be more greatly manifested in His churches.

Your advocates of discerning innovation,

Elmer Towns, Ed Stetzer and Warren Bird

EXTREME CHURCHES

Churches have gone to many extremes in order to reach people with the gospel. Following the incarnational model of Jesus Christ, who entered our world and became one of us, they try to enter the world of others. Just as Jesus used fishing illustrations for fishermen ("I will teach you how to bring in people instead of fish" [Matt. 4:19-20]), agricultural word pictures for farmers and the like, so too these churches have developed many creative ways of showing the relevance of Christ to various special-interest groups. They do so with the attitude of the apostle Paul: "I do everything I can to win everyone I possibly can. I do all this for the good news" (1 Cor. 9:22-23). They present a mix of approaches (some stand-alone churches and some really outreach ministries) and go to places we find extreme in ways that both challenge and sometimes worry us!

Actor's Church
A church in the west end of London (www.actorschurch.org) is organized around and intended to reach those in the theater community. Its name is St. Paul's of Covent Garden (built in 1633), but it is also affectionately known as The Actors' Church because of its long association with the actors, playwrights and directors. It offers regular worship services, concerts, and literary and theatrical events. As a sign reads as you come in through the church doors, "We seek to worship God as made known to us in Jesus Christ."

Cowboy Church
Cowboy Church (www.nashvillecowboychurch.org) in Nashville, Tennessee, meets in a theater, features a 10-piece country and

western band, and creates a come-as-you-are environment that draws people in jeans. Worshipers are not necessarily cowboys, but all enjoy western culture. They wear Stetson hats indoors, and ushers pass their hats to collect the offering. "I've always been a cowboy at heart," says Harry Yates, the pastor, who grew up on a ranch in west Texas. "I didn't fit in with the three-piece suit and tie bunch—and I met a lot of people who wouldn't go to church for that reason. We created an atmosphere that was appealing to those folks so that they'd listen to the Word of God."

Drive-In Church

Daytona Beach Christian Church in Daytona Beach, Florida (www.driveinchurch.net), has met at a converted drive-in movie theater since 1953. As people pull up, ushers hand them bulletins and prepackaged communion elements. They park and tune into 88.5 on their FM radio dial. In a church without walls or pews, people honk their horns instead of saying amen or clapping. Instead of traditional ushers passing an offering plate, attendants in golf carts zip around from car to car. The movie screen has been replaced with a multi-story building with a sheltered podium and choir loft. The snack shack has become the church's fellowship hall.

Hip-Hop Church

At hip-hop-oriented Crossover Community Church in Tampa, Florida (www.crossoverchurch.org), services are flavored with video clips, rappers, DJs and beat boxers—all with a Christian bent. The pastor, himself a rapper, blends musical and visual elements of hip-hop culture into spiritual messages. "At first we were like, can that work?" he said. "It worked for the youth ministry, but can we run a whole church like that? Can we bring in the turntables on Sunday?"

Motorboat Church

New Purpose Community Church in Dunedin, Washington, started in 2004 and meets in a former dockside restaurant overlooking St. Joseph Sound. A local newspaper said, "It just may be the only church in town with a tiki bar, boat slips, and a hostess stand." Instead of liquor, the church serves free Starbucks coffee and soft drinks. TV monitors are set up in front and in back near the boat docks so that people can stay outside and still attend services.

Outdoor Church

At the Church in the Woods in Stuart, Florida, a nondenominational church started in 2001, there are no pews or stained glass, and those seeking to be baptized get dunked in the horse trough. The outdoor church, located on a 138-acre cattle ranch, features only a covered stage, rows of colorful canvas-topped picnic tables, a grass-thatched gazebo, a meticulously kept portable toilet—and a weekly warning to parents to watch for alligators, boars and snakes. (No website available at present.)

Prison Church

Lake Point Church in Rockwall, Texas (www.lakepointe.org), has taken a weekly church service to a local correctional facility for years, actually holding two different services: one for men and another for women. A worship team leads inmates in music and most people chuckle when it's time to welcome any first-time guests. The teaching comes by videocast as the Rockwall team plays a DVD of a recent sermon from the church's teaching team.

Skate Church

Grace Place in Colorado Springs, Colorado (www.graceplace.org), runs what it calls a skateboarding ministry in its parking lot each week. As many as 40 skaters show up for the 90-minute,

Wednesday-night free skate sessions. The church provides equipment and supervision. "I've heard these guys say it: 'Skating is life,'" said Jeremiah McGinnis, youth pastor. "We want Christ to be their life; we want Jesus to be their life. This is a vehicle through which they can see that." After the skating session, the church hosts a 7 P.M. "U-Turn" youth service.

Surfer Church
Snow Ball Church is a new church started in 1999 by a surfer in Perdizes, Brazil. Services resemble rock shows with lots of giant screens, and the pulpit has a surfboard on the top, which is highlighted at the end of services. Rinaldo Luiz de Seixas Pereira, who started the church at age 31, says he named it Snow Ball because he wants it to get bigger and bigger as it rolls on. (No website available at present.)

Theater Church
National Community Church in Washington, D.C. (www.the aterchurch.com), which meets in the multiplex theater at Union Station, seeks to redeem today's culture that is heavily shaped by Hollywood. The restored train terminal is the most visited destination in the city, giving the church instant location recognition and direct access by a Metro stop, taxi stand and commuter parking lot. After the worship services, which use one auditorium for adults while children's ministries use another auditorium, the congregation fellowships at the nearby 40-restaurant food court.

Underground Church
Underground Church is an organization started in 2002 to minister to Christian punks in the East Village section of Manhattan, New York. The group's young members, many of whom have spiked hair or dreadlocks, gather weekly for Bible

study at the East Seventh Baptist Church, often called the Graffiti Church (www.graffitichurch.org).

For more information on new churches, visit the website at http://www.newchurches.com/public/about/index.php.

LIST OF CHURCHES MENTIONED

Name of Church	Location/Website	Senior Pastor
Alpha Church	Tulsa, OK alphachurch.org	Patricia Walker
Antioch Bible Church	Redmond, WA abchurch.org	Ken Hutcherson
Bridgeway Community Church	Columbia, MD bridgewayonline.org	David Anderson
Brooklyn Tabernacle	Brooklyn, NY brooklyntabernacle.org	Jim Cymbala
Calvary Chapel	Santa Ana, CA calvarychapel.com	Chuck Smith. Sr.
Cedar Ridge Community Church	Spencerville, MD crcc.org	Matthew Dyer (lead pastor), Brian McLaren (founding pastor)
Celebrate Recovery Ministry (Saddleback Church)	Lake Forest, CA celebraterecovery.com	John Baker
Christ the King Community Church	Burlington, WA ctkonline.com	Dave Browning
Church of Fools	Liverpool, England churchoffools.com	N/A
Church On The Way	Van Nuys, CA tcotw.org	Jim Tolle
City Bible Church	Portland, OR citybiblechurch.org	Frank Damazio
Cokesbury United Methodist Church	Knoxville, TN cclive.org	Steve Sallee, Gil Smith (small group)
Community Christian Church	Naperville, IL communitychristian.org	Dave Ferguson
Eastside Foursquare Church	Bothell, WA eastsidechurch.org	Jim Hayford, Sr.

Name of Church	Location/Website	Senior Pastor
Fellowship Bible Church	Little Rock, AR fbclr.org	Tim Lundy (directional leader), Robert Lewis (teaching pastor)
First Assembly Phoenix	Phoenix, AZ phoenixfirst.org	Tommy Barnett
First Baptist Church	Hammond, IN fbchammond.com	Jack Schaap
First Baptist Church	Leesburg, FL fbcleesburg.org	Charles Roesel
Florence Baptist Temple	Florence, SC fbt.org	Bill Monroe
Ginghamsburg Church	Tipp City, OH ginghamsburg.org	Michael Slaughter
Grace Community Church	Sun Valley, CA gracechurch.org	John MacArthur
Healing Place Church	Baton Rouge, LA healingplacechurch.org	Dino Rizzo
Journey Church	New York City, NY nyjourney.com	Nelson Searcy (lead pastor), Kerrick Thomas (teaching pastor)
Journey Church	St. Louis, MO Journeyon.net	Darrin Patrick
Lake Ridge Church	Cumming, GA lakeridgechurch.net	Phillip Nation (pastor), Ed Stetzer (co-pastor)
Life Church	Oklahoma City, OK lifechurch.tv	Craig Groeschel
Lima Community Church	Lima, OH limacc.com	Dan Huckins (lead pastor), Vince Nelson (exec. pastor)
Mars Hill Church	Seattle, WA marshillchurch.org	Mark Driscoll
Mosaic	Los Angeles, CA mosaic.org	Erwin McManus
Mosaic Church of Central Arkansas	Little Rock, AR mosaicchurch.net	Mark DeYmaz
Mt. Paran Church of God	Atlanta, GA mtparan.org	David Cooper
National Community Church	Washington, D.C. theaterchurch.com	Mark Batterson
New England Chapel	Franklin, MA newenglandchapel.org	Chris Mitchell

Name of Church	Location/Website	Senior Pastor
New Life Community Church	Chicago, IL newlifechicago.org	Mark Jobe (lead pastor), Luke Dudenhofer (campus pastor)
North Point Community Church	Alpharetta, GA northpoint.org	Andy Stanley
Northstar Community	Richmond, VA northstarcommunity.com	Theresa McBean
Redeemer Presbyterian Church	Manhattan, NY redeemer.com	Tim Keller
Saddleback Church	Lake Forest, CA saddleback.com	Rick Warren
Seacoast Church	Mt. Pleasant, SC seacoast.org/mount-pleasant	Greg Surratt
Second Baptist Church	Houston, TX second.org	Ed Young
Summit Church	Fort Myers, FL summitlife.com	Todd Milby (executive), Orlando Cabrena (teaching)
Thomas Road Baptist Church	Lynchburg, VA trbc.org	Jerry Falwell
Trinity Baptist Church	Kelowna, BC, Canada trinitybaptist.net	Tim Schroeder
United Methodist Church of the Resurrection	Kansas City, KS cor.org	Adam Hamilton
Willow Creek Community Church	Chicago, IL willowcreek.org	Bill Hybels
Xenos Fellowship	Columbus, OH xenos.org	Gary DeLashmutt

ENDNOTES

Preface

1. A revised edition of H. Richard Niebuhr's *Christ and Culture* was published by HarperSanFrancisco in 1975.

Introduction: The Church Changed, and Nobody Told Us

1. Philip Jenkins, *The Next Christendom: The Coming of Global Christianity* (New York: Oxford University Press USA, 2003).

2. In 1969, I (Elmer) wrote *The Ten Largest Sunday Schools*, which was a bestseller. Many followed the examples of those churches and grew as these Sunday Schools were growing. To read this book, see www.elmertowns.com and click the Books/Books Online on the tool bar. I wrote a second book on innovation in 1990, *Ten of Today's Innovative Churches*, which is also available at www.elmertowns.com. The methods in these two books are no longer considered innovative, which is why this present volume was written with two of the best church growth authors in America.

3. Elmer Towns, *Theology for Today* (Fort Worth, TX: Harcourt Custom Publishers, 2001), pp. 649-651.

4. Elmer Towns and Douglas Porter, *Churches That Multiply* (Kansas City, MO: Beacon Hill Press of Kansas City, 2003).

5. Wolfgang Simpson, quoted on HouseChurchBlog.org, April 25, 2006. http://sojourner.typepad.com/house_church_blog/2005/04/wolfgang_simson.html (accessed March 2007).

6. "What Is Purpose Driven?" PurposeDriven.com, 2007. http://www.purposedriven.com/en-US/AboutUs/WhatIsPD/7+Myths+of+PD.htm (accessed March 2007).

7. Elmer Towns, *Putting an End to Worship Wars* (Nashville, TN: Broadman & Holman, 1996).

8. Elmer Towns and Ed Stetzer, *Perimeters of Light* (Chicago, IL: Moody Publishers, 2004).

9. Leadership Network, a consulting group that works with large innovative churches, draws from Peter Drucker to define innovation in its *Innovation 2007* publication (p. 4) as "the effort to create purposeful, focused change." http://www.leadnet.org/Innovation2007.asp (accessed March 2007).

Chapter 1: Organic House Churches

1. "Our History: 1990-Present," Church Multiplication Associates, 2003. http://www.cmaresources.org/about/history.asp (accessed February 2007). During a six-year period, Neil Cole helped to start more than 700 churches in 32 states and 23 nations. Most are house churches that were started through Church Multiplication Associates, an organic church network he co-founded.

2. Neil Cole, *Organic Church: Growing Faith Where Life Happens* (San Francisco: Jossey Bass. 2005), p. xxii.

3. Ibid., p. xxiv.

4. Ibid., p. xxv.

5. Ibid., p. xxiv.

6. "Rapid Increase in Alternative Forms of the Church Are Changing the Religious Landscape," *The Barna Update*, October 24, 2005. http://www.barna.org/FlexPage.aspx?Page=BarnaUpdateNarrow&BarnaUpdateID=202 (accessed February 2007).

7. See the Center for Missional Research at www.missionalresearch.info.

8. Ibid.

9. "House Churches Are More Satisfying to Attenders than Are Conventional Churches," *The Barna Update,* January 8, 2007. http://www.barna.org/FlexPage.aspx?Page=BarnaUpdateNarrowPreview&BarnaUpdateID=255 (accessed February 2007).

10. Ed Stetzer, *Planting Missional Churches* (Nashville, TN: Broadman and Holman, 2006).

11. J. S. Henkel, *An Historical Study of the Educational Contributions of the Brethren of the Common Life*, Ph.D. dissertation, University of Pittsburgh, 1962. Henkel's contributions are summarized in Elmer Towns, ed., *A History of Religious Education* (Grand Rapids, MI: Baker Book House, 1975), pp. 82-88. This book is available to read on www.elmertowns.com (click on "reference").

12. "The Full Story," Lights of Christmas Worldwide Ministries. http://www.thelightsofchristmas.org/christmas/story.html (accessed September 2006).

13. Elmer Towns and Roscoe Brewer smuggled 24 Chinese Bibles to a Christian steward on a railroad passenger car in the late 1970s. The steward then delivered these Bibles from person to person over a distance of 300 miles so that churches on his circuit could have a Bible once a month.

14. T. Austin-Sparks, "What Is the Church?" The Online Library of T. Austin-Sparks. http://www.austin-sparks.net/english/000433.html (accessed March 2007).

15. For additional ways to categorize house churches, see Frank Viola, *So You Want to Start a House Church: First-Century Styled Church Planting for Today* (Gainesville, FL: Present Testimony Ministry, 2003), pp. 114-116. Available online at http://ptmin.org/movement.htm.

16. Frank Viola, "An Interview with a Modern-Day, Sunday-Morning, Church-Going Christian," TheOoze, October 15, 2005. http://www.theooze.com/articles/article.cfm?id=1255 (accessed February 2007).

17. Randy Frazee, *The Connecting Church* (Grand Rapids, MI: Zondervan Publishing House, 2001).

18. Thom Rainer and Eric Geiger, *Simple Church* (Nashville, TN: Broadman and Holman, 2006).

19. David Garrison, *Church Planting Movements* (Midlothian, VA: WIGtake Resources, 2003).

Chapter 2: Recovery Churches

1. "Salvation Army," *Encyclopedia Americana*, vol. 16, p. 136.

2. Neil Anderson, *The Bondage Breaker* (Eugene, OR: Harvest House, 2000).

3. John Baker, Celebrate Recovery website. http://www.celebraterecovery.com/index.shtml. (accessed September 2006).

4. Teresa McBean, personal interview with Warren Bird, September 1, 2006, Dallas, Texas.

5. "Teen Challenge's Proven Answer to the Drug Problem: A Review of a Study by Dr. Aaron T. Bicknese, '*The Teen Challenge Drug Treatment Program in Comparative Perspective,*'" Teen Challenge website. http://www.teenchallengeusa.com/about_studies4.html (accessed September 2006).

Chapter 3: Multi-site Churches

1. Elmer L. Towns, *10 of Today's Most Innovative Churches* (Ventura, CA: Regal Books, 1990), pp. 163-173.

2. See "Survey of 1,000 Multi-site Churches," available only as a download at www.leadnet.org.

3. Ibid.

4. Ibid.

5. Geoff Surratt, "Should Your Church Consider a Multi-Site Strategy?" *Rick Warren's Ministry Toolbox,* no. 263, June 14, 2006. http://www.pastors.com/RWMT/?id= 263&artid=9533&expand=1 (accessed February 2007).

6. Thom Rainer, "One Church, Two Locations," *Outreach,* vol. 4, no. 4 (July/August 2005), p. 18.

7. See www.multi-site.org.

8. Geoff Surratt, Greg Ligon and Warren Bird, *The Multi-Site Church Revolution: Being One Church in Many Locations* (Grand Rapids, MI: Zondervan, 2006).

9. Bill Easum and Dave Travis, *Beyond the Box: Innovative Churches that Work* (Loveland, CO: Group Publishing, 2003), p. 85.

10. Elmer L. Towns, *How to Go to Two Services* (Forest, VA: Church Growth Institute, 1989). This is a video resource packet that includes a video and information required to make an informed decision on whether to go to two services. See www.church growth.org.

11. W. Charles Arn, *How to Start a New Service: Your Church Can Reach New People* (Grand Rapids, MI: Baker Books, 1997).

12. See Mark Jobe, "Unlikely Candidates," *Leadership Journal,* July 1, 2003. http://www. christianitytoday.com/le/2003/003/6.46.html (accessed February 2007). See also Michael Pocock and Joseph Henrique, *Cultural Change and Your Church* (Grand Rapids, MI: Baker Books, 2002), pp. 179-192, and "My Patient Revolution: An Interview with Mark Jobe," *Leadership Journal,* Spring 2005. http://www.christian itytoday.com/le/2005/002/1.20.html (accessed February 2007).

13. Surratt, Ligon and Bird, *The Multi-Site Church Revolution,* p. 51.

14. Ibid.

15. "Church Franchise a Hit, but Hostile Take-overs Rattle Congregations," LarkNews. com. http://larknews.com/march_2006/secondary.php?page=1 (accessed February 2007).

16. Much of the wording of this description of campus roles comes from Surratt, Ligon and Bird, *The Multi-Site Church Revolution,* pp. 144-145.

17. Ibid., pp. 80-81.

18. Geoff Surratt, "Ideas on How to Fund a Multi-Site Ministry," Pastors.com. http://www. pastors.com/RWMT/article.asp?ArtID=9588 (accessed February 2007).

19. Surratt, Ligon and Bird, *The Multi-Site Church Revolution,* p. 113.

20. Ibid., pp. 164-165.

21. "Survey of 1,000 Multi-Site Churches," www.leadnet.org.

22. Surratt, Ligon and Bird, *The Multi-Site Church Revolution,* p. 54.

23. Thom Rainer and Eric Geiger, *Simple Church* (Nashville, TN: Broadman and Holman, 2006).

Chapter 4: Ancient-Future Churches

1. Dan Goetz, ed., ChurchLeadership.net, no. 11, June 2, 1999. http://www.christi anity.net/cln (accessed September 2006).

2. Sally Morgenthaler, *Worship Evangelism* (Grand Rapids, MI: Zondervan, 1995), p. 30.

3. From notes taken by Warren Bird at a live presentation on November 11, 1999, entitled "Church Champions" in Dallas, Texas, sponsored by Leadership Network.

4. Richard J. Mouw, "The Missionary Location of the North American Churches," cited in *Confident Witness—Changing World,* edited by Craig Van Gelder (Grand Rapids, MI: William B. Eerdmans Publishing Company, 1999), p. 8.

5. Elmer L. Towns and Warren Bird, *Into the Future: Turning Today's Church Trends into Tomorrow's Opportunities* (Grand Rapids, MI: Revell, 2000), pp. 151-158.

Chapter 5: City-Reaching Churches

1. Al Weiss, statement on the Vision USA website. http://www.vision4usa.com/index. cfm?page=7 (accessed February 2007).
2. Ibid.
3. Jerry Falwell, *Capturing Your Town for Christ* (Old Tappan, NY: Fleming H. Revell Company, 1973).
4. Ed Silvoso, *That None Should Perish* (Ventura, CA: Regal Books, 1977) and *Prayer Evangelism* (Ventura, CA: Regal Books, 2000).
5. Frank Damazio, *Crossing Rivers, Taking Cities* (Ventura, CA: Regal Books, 1999).
6. John Fuder, *A Heart for the City* (Chicago, IL: Moody Press, 2000).
7. Jerry Falwell graduated from Baptist Bible College in Springfield, Missouri, where author Elmer Towns heard a chapel speaker exhort the men students, "When you graduate, go to a town that God has put upon your heart and build a soul-winning local church and capture your town for Christ."
8. Jerry Falwell, *Building Dynamic Faith* (Nashville, TN: World Publishing Inc., 2005), p. 59.
9. Elmer Towns, *A Practical Encyclopedia of Evangelism and Church Growth* (Ventura, CA: Regal Books, 1995), p. 348.
10. "Super aggressive evangelism" is a term that Elmer Towns coined to describe the passion and faith of Jerry Falwell.
11. Elmer Towns, *The Ten Largest Sunday Schools* (Grand Rapids, MI: Baker Book House, 1969), pp. 99-104.
12. Silvoso, *That None Should Perish*, p. 32.
13. "Prayer walking" is a phrase coined by Steve Hawthorne and Graham Kendrick in *Prayer-walking: Praying On Site with Insight* (Orlando, FL: Creation House Books, 1993).
14. Silvoso, *That None Should Perish*, p. 52.
15. Ibid., p. 294.
16. Ibid.
17. Ed Silvoso, *Prayer Evangelism*, p. 127.
18. Ibid., p. 131.
19. Ibid., p. 132.
20. Frank Damazio, *Crossing Rivers, Taking Cities* (Ventura, CA: Regal Books, 1999), pp. 169-170.
21. Ibid., p. 174.
22. Ibid., p. 287.
23. Ibid.
24. Jack Dennison, *City Reaching: On the Road to Community Transformation* (Pasadena, CA: William Carey Library, 1999), pp. xiii-xiv.
25. Ibid.
26. Elmer L. Towns, John N. Vaughan and David J. Seifert, *The Complete Book of Church Growth* (Wheaton, IL: Tyndale House Publishers, 1990), pp. 61-68.
27. Larry Stockstill, *The Cell Church* (Ventura, CA: Regal Books, 1998).
28. Tim Keller, "A New Kind of Urban," *Christianity Today*, May 2006. http://www.christianitytoday.com/ct/2006/005/1.36.html (accessed September 2006).
29. Timothy J. Keller and J. Allen Thompson, *Church Planter Manual* (New York, NY: Redeemer Church Planting Center, 2002), p. 8.
30. Glenn Smith, "Articulating the Mission of God in the Large City/Regions Across the Globe: Background Paper in Preparation for the Urban Issue Group of the 2004 World Evangelization Forum" (Montréal, Québec: Christian Direction Inc., 2004), p. 3.

31. Robert C. Linthicum, "Networking: Hope for the Church in the City," *Urban Mission* (January 1987), cited in Glenn Smith, ed., *The Gospel and Urbanization* (Montreal, Quebec: Christian Direction, Inc., 1990), p. 3:42.

Chapter 6: Community Transformation Churches

1. Bob Roberts, *Transformation: How Global Churches Transform Lives and the World* (Grand Rapids, MI: Zondervan Publishing House, 2006).
2. Lianne Hart, "Churches Putting Town Out of Business," *Los Angeles Times*, September 7, 2006. http://www.latimes.com/news/nationworld/nation/la-na-churches 31jul31,0,6286040.story?coll=la-home-nation (accessed February 2007).
3. Rick Rusaw and Eric Swanson, *Externally Focused Church* (Loveland, CO: Group, 2004), pp. 28-29.
4. Charles Roesel, quoted in *World Magazine*, August 20, 2005, vol. 20, no. 32.
5. Charles Roesel, quoted in Lee Weeks, "Meeting People's Needs Yields Harvest of Souls, Pastor Says," *Baptist Press*, August 11, 2004.
6. Rusaw and Swanson, *Externally Focused Church*, pp. 20-21.
7. Robert Lewis and Rob Wilkins, *Church of Irresistible Influence* (Grand Rapids, MI: Zondervan, 2001).
8. Robert Lewis and Wayne Cordeiro with Warren Bird, *Culture Shift: Transforming Your Church from the Inside Out* (San Francisco: Jossey-Bass, 2005), p. 138.
9. Ibid., pp. 127-142.
10. William G. McLoughlin, "Revivalism," quoted in Edwin Scott Gaustad, ed., *The Rise of Adventism* (New York: Harper and Row, 1974), p. 132.
11. Stephen L. Carter, *The Culture of Disbelief: How American Law and Politics Trivialize Religious Devotion* (New York: Basic Books, 1993), pp. 23-43.
12. Tim Stafford, "The Criminologist Who Discovered Churches," *Christianity Today*, June 14, 1999, vol. 43, no. 7, pp. 35-39.
13. Rodney Stark, *The Rise of Christianity: How the Obscure, Marginal, Jesus Movement Became the Dominant Religious Force in the Western World in a Few Centuries* (San Francisco: HarperSanFrancisco, 1997).
14. Jerry Pierce, "Rick Warren: Rebuilding Always More Difficult than Building," PurposeDriven website. http://www.purposedriven.com/en-US/HurricaneRelief/ News/rebuilding.htm, (accessed September 2006).
15. Adolph von Harnack and Thomas Bailey Saunders, *What Is Christianity?* (Minneapolis, MN: Augsburg Press, 1987).
16. Walter Rauschenbusch, *A Theology of the Social Gospel* (Louisville, KY: Westminster John Knox Press, 1997).
17. Elmer Towns and Warren Bird, *Into the Future: Turning Today's Church Trends into Tomorrow's Opportunities* (Grand Rapids, MI: Revell, 2000), p. 245.
18. George Hunter, cited in Dale Galloway, *Making Church Relevant*, Beeson Series, 2nd ed. (Kansas City, MO: Beacon Hill Press, 1999), p. 255.
19. George G. Hunter, *How to Reach Secular People* (Nashville, TN: Abingdon, 1992); *Church for the Unchurched* (Nashville, TN: Abingdon, 1996); *The Celtic Way of Evangelism: How Christianity Can Reach the West . . . Again* (Nashville, TN: Abingdon, 2000).

Chapter 7: Cyber-Enhanced Churches

1. The opening illustration was adapted from Paul D. Rosevear, "10 E-Learning Questions You Wish You Had Answered, Continued." http://reference.aol.com onlinecampus/campusarticle/_a/10-elearning-questions-you-wish-you-had/2005 0829212309990001 (accessed September 2006).

2. Geoff Surratt, Greg Ligon and Warren Bird, *The Multi-Site Church Revolution* (Grand Rapids, MI: Zondervan, 2006).

3. For more on this story, see Mark M. Stephenson, "From a Single Page to Web-Empowering Churches Worldwide," The Internet Evangelism Coalition, July 2006. http://www.webevangelism.com/Brix?pageID=19155 (accessed September 2006).

4. Mark Stephenson, *Web-Empower Your Church: Unleashing the Power of Internet Ministry* (Nashville, TN: Abingdon Press, 2007).

5. Ibid., p. 88.

6. Ibid., p. 84.

7. Lee Rainie, "CyberFaith: How Americans Pursue Religion Online," Pew Internet and American Life Project, December 23, 2001. http://www.pewinternet.org/reports/toc.asp?Report=53, (accessed September 2006).

8. The results of the study by Ellison Research were published in the January/February 2006 edition of *Facts & Trends*, a publication of LifeWay Christian Resources.

9. "More People Use Christian Media than Attend Church," *The Barna Update,* March 14, 2005. http://www.barna.org/FlexPage.aspx?Page=BarnaUpdate&BarnaUpdate ID=184 (accessed September 2006).

10. Rainie, "CyberFaith: How Americans Pursue Religion Online."

11. Eric Tiansay, "Online Religion Is Bigger Attraction than Money, Report Says," Charisma News Service, December 31, 2001, vol. 3, no. 195. http://strang.com/search.php?sp=30&query=tiansay (accessed September 2006).

12. Brenda Brasher, *Give Me that Online Religion* (Piscataway, NJ: Rutgers University Press, 2001). See also John J. Shaughnessy, "Web Opens New Window on Religion," Christian.com, February 27, 2005. http://www.christian.com/ArticlesDetail. asp?id=1715 (accessed September 2006).

13. Rainie, "CyberFaith: How Americans Pursue Religion Online."

14. Mark Batterson, "Godcasting," *Christianity Today,* Spring 2006, vol. XXVII, no. 2. http://www.christianitytoday.com/le/2006/002/9.81.html (accessed September 2006).

15. Rainie, "CyberFaith: How Americans Pursue Religion Online."

16. Sherri Day, "Faithful, Church Connect Online," *St. Petersburg Times,* June 6, 2006.

17. For more information, see www.themobileword.com.

18. Batterson, "Godcasting," *Christianity Today.*

19. Neela Banerjee, "Intimate Confessions Pour Out on Church's Web Site," *New York Times,* September 1, 2006. http://www.nytimes.com/2006/09/01/us/01confession. html?_r=1&ref=us&oref=slogin (accessed February 2007).

20. The previous two paragraphs were adapted from a blog posted on October 27, 2006, by Paul Steinbrueck. http://blog.ourchurch.com/2006/10/27/the-lifechurchtv-internet-campus/ (accessed March 2006).

21. "Most Churches Did Not Answer the Phone," *The Barna Update*, January 26, 2004. http://www.barna.org/FlexPage.aspx?Page=BarnaUpdate&BarnaUpdateID=157 (accessed September 2006).

22. See Carl George with Warren Bird, *Prepare Your Church for the Future* (Grand Rapids, MI: Revell, 1991), pp. 110-111.

Chapter 8: Nickelodeon-Style Children-Focused Churches

1. Elmer L. Towns, The Ten Largest Sunday Schools and What Made Them Grow (Grand Rapids, MI: Baker Book House, 1969).

2. Elmer L. Towns, The Towns' Sunday School Encyclopedia (Wheaton, IL: Tyndale House, 1993), pp. 278-279.

3. Philip Conner, ed. *Children's Evangelism Survey Research Report* (Alpharetta, GA: North American Mission Board, 2005). This study is available at www.missional research.info.
4. Ibid.
5. Ibid.

Chapter 9: Intentionally Multicultural Churches

1. "Redmond, Washington: Demographics," Experts Archive, 2000 census data. http://experts.about.com/e/r/re/Redmond,_Washington.htm (accessed February 2007).
2. "Kirkland, Washington: Demographics," Experts Archive, 2000 census data. http://experts.about.com/e/k/ki/Kirkland,_Washington.htm (accessed February 2007.
3. Antioch Bible Church website, www.abchurch.org.
4. Bridgeway Community Church, www.bridgewayonline.org
5. David Anderson, *Multicultural Ministry: Finding Your Church's Unique Rhythm* (Grand Rapids, MI: Zondervan, 2004).
6. George A. Yancey, *One Body, One Spirit: Principles of Successful Multiracial Churches* (Downers Grove, IL: InterVarsity, 2003). See also Manuel Ortiz, *One New People: Models for Developing a Multiethnic Church* (Downers Grove, IL: InterVarsity Press, 1996).
7. Ibid., p. 15.
8. Jim Cymbala, *Fresh Wind, Fresh Fire: What Happens When God's Spirit Invades the Hearts of His People* (Grand Rapids, MI: Zondervan, 1997). See also Jim Cymbala and Dean Merrill, *Fresh Faith: What Happens When Real Faith Ignites God's People* (Grand Rapids, MI: Zondervan, 2003).
9. "Our Mission, Vision and Values," Church On The Way website. http://www.tcotw.org/landing_pages/15,3.html (accessed February 2007).
10. Scott Thumma, Dave Travis and Warren Bird, "Megachurches Today 2005 Summary of Research Findings," Hartford Institute for Religious Research. http://www.hartford institute.org/megachurch/megastoday2005_summaryreport.html (accessed February 2007).
11. Dale Galloway with Warren Bird, *Starting a New Church: How to Plant a High-Impact Congregation* (Kansas City, MO: Beacon Hill Press of Kansas City, 2003), pp. 29-31.
12. Orlando Crespo, "Our Transnational Anthem," *Christianity Today*, August 2006, Vol. 50, No. 8, p. 20. http://www.christianitytoday.com/ct/2006/008/35.32.html (accessed February 2007).

Chapter 10: Decision-Journey Churches

1. For more on the Community Christian story, see Dave Ferguson, Jon Ferguson and Eric Bramlett, *The Big Idea: Focus the Message, Multiply the Impact* (Grand Rapids, MI: Zondervan Publishing House, 2007).
2. For more on the Journey's approach to ministry, see Nelson Searcy and Kerrick Thomas, *Launch: Starting a New Church from Scratch* (Ventura, CA: Regal Books, 2007) and www.ChurchFromScratch.com.
3. Elmer L. Towns and Douglas Porter, *The Ten Greatest Revivals Ever* (Ann Arbor, MI: Servant Publications, 2000), pp. 84-85.
4. Charles Gradison Finney, *Lectures on Revival* (Minneapolis, MN: Bethany House Publishers, 1989). Finney is one of the first to systematically present the methods of revival and/or ministry in propositional form.
5. Towns and Porter, *The Ten Greatest Revivals Ever*, p. 131.
6. Ibid.

7. For more information, see "Instantaneous Salvation" on Bible.com (www.goto thebible.com/HTML/Sermons/instant.html). This sermon is one of the 10 greatest of all time because it changed the ministerial opinion about seeking salvation. Rather than having people go through a process or journey to salvation, Moody taught that people could be saved instantaneously. After this sermon by Moody, there was a slow evolution of public opinion until Billy Graham's view of "decision," in which one can be saved on the spot.

8. "Billy Graham and the Billy Graham Evangelistic Association Historical Background," Billy Graham Center Archives, Wheaton College. http://www.wheaton. edu/bgc/archives/bio.html (accessed September 2006).

9. Elmer L. Towns, *The 10 Largest Sunday Schools and What Made Them Grow* (Grand Rapids, MI: Baker Book House, 1969).

10. Dallas Billington, *God Is Real* (New York: David McKay Company, Inc., 1962).

11. Elmer Towns and Ed Stetzer, *Perimeters of Light* (Chicago, IL: Moody Press, 2004).

12. Andy Stanley, personal interview with Ed Stetzer, August 25, 2002.

Chapter 11: Attractional Churches

1. Dale Galloway and Warren Bird, *Moving from Maintenance to Ministry* (Kansas City, MO: Beacon Hill Press, 2007).

2. Doug Murren, *Baby Boomerang: Catching the Boomer Generation as They Return to Church* (Ventura, CA: Regal, 1990).

3. Doug Murren, *Leadershift* (Mansfield, PA: Kingdom Publishing, 1999), pp. 185-186.

4. Rick Rasberry, "An Analysis of the Friend Day Program, Written by Elmer Towns and Published by Church Growth Institute, Lynchburg, Virginia," Ph.D. dissertation, Liberty Baptist Theological Seminary, 1995. See also http://www.elmer towns.com/index.cfm?action=bio.

5. First Baptist Church website, http://www.fbchammond.com/schedule.php (accessed February 2007).

6. Grace Communtiy Church website, www.gracechurch.org (accessed February 2007).

7. Cedar Ridge Community Church website, http://www.crcc.org/section.php? SectionID=27 (accessed February 2007).

8. First Baptist Church of Hammond, Indiana, *The Voice,* vol. 1, no. 1. http://www.fbc hammond.com/the_voice/01%20decembervoice2003.pdf (accessed February 2007).

9. David Di Sabatino, doctoral thesis on the history of the Jesus People Movement, 1993-1994. http://www.apologeticsindex.org/13-lonnie-frisbee-and-calvary-chapel (accessed February 2007).

10. Matt Coker, "The First Jesus Freak," *Orange County Weekly,* March 3, 2005. http:// www.ocweekly.com/features/features/the-first-jesus-freak/19081/ (accessed February 2007).

11. The following titles are all by Steve Sjogren: *Conspiracy of Kindness: A Refreshing New Approach to Sharing the Love of Jesus* (Ventura, CA: Regal Books, 2003); *101 Ways to Reach People in Your Community* (Colorado Springs, CO: NavPress, 2004); *101 Ways to Reach People in Need* (Colorado Springs, CO: NavPress, 2002); and *Changing the World Through Kindness* (Ventura, CA: Regal Books, 2005).

12. Alan Hirsch, *The Forgotten Ways: Reactivating the Missional Church* (Grand Rapids, MI: Brazon Press, to be published in 2007).

13. Jake Tapper and Clayton Sandell, "Spreading the Gospel Through Pro Wrestling," *ABC News,* December 20, 20005. http://abcnews.go.com/WNT/story?id=1426365 (accessed February 2007).

14. "Fear Factor Ministry: Florence Church Youth Swallow Live Fish," *Decatur Daily*, October 7, 2005. http://www.decaturdaily.com/decaturdaily/news/051007/fear.shtml (accessed March 2007).

Conclusion: What Do These Church Types Teach Us?

1. Brian McLaren, "Bless *This* House?" *Christianity Today International/Leadership Journal*, 2004. http://www.christianitytoday.com/leaders/newsletter/2004/cln40629.html (accessed February 2007).

2. The following section is an excerpt from a longer paper that I (Ed) presented in November 2006 to the American Society for Church Growth (available at www.edstetzer.com). It emphasizes the following six marks as essentials for what makes up a church:

- **Scriptural authority.** The apostles continually appealed to the Old Testament as their authority in their preaching and teaching. Peter's sermon in Acts 2 and Stephen's sermon in Acts 7 illustrate this truth. In his itinerant ministry Paul customarily began his ministry in the synagogue, showing from the Scriptures that Jesus must be the Messiah (Acts 17:2-3). In 2 Timothy 3:15-17 Paul established for all time the authority of the Scriptures in the life of the church.

- **Biblical Leadership.** Churches need leadership . . . it is obvious in the New Testament. There are some differences of what those leadership positions, titles, and roles should be, but you cannot "innovate" leadership away. The New Testament speaks of elders, bishops, pastors, deacons, evangelists, prophets, and apostles. Probably, the church organized itself differently in different places, but the churches *were organized*. These leaders all gave themselves to equipping the believers for ministry (Eph. 4:11-12). Beyond that the Scriptures instruct the believers to accord them "double honor" (1 Tim. 5:17).

- **Preaching and teaching.** People need to hear the preaching and teaching of God's word. The lost need to hear the truth of the gospel, and the redeemed need biblical instruction so they can grow to maturity. Sadly, for many modern believers *worship* has come to mean the singing and responses that precede the sermon. True worship includes both praise and preaching. The style and length of the sermon surely will vary from culture to culture, but the preaching/teaching of God's word is a transcultural constant.

- **Ordinances.** The church at Jerusalem devoted itself to the "breaking of bread" (Acts 2:42). This is a reference to the Lord's Supper. Jesus' command to "do this in remembrance of me" and the Apostle Paul's instructions in 1 Corinthians 11 show how important the Lord's Supper was and is to the church. Jesus commissioned his disciples to baptize the nations, and the Acts and the epistles show they faithfully baptized new believers (Acts 2:41).

- **Covenant community.** Biblically, you cannot "innovate" away that there is a church and some are believers in covenant community and some are not—and they are treated differently. In fact, the letter of James insists that all the believers should be treated the same. As a covenant community, believers share several common ideals. These are found in Acts 2:42-47. First, they share common doctrinal convictions. Acts 2:42 says the believers "continued in the apostles' doctrine." This means they diligently learned the lessons taught by the apostles. They also devoted themselves to congregational prayer. They prayed for each other, bearing one another's burdens. They met the physical and financial needs of their fellow believers. When necessary they exercised church discipline.

- **Mission.** Churches are called to be a part of the mission of propagating the gospel. Scripture clearly and frequently teaches such. Mission includes the task of worldwide evangelism, social justice, human needs, and many other activities. The acts of the early Christians demonstrate their understanding of what Christ expected of them. Jesus' last words to his disciples in Acts and the four gospels all pertain to missions. Many in the churches today forget the church did mission before it did theology.

3. John Naisbitt, *Megatrends* (New York: Warner Books, 1988).

ABOUT THE AUTHORS

Elmer Towns, best known as a college and seminary professor, serves as dean of the School of Religion and vice president at Liberty University in Lynchburg, Virginia, which he cofounded with Dr. Jerry Falwell. He is widely known beyond university settings as a worldwide authority on Sunday School and church growth. He has written more than 2,000 magazine articles and published more than 50 books, including several Regal Books titles: *Fasting for Spiritual Breakthrough, Praying the Lord's Prayer for Spiritual Breakthrough, Names of the Holy Spirit, Year-Round Book of Sermon Ideas* and *What Every Sunday School Teacher Should Know*. He has created many popular church resources, such as *Friend Day*, and has received numerous awards, including the coveted Gold Medallion Award from the Christian Booksellers Association. He is also cofounder of Church Growth Institute in Lynchburg, Virginia, a resource outlet for biblical and instructional material. His academic degrees come from Northwestern College, Southern Methodist

University, Dallas Theological Seminary, Garrett-Evangelical Theological Seminary and Fuller Theological Seminary.

Ed Stetzer has planted and revitalized churches in four states, has served as a seminary professor, and has trained pastors and church planters on five continents. He currently serves as the missiologist and senior director of the Center for Missional Research at the North American Board in Alpharetta, Georgia. He has authored *Perimeters of Light: Biblical Boundaries for the Emerging Church* (with Elmer Towns), which helps churches to determine a theology of methodology; *Strategic Outreach* (with Eric Ramsey), to help churches plan to effectively reach their communities; *Planting Missional Churches,* which helps church planters to start and grow biblically faithful and culturally relevant churches; *Breaking the Missional Code* (with David Putman), to help Christian leaders think missionally about their contexts; and *Comeback Churches*, a study of churches experiencing significant revitalization. He holds an M.Div. from Southern Seminary, an M.A.R. from Liberty University, a D.Min. from Beeson Divinity School, and a Ph.D. from Southern Seminary (Missions).

Warren Bird, an ordained minister with 15 years of pastoral experience, serves as research director for Leadership Network, a highly respected think-tank that works with America's most innovative churches. His job is to research breakthrough churches and work with their leaders to multiply their evangelistic and disciple-making impact. He has served as adjunct professor at Alliance Theological Seminary for 10 years and has collaboratively authored 17 books, including *Emotionally Healthy Church,* which won the prestigious Gold Medallion Award. He has published almost 200 magazine articles, such as a 1994 cover story in *Christianity Today* on small groups. He graduated from Wheaton

College and Wheaton Graduate School in Wheaton, Illinois (B.A., M.A.), and Alliance Theological Seminary in Nyack, N.Y. (M.Div.), and earned a Ph.D. in sociology of religion from Fordham University in New York.

ACKNOWLEDGMENTS

This book has been a team effort, far more than the teamwork of co-authors Elmer Towns, Ed Stetzer and Warren Bird. Previously, Elmer and Warren co-authored *Into the Future: Turning Today's Church Trends into Tomorrow's Opportunities* (Revell, 2000). Elmer and Ed co-wrote *Perimeters of Light: Biblical Boundaries for the Emerging Church* (Moody, 2004). Both Warren and Ed are longtime fans and students of Elmer Towns, both being strongly influenced by many of his books, including *10 of Today's Most Innovative Churches* (Regal, 1990). In certain ways, this book builds on that pioneering book.

To that end, we thank Regal Books and its parent company Gospel Light for its longstanding partnership with Elmer Towns and for all they did to make this book a reality. Many people at Regal have contributed to that relationship, including Bill Greig III, Bruce Barbour, Steven Lawson, Kim Bangs, Mark Weising and Deena Davis.

We each owe a debt of thanks to our respective support staffs, in particular Linda Elliott, in Elmer's office at Liberty University, who enhanced and smoothed the final manuscript in many ways and also her student worker, Kristin Wolfe, who assisted in compiling the index.

We appreciate the many pastors who allowed us to tell their stories in this book and who have enriched our lives not only by their friendship but also by the bold and daring faith so many of them have demonstrated. We appreciate, too, the many friends who gave input, either by phone or e-mail, on a very early draft or outline of this manuscript. They include Ron Martoia, Thom Rainer, Dino Senesi and Christian Washington.

Most of all, we are thankful to God, our Savior and Lord, who is constantly doing a "new thing" (Isa. 43:19) and whose compassion and mercy "are new every morning" (Lam. 3:22-23).

ALSO BY THE AUTHORS

How to Pray When You Don't Know What to Say
Elmer L. Towns
Ventura, CA: Regal Books, 2006
ISBN 0-8307-4187-9

Did you know there are dozens of other biblical models for prayer? Never be distracted or frustrated with your quiet time again. Get excited about meeting with God.

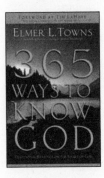

365 Ways to Know God
Elmer L. Towns
Ventura, CA: Regal Books, 2004
ISBN 0-8307-3341-8

Reflect on one name of God for every day of the year, nurturing a deep, worshipful understanding of Him so that you can come to know Him on a first-name basis.

Breaking the Missional Code:
When Churches Become Missionaries
in Their Communities
Ed Stetzer and David Putman
Nashville, TN: Broadman & Holman Publishers, 2006
ISBN 0-8054-4359-2

Breaking the Missional Code by Ed Stetzer and David Putman is a clarion call for churches in the United States to act among their local communities as missionaries would in a foreign land. For in fact, the message of Jesus Christ is still foreign to many who stand in the shadows of American steeples. As our approach to outreach changes, so can countless lives in our own backyards.

Comeback Churches
Ed Stetzer
Nashville, TN: Broadman & Holman, 2007
ISBN 0-8054-4536-6

Over time, most churches start strong, experience periods of growth, plateau and then eventually decline. Since 1991, the North American population has increased by 15 percent while the number of "unchurched" people has increased by 92 percent. To counter this trend, authors Ed Stetzer and Mike Dodson surveyed 300 churches from across 10 different denominations that recently achieved healthy evangelistic growth after a significant season of decline. What they have discovered is an exciting method of congregation reinvigoration.

Multi-Site Church Revolution
Geoff Surratt, Greg Ligon, Warren Bird
Grand Rapids, MI: Zondervan, 2006
ISBN 0-3102-7015-4

Rather than pouring millions of dollars into constructing new buildings, churches of all sizes are learning new ways to take church to the streets, reaching people in new ways. They extend into gyms and multipurpose rooms, or across town into theaters, schools and empty warehouses. From the suburbs to urban and rural settings, churches are discovering the advantage of becoming "one church, with many locations."

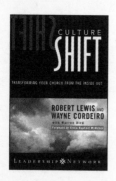

Culture Shift:
Transforming Your Church from the Inside Out
Robert Lewis , Wayne Cordeiro, Warren Bird
San Francisco, CA: Jossey-Bass, 2005
ISBN 0-7879-7530-3

Every church has its own distinct culture. This book shows churches how to develop cultures in which they and their leaders can grow into a genuine maturity that makes them more authentic and unique, less dependent on someone else's programs, and less likely to duplicate what everyone else is doing. The authors emphasize the need for leaders to understand, grow and express the ingredients of a church's special culture while reframing what it means to be a force for good in God's kingdom.

USE 11 INNOVATIONS IN THE LOCAL CHURCH AS A STUDY GUIDE FOR CHURCH STAFF, CHURCH BOARDS AND/OR ADULT CLASSES

Visit: http://www.elmertowns.com/11Churches/ or an outline of each chapter in addition to a PowerPoint to be used in presentation. This will lead to discussion that will produce health and growth for your church.

GENERAL INDEX

SCRIPTURE INDEX

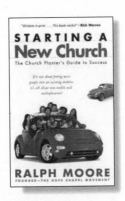
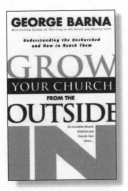

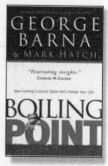

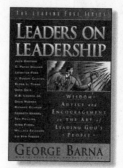

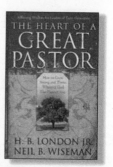